In Search of the New Woman

The 'New Women' of late nineteenth-century Britain were seen as defying society's conventions. Studying this phenomenon from its origins in the 1870s to the outbreak of the Great War, Gillian Sutherland examines whether women really had the economic freedom to challenge norms relating to work, political action, love and marriage, and surveys literary and pictorial representations of the New Woman. She considers the proportion of middle-class women who were in employment and the work they did, and compares the different experiences of women who went to Oxbridge and those who went to other universities. Juxtaposing them against the period's rapidly expanding but seldom studied groups of women white-collar workers, the book pays particular attention to clerks and teachers and their political engagement. It also explores the dividing lines between ladies and women, the significance of respectability, and the interactions of class, status and gender lying behind such distinctions.

GILLIAN SUTHERLAND is a Fellow of Newnham College and a member of the History Faculty at the University of Cambridge. She is the author of *Faith, Duty and the Power of Mind: The Cloughs and their Circle 1820–1960* (Cambridge University Press, 2006).

In Search of the New Woman: Middle-Class Women and Work in Britain 1870–1914

GILLIAN SUTHERLAND

CAMBRIDGE
UNIVERSITY PRESS

CAMBRIDGE
UNIVERSITY PRESS

University Printing House, Cambridge CB2 8BS, United Kingdom

Cambridge University Press is part of the University of Cambridge.

It furthers the University's mission by disseminating knowledge in the pursuit of education, learning and research at the highest international levels of excellence.

www.cambridge.org
Information on this title: www.cambridge.org/9781107092792

First published 2015

Printed in the United Kingdom by Clays, St Ives plc

A catalogue record for this publication is available from the British Library

Library of Congress Cataloguing in Publication data
Sutherland, Gillian.
In search of the new woman : middle-class women and work in Britain 1870–1914 / Gillian Sutherland.
    pages   cm
ISBN 978-1-107-09279-2 (Hardback)
1. Women – Great Britain – Social conditions – 19th century.   2. Women – Great Britain – Social conditions – 20th century.   3. Middle class women – Great Britain – Social conditions – 19th century.   4. Middle class women – Great Britain – Social conditions – 20th century.   5. Women employees – Great Britain – History – 19th century.   6. Women employees – Great Britain – History – 20th century.   7. Women white collar workers – Great Britain – Social conditions – 19th century.   8. Women white collar workers – Great Britain – Social conditions – 20th century.   9. Great Britain – Social conditions – 19th century.   10. Great Britain – Social conditions – 20th century.   I. Title.
HQ1593.S923   2015
305.4094109′034–dc23
                                                                2014032246

ISBN 978-1-107-09279-2 Hardback
ISBN 978-1-107-46734-7 Paperback

*For the successive generations of women teachers
in my family*

Contents

Figures and tables

Figures

Tables

Acknowledgements

Most monographs are sustained by a broad base of collective endeavour and ample and extensive scholarly exchange; the republic of letters still survives. This study is no exception. Rosalind Crone showed me how to construct the database of the Cambridge women students 1869–1914 and patiently guided my use and analysis of this. Other friends and colleagues have read all or parts of successive drafts, some several times over; and I have benefited greatly from their suggestions on bibliography, structure and argument. Their efforts in prodding me to expand and elaborate where I was understated and/or cryptic have been invaluable. I owe particular debts to Felicity Cooke, Ben Griffin, Hazel Mills, Clare Pettitt, Christopher Stray and Anne Summers and to the readers for Cambridge University Press. Needless to say, I alone am responsible for the errors and imperfections which remain.

For permission to consult and to cite copyright material in their charge, I am indebted to the Principal and Fellows of Newnham College, Cambridge, the Mistress and Fellows of Girton College, Cambridge, the Principal and Fellows of St Hugh's College, Oxford, the British Library Board, The Women's Library at the LSE, the Skinners' Company, the Metropolitan Archives, and the Governors of the Stephen Perse Foundation, Cambridge. The archivists and staff of all these institutions have been generous with their help, as were the staff at London Metropolitan University, while The Women's Library remained in their care. In the Newnham Archives, Anne Thomson first drew my attention to the Hutton Papers and has made many other fruitful suggestions, once again steering me through the photographic collection. Pat Ackerman's handlist for the Wallas Papers proved a model of clarity. Senior Members' Research Support funds at Newnham have also provided help with some of the costs of the work.

At Cambridge University Press, I am grateful for guidance to Michael Watson, the History editor, and to his deputy, Rosalyn

Scott, whose patience and good humour in responding promptly and constructively to all my questions, daft or otherwise, has been exemplary. I have benefited once again from Frances Brown's intelligent and meticulous copy-editing and also from Chris Stray's careful preparation of the index.

1   'a sort of Bogey whom no-one has ever seen'? The nature of the search

In the 1890s there was a positive media feeding frenzy in Britain and in North America both defending and attacking the 'New Woman'. Some commentators have dated the beginning of this very precisely, from March 1894, when the British novelist Sarah Grand first used the label in an article in the *North American Review*.[1] Grand hailed the New Woman as one who has at last 'solved the problem and proclaimed for herself what was wrong with Home-is-the-Woman's-Sphere, and prescribed the remedy'.[2] Other commentators have seen the term growing out of and crystallising a steadily swelling debate over several decades about the position of women of the middle classes, their scope for independence, the implications of the access to secondary and higher education which they were beginning to secure, and the legal, financial, social and psychological constraints imposed upon them by marriage.[3]

The latter is a more fruitful reading, allowing as it does a consideration of a wider literature over a longer period, not only fiction and drama but also political and social writing on the subject contemporaries came to know as the 'Woman Question' and which attracted a range of campaigning organisations. Although the structure of the English state and political system favoured single-issue campaigns, those involved were often associated, even though their primary targets differed, and they were collectively known to contemporaries as 'the women's movement'. The terms 'feminism' and 'feminist' were only just arriving in the language. Casting the net widely in these ways brings benefits. Periodical

---

[1] 'The New Aspect of the Woman Question', *North American Review* 158 (March 1894), pp. 270–6, reprinted in Carolyn Christensen Nelson, ed., *A New Woman Reader: Fiction, Articles and Drama of the 1890s* (Peterborough, Ontario 2001), pp. 141–6. For Sarah Grand, see also below, pp. 2, 75.

[2] *Ibid.* p. 142.

[3] Cf. Nelson's 'Introduction', pp. ix–x; Barbara Caine, *Victorian Feminists* (Oxford 1992), pp. 252–4 and her *English Feminism 1780–1980* (Oxford 1997), pp. 134–43.

writing was and is mostly ephemeral. Although over a hundred New Woman novels were published in the course of the decade and immediately either side of it,[4] few are now read for their intrinsic merit, even if we acknowledge the force of John Sutherland's comment that 'interest in the type enriches female characterisation in mainstream fiction of the late Victorian period'.[5] Widening the range and time-frame allows us not only to add writing which has acquired an enduring reputation and resonance but also to develop a much more complex explanatory framework for the debate itself and the challenge it represented to the ideology of domesticity, so powerful in the earlier half of the century.[6] This ideology celebrated the woman as moral authority, arbiter in the home and family standing apart from, uncontaminated by, the often sordid dealings of the public sphere, quintessentially the male sphere. The actualities of lives seldom quite matched the rhetoric or the theory; but the ideological challenge to domesticity gathered force only in the second half of the century. While the New Woman debate represents a literary peak in this challenge, it is also a curtain-raiser to the very real and practical challenge represented by the campaign for women's suffrage, gaining numbers, momentum and traction from 1900.

The style and character of writing on New Women, both for and against, may be sampled in Sarah Grand's articles and in her novels such as *The Heavenly Twins* (1893) and *The Beth Book* (1897); in Mona Caird's *The Wings of Azrael* (1889) and *A Romance of the Moors* (1891) and her articles subsequently collected in *The Morality of Marriage and other Essays on the Status and Destiny of Women* (1897); in Grant Allen's articles 'Plain Words on the Woman Question' (1889) and 'The Girl of the Future' (1890) and his novel, *The Woman Who Did*, in 1895; in Sydney Grundy's play *The New Woman* (1894) and A. W. Pinero's play *The Notorious Mrs Ebbsmith* (1895).[7] Extending the range allows us to add to these Olive Schreiner's novel *The Story of an African*

---

[4] Ann Ardis, *New Women, New Novels: Feminism and Early Modernism* (London 1990).

[5] In John Sutherland, *The Longman Companion to Victorian Fiction* (2nd edition London 2009), p. 466.

[6] For the formation of the domestic ideology, its power and the historiographical debates which have surrounded this, begin with Leonora Davidoff and Catherine Hall, *Family Fortunes: Men and Women of the English Middle Class, 1780–1850* (2nd edition London 2002).

[7] Included in *The New Woman and Other Emancipated Woman Plays*, ed. with an Introduction by Jean Chotia (Oxford 1998).

Farm (1883), George Gissing's novel *The Odd Women* (1893), and Mrs Humphry Ward's later novels, *The Testing of Diana Mallory* (1908) and *Delia Blanchflower* (1915); and to consider the context in which D. H. Lawrence began to write. It enables us to add plays such as George Bernard Shaw's *Mrs Warren's Profession* (1894), Harley Granville Barker's *The Madras House* (1910) and the first English translations and performances of Ibsen's *A Doll's House* (1889), *Hedda Gabler* and *Ghosts* (both 1891). It allows a consideration of the impact of Edward Carpenter's *Love's Coming of Age* (1896), the first volume of Havelock Ellis's *Studies in the Psychology of Sex* (1897) and the first English-language accounts of and then translations of Freud's work, from 1893 onwards.[8]

Plainly there is a great deal of noise and activity here. Its ubiquity is demonstrated in some surprising ways; in 1897 Tom Ball, later to become a regular music hall performer – and to father the British prime minister Sir John Major – won a prize for his participation in a Midlands swimming gala, dressed as 'a new woman in bloomers'.[9] More sedately, the noise and activity have sustained a thriving academic industry.[10] This study is less an addition to that industry, rather an attempt to explore the relationships between the noise and changes on the ground, changes in the ways middle-class women actually lived their lives.

Carolyn Christensen Nelson has suggested that the New Woman 'was educated at Girton College, Cambridge, rode a bicycle, insisted on rational dress, and smoked in public ... she rejected the traditional role for women and demanded emancipation'.[11] Such images proved a gift to *Punch*; and the New Woman and bicycles, often linked, were

---

[8] Ernest Jones, *Sigmund Freud: Life and Work*, vol. II, *Years of Maturity 1901–1919* (London 1974 edition), pp. 30–2 *et seq.* The political and sexual journalism and debates are treated at length in Sheila Rowbotham, *Edward Carpenter: A Life of Liberty and Love* (London 2008) but the briefer account in Sheila Rowbotham and Jeffery Weeks, *Socialism and the New Life: The Personal and Sexual Politics of Edward Carpenter and Havelock Ellis* (London 1977) remains helpful. See also Laura Schwartz, *Infidel Feminism: Secularism, Religion and Women's Emancipation in England 1830–1914* (Manchester 2012), esp. ch. 6. For the anti-suffrage women writers, see Julia Bush, *Women against the Vote: Female Anti-Suffragism in Britain* (Oxford 2007), ch. 4.

[9] John Major, *My Old Man: A Personal History of Music Hall* (London 2012), p. 297. I am indebted to Chris Stray for this reference.

[10] See for example the programme and paper abstracts for 'Women Writers of the fin-de-siècle' International Conference, Institute of English Studies, University of London, June 2010.

[11] 'Introduction' to *New Woman Reader*, p. ix.

THE NEW WOMAN.

"YOU'RE NOT LEAVING US, JACK! TEA WILL BE HERE DIRECTLY!"
"OH, I'M GOING FOR A CUP OF TEA IN THE SERVANTS' HALL. I CAN'T GET ON WITHOUT FEMALE SOCIETY, YOU KNOW!"

1 Cartoon from *Punch*, drawn by George Du Maurier, 15 June 1895

staples through the second half of the 1890s, as the examples from 1895 and 1896 above and on page 5 show. From the caricatures we can extract two lines for more prosaic further enquiry: we should be looking for women who challenged the conventions of lady-like behaviour and we should begin this search by looking at women graduates, especially those attempting to gain a foothold in Oxbridge.

The 'girl graduate' was a familiar figure in the popular fiction of the period generally. As Chris Willis remarks, 'A Girton education became the stock attribute of the intellectual New Woman of popular fiction.' Herminia Barton, 'the woman who did' in Grant Allen's novel of that name, has just left Girton, as has Bernadine Holme, the heroine of Beatrice Harraden's *Ships that Pass in the Night* (1893). Grant Allen used the character again in *The Typewriter Girl* (1897) and for his woman detective, Lois Cayley; while McDonnell Bodkin's girl detective Dora Myrl was (implausibly) 'a Cambridge Wrangler and a Doctor of Medicine'. Before taking up detection she had also been 'a telephone girl, a telegraph girl' and a 'lady journalist'.[12] These are but a sample of the

[12] Chris Willis, '"Heaven defend me from political or highly educated women!": Packaging the New Woman for Mass Consumption', in Angelique Richardson

RATIONAL COSTUME.

The Vicar of St. Winifred-in-the-Wold (to fair Bicyclists). It is customary for Men, I will not say Gentlemen, to remove their Hats on entering a Church!"
Confusion of the Ladies Rota and Iziona Bykewell.

2 Cartoon from *Punch*, drawn by George Du Maurier, 13 June 1896

caricatures, both verbal and visual, and there were many more. Albert Morrow's striking poster for Sydney Grundy's 1894 play *The New Woman*, used for the jacket and reproduced on p. 6, is perhaps the epitome. The subject was not this time a Girton girl but the New Woman novelist, George Egerton. We should note the pince-nez, the plain dress, the mass of books and papers and the cigarette, marked to suggest that the inexpert smoker had tried both ends before succeeding.[13]

Analysts of New Woman writing and writers, both for and against, generally agree that these images in pictures and in words were caricatures. Talia Schaffer sums up the prevailing view when she writes, 'By

and Chris Willis, eds., *The New Woman in Fiction and in Fact: Fin-de-Siècle Feminisms* (London 2001), pp. 53–65, at pp. 55–60, direct quotations from pp. 55 and 59. See also e.g. Annie Edwardes, *A Blue-Stocking* (1877), *A Girton Girl* (1886); Emma Frances Brooke, *Transition* (1896); L. T. Meade, *A Sweet Girl Graduate* (1891); Emily Cox, *Courtship and Chemicals* (1898); Alice Stronach, *A Newnham Friendship* (1901); 'Alan St Aubyn' (Frances Bridges), *The Harp of Life* (1908); Mrs George de Horne Vaizey, *A College Girl* (n.d. probably Edwardian).

[13] For further discussion of this see below, Chapter 4, pp. 74–6.

3 Albert Morrow's poster for Sydney Grundy's play, *The New Woman*, 1894

1895 "New Woman" had become a wildly skewed reductive media construct which did not represent the real lives and work of those people it purported to describe.'[14] There is likewise general agreement that many women active in the loosely associated campaigns of the

---

[14] Talia Schaffer, '"Nothing but Foolscap and Ink": Inventing the New Woman', in Richardson and Willis eds., *New Woman in Fiction and in Fact*, pp. 39–52, at

women's movement of the late nineteenth century disliked the caricature intensely, as intended to undermine and belittle their work, a view
the suffrage campaigner Millicent Garrett Fawcett expressed forcefully
when she reviewed Grant Allen's *The Woman Who Did*.[15]

Yet this image was a most successful literary ploy for at least a decade
and recognition of the extent to which it was a construct has not
prevented some of those analysts of New Woman writing from making
large, if rather general, claims about the relationship of the construct to
lived lives. It is an assumption which underpins Deborah Epstein Nord's
discussion in *Walking the Victorian Streets*, although she locates New
Women in the 1880s.[16] Editing a selection of New Woman plays in
1998, Jean Chotia remarks that 'women, albeit mightily slowly, were
progressing towards emancipation … Women who had access to
education … were increasingly entering the professions, notably teaching and medicine.'[17] Matthew Beaumont asserts that 'the new female
mobility ushered in by expanding educational and occupational
opportunities … afforded a feeling of confidence' but offers no evidence
to support this.[18] Teresa Mangum, in her study of Sarah Grand, claims
that after Married Women's Property legislation guaranteed women
possession of their earned income, they 'more confidently moved into
the workforce as teachers, nurses, midwives, clerks, writers and journalists'.[19] That particular claim, as we shall see, was wide of the mark.
It does however have the merit of focusing attention on money. As
Olive Schreiner, 'The Modern Woman par excellence, founder and
high priestess of the school', wrote to Edward Carpenter in October
1894, commenting on an article of his on marriage, 'You don't perhaps

---

p. 49; cf. Teresa Mangum, *Married, Middlebrow and Militant: Sarah Grand and the New Woman Novel* (Ann Arbor, MI 1998), p. 28.

[15] Mangum, *Sarah Grand*, pp. 28–9; cf. Richardson and Willis, 'Introduction' to *New Woman in Fiction and in Fact*, pp. 1–38, at pp. 25 and 28; Lucy Delap, *The Feminist Avant-Garde: Transatlantic Encounters of the Early Twentieth Century* (Cambridge 2007), p. 16.

[16] Deborah Epstein Nord, *Walking the Victorian Streets: Women, Representation and the City* (Ithaca, NY 1995), Part III, 'New Women' esp. pp. 215–16. I am indebted to Clare Pettitt for referring me to this study.

[17] Chotia, ed. *New Woman and Other Emancipated Woman Plays*, Introduction, pp. ix–x.

[18] Matthew Beaumont, 'The New Woman in Nowhere: Feminism and Utopianism at the Fin-de-Siècle', in Richardson and Willis, eds., *New Woman in Fiction and in Fact*, pp. 212–23, at p. 213.

[19] Mangum, *Sarah Grand*, p. 52.

dwell QUITE enough on the monetary independence of women as the first condition necessary to the putting of things on the right footing.'[20] To do new things, challenge established patterns of behaviour, women of the middle classes needed economic independence. If you controlled adequate resources, you had choice; you could, if you wished, challenge prevailing social conventions, especially those around marriage and sexual relationships. Without economic resources you were dependent, on either family or husband or both, and constrained by their expectations.

A crucial first step towards clarifying the relationship between the New Woman caricature, the larger attendant literature on the Woman Question and actual social change is thus to discover whether in this period new ways of acquiring independence were emerging; and whether there were new opportunities to earn a living without sacrificing social status. If there were, how many women made use of these? Only when we have some answers or part-answers to such basic enquiries are we then free to move on to look for choice about lifestyles and consider the exercise of choice and the factors influencing it more generally.

This study is therefore an attempt to re-situate the New Woman caricature and the broader debate of which it was a part, by examining the opportunities for earning money, achieving independence, available to middle-class women in Britain in the last third of the long nineteenth century, from about 1870 to the outbreak of the First World War. This is likely to prove less straightforward than it might sound, as one case-study will illustrate. The first years of Ada Radford's adult life suggested that she might become a New Woman. Born in 1859, she was sent to secondary school and then went up to Newnham College, Cambridge to read Mathematics between 1881 and 1883. After a short spell teaching in a girls' high school, she settled on her own in London, contributing occasionally to literary periodicals like the *Westminster Gazette* and the *Yellow Book*, and moving in distinctly radical circles.[21] Her brother, Ernest Radford, and his poet wife Dollie, were firm friends of Eleanor Marx and devoted supporters of William Morris's Socialist League.

---

[20] Carolyn Burdett, 'Capturing the Ideal: Olive Schreiner's *From Man to Man*', in Richardson and Willis, eds., *New Woman in Fiction and in Fact*, pp. 167–82, at p. 180, n.12, Schreiner's emphasis; the description of Schreiner is W. T. Stead's in 1894, quoted *ibid.* p. 167.

[21] One of her *Yellow Book* stories has been reprinted in Nelson, ed., *New Woman Reader*, pp. 91–100.

Ada did not share all Ernest and Dollie's political enthusiasms but stayed close and regularly contributed to their insecure finances.[22] A user of the British Museum Reading Room, like many young women writers and political activists of the period,[23] Ada was acquainted with Richard Garnett, the Superintendent of the Reading Room, and his family. Her Cambridge contemporary and lifelong friend, Constance Black, married Garnett's son Edward in the autumn of 1889; and like Garnett's daughter Olive, Ada supported the group of Russian political exiles and revolutionaries, led by Stepniak and Volkhovsky, who worked on the periodical *Free Russia*.[24]

Yet following her marriage in 1898, at the age of 39, to the Fabian political scientist Graham Wallas, the trajectory of Ada's life appeared to shift. Gradually she reduced her involvement with the Russians. She did not cease to write but her next publication in 1906 was a book of children's stories, *The Land of Play*. During the First World War she put a considerable amount of time and effort into translating and disseminating some of the work of the French philosopher Émile Chartier, writing as 'Alain'. There was a long interval before her last two books, *Before the Bluestockings*, a study of seventeenth- and early eighteenth-century learned ladies, and *Daguerrotypes*, a family memoir, both published in 1929. She chose to put most of her energy into supporting her husband in his career and public activities and into caring for their one child, May, who was born in 1899. Ada did voluntary work with the London Schools for Mothers[25] and from 1919 to 1934 served on the Council of Bedford College. Altogether she appears to have settled into a more traditional pattern of family life; and the ways in which she

[22] Newnham College Archives (NCA), Wallas Papers *passim*, but see esp. 2/7/9 John Radford to Ada Wallas 3 January 1899. For Dollie's poetry, see Ruth Livesey, *Socialism, Sex and the Culture of Aestheticism in Britain 1880–1914* (Oxford 2007), ch. 5.

[23] See Amy Levy, 'Readers at the British Museum', *Atalanta: Every Girl's Magazine* (April 1889), pp. 449–54. Reprinted as Appendix B to Levy's *The Romance of a Shop*, ed. Susan David Bernstein (Toronto 2006); Susan David Bernstein, *Roomscape: Women Writers in the British Museum from George Eliot to Virginia Woolf* (Edinburgh 2013). I am indebted to Clare Pettitt for this latter reference.

[24] NCA Wallas Papers, *passim*; *Tea and Anarchy! The Bloomsbury Diary of Olive Garnett 1890–93*, ed. Barry C. Johnson (Birmingham 1989), pp. 108–22, and *Olive & Stepniak: The Bloomsbury Diary of Olive Garnett 1893–5*, ed. Barry C. Johnson (Birmingham 1993).

[25] See Jane Lewis, *The Politics of Motherhood* (London 1980), pp. 96–7.

sustained the small family's position within the larger Radford and Wallas networks through an extensive and lively correspondence and frequent visits have established pedigrees not only through the nineteenth century but stretching back into the eighteenth century.[26]

Yet there is no indication in Ada's surviving papers that she saw her marriage as representing any kind of disjunction in her life; rather, it contributed to an evolution, a response to circumstances, but also a set of fresh choices. Graham remained immensely supportive of her activities, especially her writing, always encouraging her to do more, as did friends like Logan Pearsall Smith; and Logan and Ada exchanged drafts for critical comment. The correspondence and those volumes of her diaries which survive reveal ample evidence of shared intellectual life and friendships, perhaps the strongest and certainly the most enduring with the French historian Élie Halévy and his wife Florence, whose relationship in many ways resembled the relationship between Graham and Ada.[27]

This one example of the experience of being a New – or Newish – Woman helps us to begin to question how much the realities of life for middle-class women actually changed in the course of the whole century, let alone the last third. Ada's acquaintance Olive Garnett, whose diaries are an exceptional source for the social *mores* and activities of advanced liberal intellectual and artistic circles, recorded a discussion in October 1892 at the home of her brother Edward and sister-in-law Constance about the invitation issued in 1814 by Shelley and his new love, Mary Godwin, to Harriet, his wife, to share a home. The Garnetts' friend, the exiled Russian revolutionary and journalist

---

[26] See e.g. Christopher Tolley, *Domestic Biography: The Legacy of Evangelicalism in Four Nineteenth-Century Families* (Oxford 1997); Naomi Tadmor, *Family and Friends in Eighteenth Century England: Household, Kinship and Patronage* (Cambridge 2001); R. J. Morris, *Men, Women and Property in England 1780–1870* (Cambridge 2005).

[27] For Graham, see Martin J. Wiener, *Between Two Worlds: The Political Thought of Graham Wallas* (Oxford 1971) and Peter Clarke, *Liberals and Social Democrats* (Cambridge 1978). The personal papers of the Wallases are held in the Archives of Newnham College Cambridge. Ada's papers form series 2 in this collection; Graham's form series 1. As these show, they wrote to each other almost daily when apart. Ada's First World War diaries, 2/1/3 to 2/1/6 also survive. For exchanges with Logan Pearsall Smith, see e.g. 2/7/11, Logan Pearsall Smith to Ada Wallas 8 August 1908; 2/7/13, Logan Pearsall Smith to Ada Wallas 11 March, 28 March, 11 April and 15 August 1915. The folders 2/5/1 to 2/5/12 contain letters from Florence Halévy 1913–34.

Stepniak, perhaps tongue-in-cheek, described the invitation as 'a delightful piece of nature & quite after the Russian heart. I could only say that I thought it showed a singular lack of appreciation of Harriet's character. Then he said "why doesn't someone in England attack the marriage institution?" I said "well someone did, Mrs Mona Caird, & as she was a person for whose judgement no-one cared a fig, she got laughed at for her pains"'.[28] In other words, some of the media comment was froth; or, as a Cambridge schoolgirl debater would put it in 1898, '"the New Woman", a sort of Bogey whom no-one has ever really seen'.[29]

Although marriage reshaped the trajectory of Ada Radford's life, she had begun with all the right New Woman credentials, formal secondary schooling then an Oxbridge college before involvement in the circles of advanced radicalism in London. In examining whether the media noise of the 1890s reflected an accomplished change in the position of women in nineteenth-century Britain, we too must begin with education. There were major changes in the provision of education for middle-class women in the course of the nineteenth century and among the battery of questions in our enquiry must be how far those changes were catalysts. Was Ada's experience typical? How does it compare with the experience of her peers? Chapter 2 examines the lives of those women who did receive a formal secondary schooling and then some higher education. It focuses in partic-ular on those, usually assumed to be the elite group, who had attended the fledgling women's colleges of Oxford and Cambridge, the Girton Girls of the caricature and their peers. How many of them went on to paid employment and what was that employment? How many of them mar-ried and did they go on working? The survey is extended in Chapter 3, which looks at the opportunities for women in the public service and in various other kinds of 'caring' work, traditionally a feminine preserve.

What emerges from these two chapters is the continuing dominance of teaching as a source of employment for 'ladies', as important at the end of the century as it had been at the beginning. Yet formal schooling and higher education provided no royal road to new, exciting or

---

[28] *Diary of Olive Garnett 1890–93*, ed. Johnson, p. 125. 'Delightful piece of nature' hardly does justice to the fraught drama of those weeks in 1814 – see Richard Holmes, *Shelley: The Pursuit* (first published London 1974, pbk edition 1987), pp. 232–4.

[29] *The Persean* (the magazine of the Perse School for Girls, Cambridge), 2 (autumn 1898), p. 216.

extensive opportunities for women. And those who made their careers
working within the new educational institutions were expected to
exhibit a rigid outward conformity to prevailing social norms of behaviour – their livelihoods might depend upon it. Paradoxically the price of
economic independence for teachers was likely to be an extended obei-
sance to traditional models of behaviour.

'Caring' roles were celebrated by proponents of the domestic ideology
as distinctively women's work. Some historians have seen them also as
providing crucial bridges into work in the public sphere.[30] Yet exploration of opportunities for women in medicine, nursing, government-
regulated social work and charitable work shows how long-drawn-out,
fraught and complex this process was, how powerful and durable
assumptions about social class remained, how seductive and enduring
the image of the Lady Bountiful proved, inhibiting the development of
professional social work yet at the same time enriching the associational
life of the society. There is more than a whiff of atavism about prime
minister David Cameron's vision of the 'Big Society'. The continuing
power of stereotypes of lady-like behaviour and the relatively small
numbers of women involved in these employments, whether as teachers
or as other sorts of carers, do not provide secure foundations on which to
build a narrative of change accomplished.

The other paid activity besides teaching in which a lady had been able
to engage at the beginning of the nineteenth century without losing caste
was writing and this too maintained its attraction. Chapter 4 looks at
the routes for women into creative work, in literature, in art and in the
theatre. It becomes immediately apparent that higher education was not
the way in to any of these means of earning a living. Actresses had a
desperate struggle both to survive economically and to assert their
status as 'ladies'. Aspiring writers found that the hard graft of journalism, a field rapidly expanding in the last third of the century, offered the
best opportunities. While it did help to have a cushion of private money
as one got going and fought for recognition, it was possible to make it
without; and there are some signs that by the end of the century women
writers were a larger and more socially diverse group than they had
been at the beginning. Social and professional expectations of the

---

[30] E.g., Simon Morgan, *A Victorian Woman's Place: Public Culture in the
Nineteenth Century* (London 2007).

growing tribe of women writers were also different from those of teachers and women in other caring roles; high visibility and metropolitan contacts were all-important. The translation of visibility into notoriety had its social costs; but it was a choice made by some. There are some women whose lives appeared to fuel the caricature, but hardly enough to suggest a major shift in social conventions and patterns of behaviour.

Where else then should we look in the search for change in the lives of middle-class women? Expanding employment opportunities for the daughters of the labour aristocracy and lower middle class – burgeoning white-collar work in offices both private and government, and, most important, elementary school teaching and then after 1902 the new maintained secondary schools – are not usually considered in discussing the New Woman. Yet numerically these women, in search of respectability rather than ladyhood, were, like the journalists, far more significant than the graduates, far more visible and often working in heterosocial environments, in ways that many graduate women in employment were not. Chapters 5 and 6 are a first attempt to pull together what is known about white-collar work for women and its growth up to 1914. So far these women have been neglected in the secondary literature, whether that of the women's movement in general or that of the campaigns for women's suffrage gathering pace after 1900. Yet women white-collar workers are present in the workforce in far greater numbers than women graduates and some of them can be found in campaigning groups. If we are looking for the beginnings of a real shift in women's lives and opportunities in England in this period, the most plausible candidates to experience this are to be found amongst white-collar workers.

At this stage too, it becomes important to separate out the Oxbridge students from the women who attended the burgeoning new universities and university colleges elsewhere in the UK. The secondary literature is still fragmentary; but the social backgrounds and work experiences of the latter were often closer to those of maintained school teachers, some clerks and some journalists than they were to those of the Oxbridge women. These distinctions in turn raise questions about the relations and interactions between ladies and women. Both these terms have been used in this chapter. However even now they are not straightforwardly interchangeable; and in the period under discussion, as will become clear, they had very different resonances.

At the beginning of the twenty-first century 'woman' is generally used as a generic, relatively neutral description. The term 'lady' is more likely to carry pejorative overtones. An obituary of the journalist Arline Usden, credited with the transformation of the weekly magazine *The Lady*, first published in 1885, quoted her description of its editorial content when she took over in 1991 as 'almost entirely made up of amateur features sent in on spec, and odds and ends by staff' – in other words dilettante and distinctly unprofessional.[31] In the nineteenth century, however, both terms, lady and woman, carried powerful and complex meanings, saying much about the standing of those they described in the social structure. Women were expected to work, had to do so; ladies did not have to work, indeed were in general not expected to do so, and were expected to look and behave very differently from women. The lady was essentially the creature whose role was celebrated by Ruskin in 1864 as one of 'sweet ordering, arrangement, and decision. She sees the qualities of things, their claims, and their places. Her great function is Praise: she enters into no contest, but infallibly adjudges the crown of contest. By her office and place, she is protected from all danger and temptation.'[32] The gulf between such a creature and the working woman was absolute – the latter's life might fairly have been described as one long contest for survival. It was a divide perceived to be greater than that between gentleman and man, for the male animal, whatever his status, was expected to engage with the world at large and for him work was not taboo. As Ruskin put it, 'in his rough work in open world [he] must encounter all peril and trial: – to him, therefore, the failure, the offence, the inevitable error; often he must be wounded, or subdued, often misled, and *always* hardened'.[33] Ruskin developed this contrast to present the female as the presiding deity of the home, the private sphere, making in the process a powerful and oft quoted statement of the domestic ideology already mentioned.[34]

The chapters which follow explore both the power and the resonances of the divide between ladies and women and the possibilities for

---

[31] *The Guardian*, 19 August 2013.

[32] John Ruskin, *Sesame and Lilies*, Lecture II, *Lilies: Of Queens' Gardens* (first delivered and published 1864, Everyman edition 1907), p. 59.

[33] *Ibid*. his emphasis.

[34] Above, p. 2, note 6. In *A Man's Place: Masculinity and the Middle-Class Home in Victorian England* (London 1999), John Tosh launched a discussion of the burdens these notions might represent for men.

narrowing and crossing it. Was the power of the ideal of the lady beginning to be diluted? Does the notion of respectability play a part in this process? Did ladyhood begin to give way to respectability? On the eve of the First World War does it begin to look as though achieving a respectable independence might prove more empowering than having to secure one's position as a lady? When do training, experience and demonstrable professional competence begin to count in defining women's social position? Such questions go to the heart of complex relations between class, status and gender. Chapter 7, 'Ladies and women', represents an attempt both to tease out the implications for such relations of the material in earlier chapters and to confront and explore them directly. If the search for actual changes in the position of women in this period is to advance fruitfully, they have to be faced. The net effect, however, is to suggest that the media outpouring of the 1890s reflected not a shift accomplished, but rather one beginning slowly and painfully to get under way.

In an ideal world this exploration would take in both sides of the Atlantic. Sarah Grand's article was after all published in the *North American Review* and an equally celebrated rebuttal of her arguments by Ouida followed in the same journal two months later, in May 1894.[35] Certainly traffic across the Atlantic was in full swing by this stage, involving not only Americans and British but also many European women. Its range and complexity were symbolised by the formation of the International Council of Women in 1888, which took the decision to hold an International Congress every five years.[36] Margaret McFadden has made an excellent job of charting the growth of 'a pre-organisational matrix (or network or web) made up of complex lines of international contact, association, friendship, argument and correspondence'. Yet such a chart seldom tells you precisely what passed between people or what they talked about. The existence of such networks is a precondition for influence but not evidence itself of influence. As McFadden herself puts it, 'I am constrained to assume that such contacts and relations were contributory rather than negligible or evanescent. It falls to future researchers

[35] Nelson, ed., *New Woman Reader*, pp. 153–60, reprints the article; the original was in the *North American Review* 158 (May 1894), pp. 610–19. For Ouida (Marie Louise de la Ramée), see also Nelson, ed., *New Woman Reader*, pp. 140–1 and Sutherland, *Companion to Victorian Fiction*.

[36] Margaret H. McFadden, *Golden Cables of Sympathy: The Transatlantic Sources of Nineteenth-Century Feminism* (Lexington, KY 1999), pp. 172, 176.

to refine or challenge such an assumption.'[37] Colouring in the chart, establishing who influenced whom, what passed and in which directions along these channels takes a great deal more work at the individual and group level, contingent as always on the survival of sources.

Sheila Rowbotham has made one such attempt in her study, *Dreamers of a New Day*, presenting women's thought and activism on a range of themes, through reformist to radical, to utopian, juxtaposing publications and campaigns in the UK and US, one against the other.[38] However, coincidences, similarities and congruities do not translate automatically or straightforwardly into patterns of causation or even correlation. As Rowbotham cautions, 'though a similar impulse for change appears both in Britain and in the United States, the contexts in which they operated differed markedly'. She sketches the different patterns of the economic and social development in the two societies, resulting in very different structures and organisations for change, and points to two further great differences: deep divisions between the two societies over the role of the state in change and the power of the fault line of race in the US, largely absent in the UK.[39] Her subsequent exposition of arguments and campaigns over a range of issues serves to underline these themes.

The existence of English-speaking audiences on both sides of the Atlantic brought the obvious gain of a larger market overall to writers and journalists; and awareness of other campaigns and campaigners could diminish the sense of any individual group that they were but voices crying in the wilderness. Charlotte Perkins Gilman's journal, *The Forerunner*, for example, was read in the UK as well as in the US; and she referred her readers to UK periodicals such as *The Englishwoman*.[40] However, to move from such shared awareness to issues of imitation, let alone influence, is to face tangled knots. It may be possible to unravel specific tangles in such knots, but only if the sources are plentiful. Moreover the central focus of this study is the investigation of economic autonomy and the freedom of choice it might bring. If women did not inherit money, how might they earn it? As will become clear, there were significant differences within the UK, between occupational structures and between areas. How much greater were the differences within the

---

[37] *Ibid.* pp. 171, 132.
[38] Sheila Rowbotham, *Dreamers of a New Day: Women who Invented the Twentieth Century* (London 2010).
[39] *Ibid.* pp. 5–12, direct quotation from p. 5.
[40] *Ibid.* p. 13; cf. Delap, *Feminist Avant-Garde*.

US, between East Coast and West, between New York, Chicago, San Francisco and Los Angeles, between these exploding cities and the sparsely populated farming areas of the Midwest, or of the Texas hill-country, or the depressed cotton-growing areas of the Old South. Any generalisations about the scope for economic autonomy and independence for American women must be even more open to question than those about the independence possible for British women. These are huge issues, deserving of at least another book or even several. The present study represents a first attempt to explore the issue for Britain.

2 'all that she sees before her . . . is teaching': formal schooling and its opportunities

From the beginning of the nineteenth century teaching had represented a well-trodden route to self-sufficiency for the daughters of those parents with pretensions to gentility but without the resources to secure them good marriages. It had been a route taken by the Byerley sisters, members of the Wedgwood family, in Warwickshire, by the Franklin sisters, whose school in Coventry was attended by the young Marian Evans (George Eliot), by Rebecca Martineau in Liverpool, by Anne Jemima Clough first in Liverpool then in Ambleside, by Elizabeth Sewell on the Isle of Wight. It provided the solution for 'Agnes Grey' and her widowed mother in Anne Brontë's 1847 novel of that name. It was what the Brontë sisters had planned to do at Haworth; it was how the Clergy Daughters' School at Casterton, the original of 'Lowood' in *Jane Eyre*, justified its existence. However, the rhetoric of 'separate spheres', which encompassed within it the view that a gentlewoman was best educated at home by her mother, still dominated; and these schools, with the exception of the Clergy Daughters', acknowledged the force of this rhetoric by stressing their small domestic nature, by implication the ephemeral nature of their existence, by presenting and marketing themselves as surrogate homes rather than professional enterprises. In 1868 the Schools Inquiry Commission reported that girls' schools were 'often spoken of as intended to be more a home than a school'.[1] Implicit in all this too was their relatively ephemeral nature.

---

[1] Quoted in Christina de Bellaigue, *Educating Women: Schooling and Identity in England and France 1800–1867* (Oxford 2007), p. 19; see also esp. pp. 43–56 and her 'The Development of Teaching as a Profession for Women before 1870', *The Historical Journal* 44 (2001), pp. 963–88; Gillian Sutherland, *Faith, Duty and the Power of Mind: The Cloughs and their Circle 1820–1960* (Cambridge 2006), pp. 30–6.

The inclusion of girls' schools besides boys' schools in the investigations of the Schools Inquiry Commission signalled the beginning of a shift in these attitudes and in the types of provision for girls. In her modest memorandum of evidence to the Commission, subsequently published in an expanded form in *Macmillan's Magazine* in 1866, Anne Jemima Clough tackled head-on this domestic model for the education of girls, asking what was wrong with a little competition between peers and arguing that larger, more institutional and structured provision would provide the resources to allow the employment of better-trained, specialist teachers.[2] Three examples already existed in the country: two day schools, Queen's College, Harley Street (1848) and the North London Collegiate School (1850), and one boarding school, Cheltenham Ladies' College (1854). More were to follow. The Endowed Schools Act of 1869 gave the Statutory Commission thereby created power to remodel endowments to make provision for girls as well as for boys. The Charity Commission, which succeeded the Statutory Commission, continued the work, albeit at a slower pace, and by 1903 sixty-one schools had been established, using these powers. In 1872 a Girls' Public Day School Company (GPDSC) was formed, which by 1880 had opened eleven proprietary schools in London and eleven elsewhere in other towns around the country.[3]

Not all of the GPDSC schools proved financially viable in the longer term and the domestic model took a long time to lose its resilience. In her family memoir *Daguerrotypes*, long in the writing and only published in 1929, Ada Radford recalled the anxious discussions that had taken place in her circle of family and friends in Plymouth in the late 1870s, as they awaited the opening of the new girls' high school. The Congregational minister was 'a very enlightened man', and 'having satisfied himself that each one of his daughters could make a bed, a pudding, and a shirt, he thought that the higher education would do them good rather than harm'. The elder Miss Clatworthy, however, worried about the size of the school. 'She doubted whether it would be possible to be educated in such a crowd and to retain the refinement of a gentlewoman.' On the other hand another friend 'thought that the tone

---

[2] Sutherland, *Faith, Duty and the Power of Mind*, pp. 73–7.

[3] Sheila Fletcher, *Feminists and Bureaucrats: A Study in the Development of Girls' Education in the Nineteenth Century* (Cambridge 1980), Appendix 3; Josephine Kamm, *Indicative Past: A Hundred Years of the Girls' Public Day School Trust* (London 1971), Appendix.

of a school depended more on *esprit de corps* than on the actual numbers and social position of those who attended it'. For Ada, the matter was settled by her father, a prosperous Plymouth draper, who was strongly in favour. Moreover he took the view, radical for the day, that girls could be taught the same subjects as boys; and to the new Plymouth High School Ada duly went.[4] When in 1881 Molly Hughes and her newly widowed mother concluded Molly should prepare to earn her own living rather than depend on the charity of her brothers, her aunt weighed in with the money for the fees at the North London Collegiate School.[5] Cumulatively such individual family decisions began to make an impact, bringing an upward trend in institutional provision for girls.

Gradually schools in which women who had to plan to support themselves could receive some formal schooling were proliferating. But who was to teach in these new institutions? How were the women staff to do better than stay a chapter of the textbook ahead of their charges? There was a chicken-and-egg problem here, clearly perceived by Anne Jemima Clough, who had coupled her challenge to the domestic model with a proposal for programmes of lectures for ladies, which contained the germ of the University Extension Movement.[6] The very first attempt to provide a truly higher, as distinct from secondary, education for women had been Elizabeth Jesser Reid's Bedford College in 1849. This, however, had nearly foundered because the women who came were so ill prepared. In the end the enterprise was split, to create a school and a college;[7] and this proved to be the right model for the future. Institutions of higher education for women developed in symbiosis with secondary schools for girls, each feeding off the other. They were founded at the same time and expanded at roughly the same pace. Girton College opened its doors at Hitchin in 1869 and moved to Cambridge in 1873. Newnham College began as a house for five students in Cambridge, presided over by Anne Jemima Clough, in 1871. The first two women's colleges in Oxford, Somerville and Lady Margaret Hall, began admitting students in 1879. Three more institutions would join them in the next two decades. Westfield and Royal

---

[4] Ada Wallas, *Daguerrotypes* (London 1929), pp. 115–18.
[5] M. V. Hughes, *A London Girl of the 1880s* (Oxford 1946; part of the trilogy *A London Family 1870–1900*, pbk edition 1978), pp. 6–9.
[6] Sutherland, *Faith, Duty and the Power of Mind*, pp. 77–80.
[7] Margaret Tuke, *A History of Bedford College for Women 1849–1937* (London 1938), chs. II–IV.

Holloway joined Bedford College in the 1880s while both University College London and King's College London took steps to admit women. The new university colleges developing around the country and initially taking London External degrees admitted women from the first, and the Scottish universities followed suit in the 1870s. In 1900–1 there were just under 600 women students at the Oxbridge colleges and not quite 3,000 elsewhere in England, Wales and Scotland.[8] These initiatives and the proliferation of formal secondary schools for girls coincided exactly.

By the end of the nineteenth century, therefore, there were institutions for the formal secondary and higher education of women. The daughters of gentlemen and those parents aspiring to gentility could receive extended formal schooling and, if the resources could be mustered, a higher education as well. Did these changes in provision widen employment opportunities for women more generally, or did they simply change the nature and number of teaching posts? Did the situation remain a closed and narrowly virtuous circle? An initial investigation indicates the latter.

Before such an investigation can proceed further, however, an important caveat needs to be entered, about the ways in which we might generalise about women graduates. They cannot easily be treated as a single whole. We need to distinguish between the minority, the Oxbridge women, the 600 of 1900, and the majority, the 2,749 attending other institutions of higher education. Their social backgrounds and experiences might overlap but could also be markedly different. We need also to remember that these two elite groups were very tiny indeed. Although behind the approximately three and a half thousand women students in 1900–1 there were the gradually growing ranks of those who had attended these institutions in earlier years, such figures must be

---

[8] Gillian Sutherland, 'Education', in F. M. L. Thompson, ed., *The Cambridge Social History of Britain 1750–1950* (3 vols. Cambridge 1990), vol. III, pp. 119–70, at pp. 154–8. For more detail, Gillian Sutherland, '"The Plainest Principles of Justice": The University of London and the Higher Education of Women', in F. M. L. Thompson, ed., *The University of London and the World of Learning 1836–1986* (London 1990), pp. 35–56, at pp. 39, 40; Tuke, *Bedford College*; Janet Sondheimer, *Castle Adamant in Hampstead: A History of Westfield College: 1882–1982* (London 1983); Rita McWilliams Tullberg, *Women at Cambridge* (2nd edition Cambridge 1998). For university colleges elsewhere in the country, see Carol Dyhouse, *No Distinction of Sex? Women in British Universities 1870–1939* (London 1995).

set against a total UK population in 1901 of just over thirty-eight million, roughly half of whom were female.[9]

To complicate the picture further, we know at present more about the minority, the Oxbridge women, than we do about the majority, women graduates elsewhere in England and Wales and in Scotland. In part the extent of this knowledge is an artefact of the sources. Before 1914 both Oxford and Cambridge refused to admit women to degrees; the individual colleges had therefore to act as institutions of record for their students and the product has been biographical registers of exceptional quality, facilitating prosopographical analysis. In part also this minority group deserve attention because they attracted so much attention from their contemporaries. The society as a whole regarded Oxford and Cambridge as the elite institutions in the developing structures of all higher education; thus the efforts of women to join this elite were especially newsworthy, a symbolic challenge. As we have already seen, the 'Girton Girl' was firmly part of the New Woman caricature.[10] The social backgrounds and subsequent experiences of the Oxbridge women are therefore intrinsically deserving of some detailed study; but in engaging in this and seeing how far it might support the stereotypes and caricatures, it is important not to forget the larger group of women graduates elsewhere, in the wings, as it were. Much more work needs to be – and could be – done on them. What has been done so far suggests first that their social backgrounds differed, more lower middle class than middle class, and second that far more of them went into employment. The articulation of the stereotypes and caricatures must have afforded irritation and ironic entertainment in almost equal measure. We shall return to them and their importance below.[11]

The experience of the 959 women who went to Oxford between 1881 and 1913 has been well surveyed by Janet Howarth and Mark Curthoys in two chapters in the magisterial volumes of *The History of The University of Oxford*.[12] To match this I have used the

[9] For details, see B. R. Mitchell and H. G. Jones, *Second Abstract of British Historical Statistics* (Cambridge 1971).

[10] Above, pp. 4–5.   [11] Below, chapter 6, esp. pp. 121–8.

[12] Janet Howarth, '"In Oxford but ... not of Oxford": The Women's Colleges', ch. 10, pp. 237–310, and Janet Howarth and M. C. Curthoys, 'Origins and Destinations: The Social Mobility of Oxford Men and Women', ch. 14, pp. 571–95, both in M. G. Brock and M. C. Curthoys, eds., *The History of the University of Oxford*, vol. VII, *Nineteenth-Century Oxford, Part 2* (Oxford 2000).

exceptional biographical *Registers* of Girton and Newnham to compile a database of the lives and work of the women attending these two Cambridge colleges, recording the details of every student entering in every fifth year – 1869, 1874, 1879 etc. down to the students entering in 1914. This produces a total sample of 782 women; and Tables 2.1 and 2.2, show what if anything they went on to do.[13] Over three-quarters (617) were recorded as engaging in work of some kind after college. Some of this was unpaid voluntary work; the two colleges' records, exceptional though they are, do not make it easy to separate out paid and unpaid charitable work. Of those recorded as working, however, over 70% (443) worked at some stage as teachers of one kind or another, a handful in the newly emerging institutions of higher education for women but the majority in schools, mostly secondary. Although in the analysis permitted by the database there can be multiple counting – some people did several things – other occupations barely feature. The post-1900 generations plainly made their contributions to the war effort, yet in only a minority of cases does it look as if this experience may have had consequences for their post-war trajectories.[14]

The experience of the Oxford women was similar. Teaching dominated, not as strongly as in the Cambridge profile; but the standard question at student cocoa parties at the turn of the century was said to be, 'Are you going to teach when you go down, or be a Home Sunbeam?'[15] Nor does it seem to have been that different elsewhere. Thomas Holloway had expressed the wish that his magnificent red brick college at Egham, modelled on the chateau of Chambord, 'shall neither be considered nor conducted as a mere training college for teachers and governesses'; nevertheless teaching was the occupation followed by a high proportion of Royal Holloway graduates to 1914 and beyond. Westfield College was exceptional in producing a sizeable number of missionaries – as its founder had hoped; but again the largest single group amongst those of its early students who subsequently

---

[13] The *Girton Register* is exceptionally full and consistent from the beginning; the *Newnham Register* is patchier for the first two decades but then begins to catch up. I am indebted to Rosalind Crone for generous help in constructing and analysing this database.

[14] See below, p. 44 for a fuller discussion.

[15] Howarth, 'In Oxford but … not of Oxford', p. 297, Table 10.2, p. 293.

Table 2.1 *Girton College: occupations of former students 1869–1914*

Year mat.	Total students	Total occupations recorded	Teacher	Academic	Writer	Artist	Vol. work	Relig. profession	War work	Medicine	Civil service	Industry	Other
1869	7	7	3	0	1	1	2	0	0	0	0	0	0
1874	6	4	3	1	0	0	0	0	0	0	0	0	0
1879	25	19	15	3	0	0	1	0	0	0	0	0	0
1884	25	17	12	0	2	0	3	0	0	0	0	0	0
1889	33	27	15	4	2	0	2	0	1	1	1	0	1
1894	31	24	15	2	0	0	5	0	2	0	0	0	0
1899	41	34	22	0	0	0	5	1	3	1	0	0	2
1904	42	30	19	2	0	0	6	1	1	0	0	0	1
1909	49	38	21	2	1	0	3	0	3	1	2	0	5
1914	56	44	23	0	0	0	2	1	11	3	0	0	4
TOTAL	315	244	148	14	6	1	29	3	21	6	3	0	13

Table 2.2 *Newnham College: occupations of former students 1869–1914*

Year mat.	Total students	Total occupations recorded	Teacher	Academic	Writer	Artist	Vol. work	Relig. profession	War work	Medicine	Civil service	Industry	Other
1869	n/a												
1874	13	11	7	2	4	0	2	0	1	0	0	0	1
1879	46	38	29	1	2	0	2	1	0	1	0	0	1
1884	45	36	25	4	0	0	5	0	0	0	0	0	2
1889	54	35	27	1	0	0	4	0	2	0	1	0	3
1894	65	50	39	3	1	1	4	3	1	1	0	0	0
1899	51	39	27	3	0	0	3	1	1	0	1	0	4
1904	51	44	33	0	2	0	7	0	0	0	1	0	1
1909	61	52	30	7	0	0	3	0	10	0	0	0	2
1914	81	68	37	6	5	0	14	3	11	4	7	3	13
TOTAL	467	373	254	27	14	1	44	8	26	6	10	3	27

sought employment did so as teachers.[16] As Clara Collet, the labour investigator, summed it up: 'all that she sees before her, unless she has exceptional talent, is teaching'.[17] Mrs J. E. H. Gordon, writing in the periodical *Nineteenth Century* in 1895, agreed: 'The careful study of the reports published by the women's universities will, I think, incline parents to question if a university training has yet succeeded in opening the doors of any other profession.'[18]

Against such a background Ada Radford's year teaching at Wimbledon High School 1883–4 and two years acting as (honorary) Lady Superintendent of the College for Men and Women in Queen Square in Bloomsbury 1893–5 begin to look typical. Can the same be said of her occasional contributions to the *Westminster Gazette* and the *Yellow Book*?[19] These, however, have a dilettantish flavour, as do her later books, the children's stories in *The Land of Play* (1906), the historical essays *Before the Bluestockings* and the family memoir *Daguerrotypes* (both 1929). They are not the work of someone who has to earn her living by her pen; and the very small numbers of authors and journalists emerging from the Oxbridge women – thirty from Oxford, twenty from Cambridge – make it plain that a higher education was not the obvious route to success in writing or journalism; that lay elsewhere, as we shall see. Ada could write what she chose, when she chose, because she had a modest private income from a family inheritance. This made all sorts of choices possible: to quit school teaching, which she did not enjoy, and to leave the College for Men and Women after she had failed to convince their Council that, in order to be more than 'a pleasant club', they should charge a modest fee and pay their teachers.[20] She could act unpaid as assistant editor of *Free Russia*,

---

[16] Caroline Bingham, *The History of Royal Holloway College 1886–1986* (London 1987), pp. 54, 78; Sondheimer, *Castle Adamant*, pp. 67–8.

[17] Clara Collet, *Essays on the Economic Position of Women Workers in the Middle Classes* (London 1902), p. 13; this first essay reprints an address on 'The Economic Position of Educated Working Women' which she gave at the South Place Ethical Society in 1890.

[18] Mrs J. E. H. Gordon, 'The After-Careers of University-Educated Women', *Nineteenth Century* 37 (June 1895), pp. 955–60, at p. 959.

[19] Her 1896 *Yellow Book* short story, 'Lot 99', has been reprinted in Nelson, ed., *New Woman Reader*, pp. 91–100.

[20] NCA, *Wallas Papers*, 2/4/1 Ada Radford to George Radford 27 July 1893, 17 April 1895 (the phrase quoted comes from the latter) and 22 November 1895; for the Men and Women's College, see June Purvis, *Hard Lessons: The Lives and*

which always existed on a shoe-string.[21] It also inverted a more usual situation in making it possible for Graham Wallas to marry her. After their marriage Graham confessed that having himself chosen a course which would not make him rich (political activism while teaching at a series of boys' preparatory schools of greater and lesser degrees of respectability) he had given up all thought of marriage and children. When Ada asked him 'whether he would in fact have proposed to her if she had not possessed a moderate unearned income of her own, he answered very simply: "I should have tried not to."'[22]

What did those without the freedom to choose do? For Ada's friend Constance Black, there was never any question but that she would have to earn her living after completing her Cambridge course. She began as a governess in the household of a London cement manufacturer, Robert White; gradually she added other pupils, including the children of the social scientist Charles Booth. It was not work she enjoyed and, recognising this, in 1887 Booth recommended her for the newly created post of Librarian at the People's Palace in Mile End Road. This she enjoyed much more. She gave the post up however in 1889, ostensibly on marriage to Edward Garnett but probably because she was already pregnant. Subsequently the Garnetts found it hard to make ends meet on Edward's salary as a publisher's reader alone. In the early 1890s Constance began the work of Russian translation by which she is best known; but the rewards from this were small and sporadic. Although Edward was angry, she was not too proud to accept a Civil List pension of £70 a year from 1910, after a group of her friends, organised by Ada Radford's brother Ernest, had successfully petitioned the prime minister.[23]

What else was on offer to those women who did not have choice, who were not cushioned by modest private means, who did not have the good fortune to encounter a perceptive patron, who did not or did not choose to marry? What salaries could they expect, what kind of life as they embarked on teaching in the new girls' high schools mushrooming across the country? The salaries were never princely. Without any sort

Education of Working Class Women in Nineteenth Century England (Cambridge 1989), pp. 173, 183–95.

[21] NCA, *Wallas Papers*, 2/7/6 F. Volkhovsky to Ada Radford 21 October 1893; *Diary of Olive Garnett 1893–5*, ed. Johnson, pp. 2–4, 25–6.

[22] NCA, *Wallas Papers*, 4/3/2 May Wallas draft, p. 210.

[23] Richard Garnett, *Constance Garnett: A Heroic Life* (London 1991), pp. 36, 47, 55–6, 64–6, 72, 247–50.

of higher education, one started at the bottom: Clara Collet began teaching at Wyggeston Girls' Grammar School in Leicester in 1878, aged 18, straight out of North London Collegiate School (but hand-picked for the post by Miss Buss), on £80 per annum.[24] Only gradually, as the equally newly mushrooming institutions providing some higher education for women began to send forth their students, was it possible to employ teachers who were more than a jump ahead of their pupils. The new Girls' Public Day School Company (GPDSC) school in Brighton, opening in 1876, was exceptionally fortunate in being able to appoint as its first headmistress Edith Creak, just short of her twenty-first birthday and the child prodigy among the first five students of Newnham College, Cambridge.[25]

More typical was the pattern of working one's way up, securing a variety of experiences, exhibited elsewhere. Kate Harding Street, the first Headmistress of the Perse School for Girls in Cambridge, which opened its doors in 1881, had begun as a student teacher aged 16 at a private school in London. Next she moved to a residential full-time post at the Clergy Daughters' School at Casterton in Westmorland. There she met and befriended Hannah Osborn, who encouraged her ambition; and pooling their savings they moved to London, living 'in an attic', while Kate attended university lectures and studied hard. Both then secured posts at the Grey Coat School in Westminster, from which Kate was recruited to the Cambridge post.[26] In similar fashion Mary Hannah Page, appointed in 1890 as the first Headmistress of the Skinners' Company School for Girls on Stamford Hill in London, had begun by helping out in the school run by her father, a missionary in India. From there, at 19 she came to a post in a private school in Plymouth; but she too saw the case for some higher education and in 1879 managed to afford a year at Newnham College, Cambridge. This was enough to secure her an assistant's post at the GPDSC school in Nottingham; from which she was speedily promoted in 1883 to a headship at the GPDSC school in Clapham.[27]

---

[24] Jane Miller, *Seductions: Studies in Reading and Culture* (London 1990), p. 83.

[25] Garnett, *Constance Garnett*, pp. 26–9.

[26] M. A. Scott, *The Perse School for Girls: The First Hundred Years 1881–1981* (Cambridge 1981), p. 7.

[27] Obituary of M. H. Page in *Our Chronicle* (*OC*) [the magazine of the Skinners' Company School for Girls] October 1900.

Clara Collet used a route like this as a way out of teaching. While she was teaching at Wyggeston in Leicester she had worked hard to secure an external London B.A. and scrimped and saved enough to keep herself in London during the years from 1885 to 1887, while she worked for an M.A. in Political Economy at UCL. For the next four years she worked for that perceptive patron of educated middle-class women, Charles Booth, on his survey of London life and labour. Then in 1891 she secured appointment as one of the four Women Assistant Commissioners gathering data for the Royal Commission on Labour and the next year became Labour Correspondent of the Board of Trade, where she continued to work until her retirement.[28]

By the 1890s the GPDSC, the governors of the newly formed endowed schools and the governors of the handful of big boarding schools, were beginning to pride themselves on employing graduates only; and a decade later they were beginning to look for a year's professional training as well.[29] At the beginning of the 1890s Collet reckoned that Girton and Newnham students with good degrees could hope for initial salaries between £105 and £120 per annum, slowly rising by degrees to £140–150 p.a. Posts in these schools, whether as heads or assistants, did not offer security of tenure or pensions; and in the mid 1890s Collet also calculated that it was not possible for the woman teacher to save for her old age on a salary of less than £120 p.a.[30] Promotion to a headship could bring more; in 1900 the Governors of the Skinners' Company School for Girls determined to offer their second head, Emily Newton, Mary Hannah Page's successor, a basic salary of £120 p.a. plus substantial capitation fees, linking financial reward to recruitment. Seventy-three candidates applied for the post.[31] By 1912 the Association of Assistant Mistresses (AAM), founded in 1884, was recommending a salary scale for assistant mistresses which started at £120 p.a., rising over ten years to £220 or to

---

[28] Miller, *Seductions*, pp. 74–5, 82–3, 88, 90–2. It is a matter of regret that up to the time of writing it has not so far been possible to access the papers of Clara Collet and her family, now on deposit at The Women's Library but awaiting cataloguing.

[29] Lis Whitelaw, *The Life & Rebellious Times of Cicely Hamilton* (London 1990), pp. 18–19; Morley, ed., *Women Workers*, pp. 28, 31.

[30] Collet, *Economic Position of Women Workers*, pp. 59–60.

[31] Metropolitan Archives (henceforward MA) 30741, Skinners' Company Schools Committee Minutes Books (in effect the minutes of the Girls' School Governing Body by this stage), vol. 2, minutes of 11 October and 13 November 1900.

£250 where special responsibilities were carried. The Headmistresses' Association, founded 1874, recommended a minimum salary of £300 for heads; but in reality there was huge variation, some getting as little as £200 and one, at the other extreme, said to be being paid £1,500. Overall, the range of salaries for heads was comparable with the range being paid to the tiny number of women teaching at university level.[32]

The GPDSC, however, was notorious for underpaying its staff[33] – and getting away with it – in what was, to begin with, a wholly unregulated market. The two professional associations had few bargaining counters and were slow to recruit. Collet estimated there to be some 1,500 assistant mistresses in the mid 1890s; but by 1900 the AAM still had only 623 members.[34] The Association's hand was strengthened by the creation of maintained secondary schools under the 1902 Education Act and the AAM hastened to offer membership to women secondary school teachers in local authority employment. Already by 1912, the London County Council, the pace-setter among local education authorities, was offering assistant mistresses starting salaries of £120, rising to £220/250, and women heads starting salaries of £300, rising to £450/600.[35] However, the full impact of the arrival of local authorities as competing employers would be felt only after the First World War and the creation of national machinery, the Burnham committees, for pay negotiations. In 1921 for the first time over half the women teaching in secondary schools would be AAM members.[36]

The GPDSC, in 1906 becoming the Girls' Public Day School Trust (GPDST), also stood out as controlling its early heads very tightly indeed – even the house history writes of 'rigid control'.[37] They moved them around the country at will, could and did intervene to dismiss staff, controlled admissions and expulsions, had to authorise textbooks and every single book purchased for the school library. Heads had to account for every penny spent in the school. One wonders whether among the reasons for moving from the employ of the GPDSC/T to that of the Skinners' Company in 1890 was Mary Hannah Page's

---

[32] Morley, ed., *Women Workers*, pp. 17–19, 32.

[33] Kamm, *Indicative Past*, pp. 84–6; Morley, ed., *Women Workers*, pp. 32, 104–6.

[34] Collet, *Economic Position of Women Workers*, p. 57; Alison Oram, *Women Teachers and Feminist Politics 1900–39* (Manchester 1996), pp. 101, 105–6.

[35] Morley, ed., *Women Workers*, p. 32; on the impact of the 1902 Act see also below, Chapter 6.

[36] Oram, *Women Teachers*, p. 105.   [37] Kamm, *Indicative Past*, p. 63 *et seq.*

wish for a little more autonomy and scope, as well as stability. She too had to submit detailed accounts and communicated with her governors by letter, rather than being in attendance at governors' meetings. But more generally she seems to have been allowed to exercise her discretion. She was well aware that she was shaping an institution from scratch; and early in 1891 she was At Home after school to senior staff and senior girls to take tea, share suggestions and consider how to do this: should they have a school magazine, should they have prefects, should they choose special charities to support? It was a cooperative, consensual way of working which was well ahead of its time. By the spring of 1893 her Governors were sufficiently confident about the enterprise she was shaping and leading to grant her leave of absence for three months to use a Gilchrist Scholarship to travel in the United States and observe educational methods there.[38]

At the Perse School for Girls in Cambridge, Kate Harding Street subscribed herself 'Your obedient servant' in her reports to her managers, but as the school historian, herself the head almost a century later, observed, 'she usually seemed to ensure that the instructions their servant received were those she wished to receive'; and control of staff was firmly in her hands.[39] Working relationships between heads and governors depended hugely on the personalities – and could go horribly wrong. Mrs Withiel, the second mistress at Notting Hill GPDSC/T school, had hoped to be appointed to the headship in 1900, but was not, and was not offered anything anywhere else, so resigned, only to be appointed as one of the first women among His Majesty's Inspectors of Schools in the wake of the 1902 Education Act. The GPDSC/T did its best to persuade the Board of Education to withdraw the nomination – but failed; although the Board had the tact not to send Mrs Withiel to inspect her old school.[40] In individual, free-standing schools it was probably easier for a sense of shared enterprise and trust to develop, and for a well-established head to be given considerable scope and discretion, than it proved to be in the highly centralised GPDSC/T.

For those teachers and heads who served their apprenticeships, buckled down and learned to negotiate the domestic politics of their management committees and governing bodies, the work could bring

---

[38] OC, July 1891, June 1893; MA 30715, Skinners' Company Schools Committee Minutes Books, vol. 1, 8 May 1890–14 March 1895.
[39] Scott, *Perse School for Girls*, p. 8.   [40] Kamm, *Indicative Past*, p. 100.

some rewards. Financially heads at least were likely to be comfortable,
if not rich. In constructing budgets for middle-class working women,
Clara Collet regarded it as essential for teachers to be able to afford
proper holidays – and in these she included foreign travel – although
she reckoned they would need to spend less on clothes than women
with office jobs.[41] Within their local communities they had some
standing: at the Perse School for Girls Kate Harding Street was invariably known to her pupils, little boys in the prep school as well as all
the girls, as 'Madam' – and no doubt known likewise to their parents,
who included a sizeable sprinkling of distinguished academics, the
Keynes family among them.[42] The post-retirement work of many of
the heads and teachers in voluntary organisations and local government is a further, more general testimony to this. However, the con-
comitant of social standing was the expectation that women
secondary school teachers and heads would conduct themselves as
'ladies' in school and out, in deportment, dress (even if dowdy) and
associations.

The vastness of London – and having the LCC as employer – could
offer some opportunities for anonymity and escape from social censure.
An Oxford (St Hugh's) old student Margaret Tew reported to her
college's *Club Paper* in 1912, that

For the last three years I have been very busy discovering the inexhaustible
delights of London life. These seem to range from the supreme joy of a flat of
one's own, to the surprise of meeting St Hugh's friends in the most unexpected
places. I have not yet got used to sitting down in a bus next to someone I last
saw seven years ago, or to 'lining-up' in a Suffrage procession with one of my
own year. Another joy of London seems to be that of finding oneself doing the
most unnatural things in the most natural way, such as spending the night on
a friend's drawing-room floor in order to 'resist the Census', or crowded into a
very sturdy gallery at the Old Bailey. In the summer holidays I went for a
bicycling tour in Normandy, and had the most glorious time ... Incidentally I
teach history at Graham Street High School, manage the games and edit the
magazine.[43]

[41] Collet, *Economic Position of Women Workers*, pp. 78–9.
[42] Scott, *Perse School for Girls*, pp. 7, 54.
[43] *St Hugh's Club Paper* No. 20, August 1912, and quoted in Laura Schwartz, *A Serious Endeavour: Gender, Education and Community at St Hugh's 1886–2011* (Oxford 2011), p. 41. Miss Tew's lively contributions – No. 14, August 1906, No. 17, August 1909 and No. 18, August 1910 – stand out.

The responses of other St Hugh's old students to the regular invitation to supply 'postcards' or bulletins on their doings suggest that for many a teaching post in the London area was a long-term goal. Margaret Tew had moved from a first post in Swansea. In August 1909 Zoe Eppstein, whose first post had been in Salisbury, commented, 'like so many other sensible members of the Hall, I have made my way to London ... It is very delightful being at the heart of everything.' And Hilda Fear, reporting her move from a post in East Grinstead to the Grey Coat Hospital in Westminster, continued, 'My play is "compact of many sweets" – concerts, picture galleries, suffragist riots, aimless wanderings.' Others joined her and Margaret Tew in suffrage activities.[44] Even so, it is difficult to imagine some of these activities escaping gossip, criticism and possible censure if engaged in by GPDSC/T staff in London; and criticism and censure were very likely in the provincial towns and cities where many of the women graduates had to seek their first teaching posts and where some of them stuck.

There was also a firm expectation that women secondary heads and teachers would resign their posts on marriage. The correlation between such an expectation and the outcome is clear enough: relatively few of all early Oxbridge women students married. Just over 30% of the early women students at Oxford married, although the proportion was beginning to rise in the early twentieth century.[45] The pattern in Cambridge was not dissimilar: 32% of the students coming up to Newnham in the years up to 1914 would marry; for Girtonians, the proportion was higher, at 39%, although there are fewer signs of a rise in the early twentieth century. Causal connections, however, are much less clear: were women graduates prevented from marrying because of the career paths they had chosen or did they choose not to marry? Did some of them agree with the American writer Louisa May Alcott that 'liberty is a better husband than love to many of us'?[46] In 1889 the *Englishwoman's Review* asserted, 'whatever may be said by narrow-minded biologists, who apparently cannot regard a woman except as a

---

[44] Direct quotations from *St Hugh's Club Paper* No. 17, August 1909; see also No. 18, August 1910. Biographical details from the *St Hugh's College Register 1886–1959* (published for the college, Oxford 2011).

[45] Howarth, 'In Oxford ... but not of Oxford', p. 295; Howarth and Curthoys, 'Origins and Destinations', p. 594.

[46] Alcott quoted as epigraph by Lee Virginia Chambers Schiller, *Liberty a Better Husband: Single Women in America: the Generations of 1780–1840* (New Haven and London 1984).

female animal, we maintain that facts reveal to us the existence of a certain number of women who, in their own estimation at least, are happier and better as spinsters than wives'.[47]

Did women with higher education intimidate or repel potential marriage partners, as late nineteenth-century cartoonists claimed?[48] Mrs Gordon in the *Nineteenth Century* worried that university education might incline women 'to look upon married life as a rather dull and unintellectual career' and considered a university training ill-adapted for developing the prosaic virtues needed in marriage, 'careful housekeeping, motherhood and thrift'.[49] Or did these women seek training and qualification *because* they and their families knew they were unlikely to marry and would need to support themselves? Already from the beginning of the century this latter pattern had been a familiar one;[50] and as the century wore on, it became more pronounced. This was the era of the 'surplus woman', when women outnumbered men, and Howarth and Curthoys have written of 'a crisis of nuptiality [which] was of particular concern to professional and business families who relied on earned or precarious income' – the very group prominent among the parents of these early women students.[51] Extended education and training for their daughters was the best they could do if they could not supply the capital for a marriage settlement. All of these factors might come into play, the relative weight of each varying from one family situation to another.

Even so, the conventional wisdom was plain: ladies *either* married *or* pursued paid employment. A tiny 3% of the Oxford women students remained in paid employment after marriage;[52] proportions in the Cambridge sample were similar. Eight Girtonians (3%) and fourteen Newnhamites (almost 4%) remained in, took or returned to paid employment after marriage. One of these was an academic, one an artist and craftswoman and three became doctors, a distinctive group in various respects; all of these are more fully discussed below.[53] Two of

---

[47] Quoted in Susan Kingsley Kent, *Sex and Suffrage in Britain 1860–1914* (Princeton, NJ 1987), p. 83.

[48] Howarth, 'In Oxford … but not of Oxford', pp. 253–5.

[49] Gordon, 'After-Careers', p. 960.

[50] Bellaigue, *Educating Women*, pp. 48–50.

[51] Howarth and Curthoys, 'Origins and Destinations', p. 581.   [52] *Ibid.* p. 594

[53] For Constance Herschel, the academic (GC 1874), see p. 37; for Leila Legg, the artist (NC 1894), see p. 59; for the doctors Nolini Bonnerjee (GC 1889), Norah Lenwood (NC 1894) and Marian Mayfield (GC1899) see below, pp. 45–8.

the women appear to have come to Newnham as widows, that is, they entered the college under their married names. Elizabeth Farman came in 1889, at the age of 42, remained until 1892, although not taking any Tripos-level examinations, and thereafter was employed first as a typist and subsequently as a teacher of typing. Ellen Elizabeth Travers arrived in 1904, aged 41; again, she took no Tripos-level examinations, departing after four terms. In her case there seem to have been some additional resources; for the post she then took at a college of physical education is described as honorary. In 1909 she married again and in the immediate post-war period was describing herself as a farmer, whether with or without her second husband. Three more, Jessie Deed (GC 1894), Lucy Blakiston and Barbara Carpenter (NC 1909) returned to teaching in widowhood; while Olga Ericson (NC 1909), having fled Russia following the Revolution and then divorced her husband, supported herself in Paris as a technical translator and language teacher.

Three, Lucy Bartlett (GC 1894), Kathleen Coates (GC 1909) and Agnes Ward (NC 1909) wrote and published extensively. None of the three appears to have depended for her livelihood on her writing, although the timing suggests that Kathleen Coates may have been supplementing a pension. These three apart, it is only at the very end of the period that there are the first pointers to patterns which would become much more pronounced in the third and fourth quarters of the twentieth century. Two worked with their husbands: Edith Rowntree (NC 1889) and her husband headed a residential institution; after a break from teaching following her marriage, Fanny Moore (NC 1894) took up a technical post in her husband's firm in 1916 – war work initially perhaps, but she remained working there until 1944. Four, Phyllis Jewson and Dorothy Revell (NC 1909), Annie Fraser (NC 1914) and Dorothy Edwards (GC 1914) took breaks from teaching following marriage and then returned to paid work, although both Revell and Edwards took the opportunity to reshape their careers in the direction of child guidance and counselling, profiting from the fact that their families were not dependent on their earnings.[54] Only two women out of the twenty-two thrown up by the sample worked on after

---

[54] On the rise of child guidance as a specialism, see Deborah Thom, 'Wishes, Anxieties, Play and Gestures: Child Guidance in Inter-war England', in Roger Cooter, ed., *In the Name of the Child: Health and Welfare 1880–1940* (London 1992).

marriage with no obvious break or change of direction. Phyllis
Hammond (NC 1909) continued to teach; while A. C. Stuart Palmer
(GC 1914) worked steadily through as a member of the technical staff
of first the Ministry of Munitions, then the Imperial Institute and subsequently the Imperial Mineral Resources Bureau. In 1931 she became
a teacher at St Felix, Southwold and from 1942 a war-time civil servant.
Altogether this handful, twenty-two women, seems to represent exceptions proving the general rule: ladies either worked for money or
married.

Institutions of higher education for women could also constitute
employment opportunities. For those who thrived on this particular
educational track, there was the possibility of teaching not only in the
new high schools but also in universities. Ada and Graham Wallas's
only daughter, May, would read Modern Languages at Newnham
1917–20, take her doctorate in the University of London in 1926 and
go on to teach in the Universities of London and Cambridge. Her
cousin, Helen Wodehouse, would read Mathematics and Moral
Sciences at Girton 1898–1902, take a doctorate in Birmingham in
1906, teach there and at Bristol, and return to Girton as Mistress in
1931.

Was there then any more flexibility in attitudes towards and the
treatment of marriage among the small minority of women who did
well enough in their academic studies to go on to university teaching? In
the Cambridge sample, university teachers numbered just over 6% of
the total number who went on to any sort of employment and 9% of
those who taught.[55] However the answer to the question about marriage has to be a somewhat qualified 'no'. Outside Oxbridge the expectations of resignation on marriage were as powerful as those brought to
bear on heads and secondary teachers. The services of women lecturers
were usually dispensed with following their marriages; although the
only university which sought to impose a formal marriage bar, in the
1930s, was Liverpool.[56]

In Oxbridge a little greater flexibility was provided by the importance
of small-group teaching, tutorials and supervisions, within the whole
package of teaching provision. Such teaching could be part-time and

[55] For the raw data behind this, see above pp. 24–5, Tables 2.1 and 2.2.
[56] Dyhouse, *No Distinction of Sex?*, pp. 161–9, 243–4; cf. Edith Morley's
impassioned plea against the practice, *Women Workers*, pp. 23–4.

was paid at piece-rates. This could allow the married woman who chose so to do to eschew a formal post and full-time work but at least keep her hand in and earn some pin money. Mary Paley, the economist (NC 1871), married Alfred Marshall in 1877, having resigned her Newnham Lectureship. In search of a stipend for him they went off to run the fledgling university college at Bristol. There Mary managed to insert herself into some of the lecturing and became tutor to the women students. In 1883 Alfred was appointed to a post in Oxford and Mary gave lectures and tutorials to the women students there. When in 1885 Alfred was elected to the Chair of Political Economy and they returned to Cambridge, Mary promptly resumed supervising and lecturing for Newnham and Girton.[57] A similar pattern marked the life and work of Margaret Merrifield, Newnham Lecturer in Classics 1880, who married Arthur Verrall, Fellow of Trinity, in 1882; she resigned her College Lectureship but continued to supervise. Constance Herschel, Lecturer in Natural Sciences and Mathematics at Girton, unusually, continued in this post for six years after her marriage to Sir Nevile Lubbock, relinquishing it only after his work took them to the West Indies.

An even larger exception – but perhaps again one proving the rule – was the career of Eleanor Balfour, married in 1876 to the Cambridge philosopher Henry Sidgwick. Nora Sidgwick, as she was always known, became Treasurer of Newnham in 1878, Vice-Principal 1880–82, during which time she and Henry lived in college, and Principal 1892–1911, remaining Treasurer until 1920. From 1894 until Henry's death in 1900 they lived in college once more. However, married to one of the founders of the college, herself one of the college's major benefactors, niece of Lord Salisbury, and elder sister of a future prime minister (Arthur Balfour), Nora, with Henry, was sufficiently secure financially and socially to make her own rules. Even so, the Sidgwicks had taken care to consult the rest of the Newnham Council in May 1880 about the propriety of the proposed residential arrangements.[58]

More common still was the pattern after marriage of turning one's hand to occasional writing and energetic voluntary work, sometimes on behalf of the institution where one had been employed. This was the

---

[57] Mary Paley Marshall, *What I Remember* (Cambridge 1947), pp. 23, 44; *NC Register*.
[58] Sutherland, *Faith, Duty and the Power of Mind*, pp. 105–6.

course followed by Ellen Crofts, Newnham Lecturer in Literature 1878–83, who married Francis Darwin in 1883, and by Marion Greenwood, Lecturer in Physiology and Botany at both Girton and Newnham 1888–99, who married George Bidder in 1899. Such a pattern was not confined to women university teachers; it was that followed by Ada Radford after her marriage to Graham Wallas. Howarth and Curthoys have identified a similar pattern among the Oxford women, offering Barbara Hammond, Rachel Lane Poole and Lettice Fisher as examples.[59] Constance Garnett's engagement with translation from the Russian might be construed as an extreme version of such a pattern.

Widowhood, especially if penurious, could also qualify teachers at a variety of levels for entry or return to the labour market, as we have seen. When Arthur Strong, the husband of Eugénie Sellers (GC 1879), died in 1904, she succeeded to his post as Librarian and Keeper for Collections to the Duke of Devonshire, before going on to become Assistant Director of the British School at Rome in 1909.[60] Likewise the GPDSC/T was prepared to employ as teachers and as heads some women widowed young.[61]

What emerges from all this is that combining continuous employment with marriage was rare and presumably difficult. Even where there were no formal barriers, there were very powerful social conventions and expectations. The view expressed by Anthony Trollope in *The Vicar of Bullhampton* at the beginning of the 1870s still held sway:

> When a girl asks herself that question, – what shall she do with her life? it is so natural that she should answer it by saying that she will get married, and give her life to somebody else. It is a woman's one career – let women rebel against the edict as they may; and though there may be word-rebellion here and there, women learn the truth early in their lives. And women know it later in life when they think of their girls; and men know it, too, when they have to deal with their daughters.[62]

---

[59] Howarth and Curthoys, 'Origins and Destinations', p. 594; for more on Crofts and Fisher, see below, pp. 55–6, 71.

[60] Mary Beard, *The Invention of Jane Harrison* (Cambridge, MA 2000), pp. 23–5.

[61] Kamm, *Indicative Past*, p. 68, Appendix II.

[62] Anthony Trollope, *The Vicar of Bullhampton*, serialised 1869–70, published 1870, ch. xxxvii (Oxford World Classics edition 1924, p. 259).

In the last years of the century, too, these social expectations were reinforced by sexual slur and innuendo. On the eve of the First World War Edith Morley led a Fabian Society Women's Group in surveying women's work, a survey which is a mine of information, heavily used in these chapters. Morley, and her contributor on secondary teaching Mrs O'Brien Harris, head of an LCC secondary school in south Hackney, together made an impassioned plea 'that continuance in the profession after marriage should be more usual than it is'. They made their plea, however, not on grounds of equality of opportunity, but on the ground that women secondary teachers 'need not abandon either the career they have chosen or the prospect of their fullest development as women'.[63] It is an early sign of a defensiveness in the face of a challenge to spinsterhood and single women which would rise to a shrill crescendo between the Wars. Alison Oram has characterised the developing set of beliefs which were to generate a Catch 22 situation for many women thus: 'Economic independence, sexual expression and motherhood could not be achieved *together*, either within marriage or outside it, without forfeiting respectability or femininity.' What has been characterised as the 'pathologising of spinsterhood' in these years also brought a more critical and censorious attitude to the enduring female friendships which were a feature of many spinsters' lives, whether employed in teaching or in other occupations.[64]

Finally it is important to recognise how narrow and self-contained these particular educational and career ladders were. It was not as if single women commonly achieved careers which amply fulfilled their talents. For decades women expected and were expected to teach women only. Despite distinguished support, the classicist Jane Harrison was twice disappointed in her efforts to gain a professorship in the University of London. She could keep going in London through public lecturing, underpinned by a small private income; but the opportunity to return to university teaching in Cambridge at the end of the 1890s came about only because Newnham invented a special Lectureship for

---

[63] Morley, ed., *Women Workers*, pp. 35–7; cf. also earlier comments in respect of women university teachers, pp. 36–7.

[64] Oram, *Women Teachers*, pp. 47–57, 185–98, direct quotations from pp. 57, 187. Aspects of the context for this development are sketched in Kent, *Sex and Suffrage*. Sheila Jeffreys first made a number of these points, although in a selective and polemical fashion, in *The Spinster and her Enemies* (London 1985), esp. ch. 5.

her.[65] For scientists it was harder. Their male colleagues controlled not only appointments but also the resources needed for increasingly expensive laboratories, equipment etc. In 1923 the astronomer Cecilia Payne-Gaposchkin concluded there was no future beyond school teaching available to her in England and took herself off to the United States.[66] As late as 1945, when May Wallas was applying for a university post in Cambridge, the Principal of Newnham made a note of a conversation with the Professor of French about the shortlist, in which he acknowledged May's scholarship but felt that the claims of 'ex-service men with families to maintain had to be considered'.[67]

Teaching in the girls' secondary schools and the university colleges which were springing up from 1869 onwards thus represented a quasi-professional occupation for women with higher education. It could bring them modest economic independence and some assured social status. It was, however, so very firmly anchored in existing social conventions about appropriate behaviour for ladies that such teachers do not look a likely group to whom to apply the label 'New Woman'. Some of these women may well have nurtured more radical ambitions about work and/or relationships in their hearts. But they had to keep quiet about such notions and above all take no steps to act them out. If they did so, they were at real risk of losing their jobs, the measure of independence the employment brought and their social position. It was indeed a closed, narrowly virtuous circle.

---

[65] Sutherland, *Faith, Duty and the Power of Mind*, p. 145.

[66] Katherine Haramundanis, ed., *Cecilia Payne-Gaposchkin: An Autobiography and Other Recollections* (2nd edition Cambridge 1996), pp. 25–7, 124.

[67] NCA, Wallas Papers, MGW personal file, undated note, probably by Dame Myra Curtis, Principal 1942–54.

3 'the exercise of what may be termed her maternal faculties': public service and 'caring' occupations

Clara Collet had eventually escaped from teaching into a civil service post. From 1903 she was styled Senior Investigator for Women's Industries at the Board of Trade and paid £450 per annum in what was a pensionable post. She had enough money comfortably to live an independent life, she travelled, served on the Council of the Royal Statistical Society and was among the founder members of the Royal Statistical Society and the Royal Economic Society. Jane Miller, her great-niece and biographer, describes her life as being essentially similar in all outward respects to that of a professional man. What was less obviously masculine was Collet's involvement in and sense of responsibility for the affairs of the rest of her family and the ambivalence of her own feelings. Representative was her comment that 'Most women ... who look forward to a long working career must have an occupation to which they can give heart and mind. The reason is simple. The woman is living an isolated life; unless her work involves the exercise of what may be termed her maternal faculties, she is living an unnatural life.'[1] Here was someone already both acknowledging and vulnerable to a challenge to spinsterhood.

Yet Collet had quit teaching, supposedly one of the occupations which offered most opportunity for the exercise of maternal faculties, was earning a good salary with a pension and was pursuing an intellectually demanding career path. Her trajectory generates the question, did the upper ranks of the civil service represent a more general opportunity or was Clara Collet's career primarily a product of particular abilities, contacts and sheer good fortune – a fluke? Tables 2.1. and 2.2 above suggest the latter.[2] The sample of Cambridge women students produced

[1] Morley, ed., *Women Workers*, p. 242; Miller, *Seductions*, pp. 75–6, 104–7.
[2] Above, pp. 24–5.

precisely thirteen civil servants (1.6% of the total) over the whole period
and seven of those were Newnhamites of the 1914 entry, sucked into
government service during the First World War. The Oxford analysis
groups occupations on a slightly different basis; but the overall picture is
similar: 2% were employed in central or local government and 3% did
war work.[3] Only a handful of senior posts were designated as specially
needing a woman's touch and mindset; and appointment to these posts
was either by patronage or by nomination and limited competition, that
is, having secured a nomination, the woman had then to meet a minimum
standard of competence. Women graduates would not be allowed to enter
open competition for the higher-ranking civil service posts until 1925.

To stress this is not to suggest that government set its face outright
against the employment of women; rather, it points towards the divide
which characterised a number of occupations, that between 'ladies' and
'women'. Government in the last quarter of the long nineteenth century
employed increasing numbers of women, but only a handful of ladies.
The initial employment of women by the government had been almost
inadvertent. In 1870 the state took over all telegraph services and these
were already employing women. Experience of these reliable and dex-
trous employees encouraged the Post Office to copy the practice more
generally; and gradually other departments followed suit. By 1914
7,000 women were being employed by the GPO alone, recruited by
open competition. Elsewhere in the government service there were
another 3,000. They were however paid less than their male colleagues
and a marriage bar operated.[4]

Recruitment to supervisory and more senior posts was a different
matter. The first Superintendent of Women Workers in the Post Office
Savings Bank, appointed in 1875, was Miss M. C. Smith, aged all of
twenty-three, educated entirely at home and the niece of the distinguished classicist Sir William Smith. She was emphatically a lady,
although she also proved far-seeing and doughty in advancing the
careers of her charges. A first female poor law inspector was appointed
at the Local Government Board in 1873 – the widowed Mrs Nassau
Senior, sister of the novelist Thomas Hughes and daughter-in-law of the
economist. Illness forced her resignation in 1877 and she was not
replaced until 1885. By 1910 there would be seven women poor law

[3] Howarth, 'In Oxford ... but not of Oxford', p. 297, Table 10.2.
[4] Morley, ed., *Women Workers*, pp. 252–5, 261–73.

inspectors. The first female factory inspectors, specialising of course in trades which employed women, were appointed by the Home Office in 1893. By 1913 there would be twenty, along with one woman inspector of prisons and one woman inspector of industrial and reform schools. In 1911 one of the five Insurance Commissioners appointed for England would be a woman, Mona Wilson (NC 1892), social investigator and former Secretary to the Women's Industrial Law Committee and Women's Trade Union League.[5] The Education Department appointed a Directress of Needlework in 1884, a Directress of Cookery in 1891 and a Directress of Laundrywork in 1893. The first women were recruited to HM Inspectorate only in 1904, including not only Mrs Withiel, the bête noire of the GPDSC/T, but also the Hon. Maude Lawrence, who the next year was made Chief Woman HMI. Once there, however, the group expanded quite rapidly and there were forty-five women HMIs by 1913–14. By comparison with women secondary school teachers, heads, and university teachers, these senior women civil servants tended to be better paid, on scales between £200 and £650, although ones invariably lower than the scales on which their male counterparts were paid. They had greater security of tenure than teachers; but a marriage bar operated for ladies as for women.[6]

By 1914, however, there were in total fewer than a hundred such senior women in the civil service, compared to 10,000 or so in the lower grades. The modes of appointment, patronage, nomination and limited competition meant too that they had to be well connected and in the right place at the right time. Hilda Martindale, who in 1901 accepted appointment to the factory inspectorate, left Royal Holloway College in 1895 determined to do social work with children. Since there was no dedicated training, she devised her own – with the advice and help of Graham Wallas. After courses in hygiene, public health and the social sciences, she used her family's considerable financial resources to make investigatory visits to a whole range of institutions not only in the UK but also in Europe and other parts of the world. She could afford to wait until the right opening came up for her.[7] Mona Wilson likewise had private money, enough to abandon social investigation in 1919 and

---

[5] *Newnham College Club Letter (NCCL)* [the magazine of the Old Students' Club, begun 1881] 1911, p. 61; see also her entry in the *NC Register*.

[6] Morley, ed., *Women Workers*, pp. 236–45; Hilda Martindale, *Women Servants of the State* (London 1937), pp. 15–65, 176–80, 182–6.

[7] Hilda Martindale, *From One Generation to Another* (London 1944), pp. 46, 65–7.

take her chance as a writer.[8] This handful of senior posts could hardly be said to represent a substantial and expanding set of opportunities for women graduates. A few women were lucky; but they were more likely to be those who, like Hilda Martindale and Mona Wilson but unlike Clara Collet, did not have to earn their own living and could wait and prepare for the opportunity to occur.

Examining opportunities for women in public service, it seemed also worth trying to establish whether the experience of government war-related work during the First World War might have been associated with any change of direction in women's post-war occupational trajectories. Analysis of the Cambridge sample showed that 107 women in total, sixty from Newnham and forty-seven from Girton, engaged in activities which could be identified as war work. In twenty-eight cases, fourteen from each group, there were observable changes in their post-war trajectories, that is, for just under a quarter in the case of the Newnhamites and slightly under a third in the case of the Girtonians. Whether these were triggered by the war-time experience, however, or by shifting post-war boundaries, or a combination of both, it is impossible to say. Moreover, there is no observable pattern in these changes; the linked hypotheses that war work might have led into greater employment in the civil service itself and/or industrial research proved without foundation when tested against the database.

It was recognised at the time and has become conventional wisdom in the historiography that the work of caring, seen as peculiarly feminine and initially honed in a domestic, essentially private setting, could be developed and expanded to provide a route for middle- and upper-class women into the public sphere; and, for those whose incomes were insufficient to support their status, such work could provide a route into paid employment. By the eve of the First World War there was seen to be, as E. M. Stopford (NC 1908) put it, 'a distinct "women's work" outside the home', namely 'the supervision and care of women and children, the tending of the sick, the inspection of conditions under which women and children were working'.[9] Yet the slow and uneven

---

[8] *NC Register.*

[9] *NCCL* 1914, pp. 28–30 'Careers for University Women'. Stopford herself was then working as an organiser of women's work for the new Labour Exchanges – see *Register.*

penetration of the public service by women with professional ambitions suggests that this transition, if it occurred, was seldom straightforward. Such an impression is strengthened by an exploration of opportunities for women in medicine and nursing – quintessentially caring occupations – and the transmogrification of philanthropy and charitable endeavour into social work.[10]

Two important clues to the tortuousness of the processes in these occupations are to be found in the tables presented above, of the post-college occupations of the sample of Cambridge women 1869–1914.[11] The first clue is the very small numbers who went on to qualify as doctors and to practise, a total of twelve, six from each college. The second clue is the consistent blurring in the original record of distinctions between voluntary charitable work and paid social work. Let us begin with the opportunities in medicine.

One of the reasons for the very small number of women doctors was a prolonged battle with the male medical establishment, who fought hard to keep them out. In January 1882 twenty-six women were registered as having medical qualifications, only one of them, Elizabeth Garrett Anderson, with that qualification gained in England. By 1895 there were 200 such women and in 1911 477. Pre-clinical teaching open to women was provided by the London School of Medicine from 1874 and the Royal Free Hospital opened its wards to women clinical students in 1877. Opportunities for house jobs came only from 1898, when the two merged to form the Royal Free Hospital School of Medicine for Women.[12] The other clinical schools would only be forced by government formally to agree to admit women in the course of the First World War and already by 1921 some of them were reversing that decision, arguing that the emergency was now over.[13] In Cambridge women were

---

[10] I am grateful to Anne Summers for bibliographic guidance and fruitful discussion in preparing the section which follows.

[11] Tables 2.1 and 2.2, above, pp. 24–5.

[12] Jenifer Glynn, *The Pioneering Garretts: Breaking the Barriers for Women* (London 2008) pp. 102, 106–7; Catriona Blake, *The Charge of the Parasols: Women's Entry into the Medical Profession* (London 1990), p. 193, Appendix II; Vera Brittain, *Women's Work in Modern England* (London 1928), p. 14; see also the very useful summary at the beginning of the article by J. F. Geddes, 'The Doctors' Dilemma: Medical Women and the British Suffrage Movement', *Women's History Review* 18:2 (2009), pp. 203–18, at pp. 204–6.

[13] Cheryl Law, *Suffrage and Power. The Women's Movement 1918–1928* (London 1997), p. 105; Carol Dyhouse, 'The Citadel Storms Back: Women's Medical

not admitted to pre-clinical medical courses until the inter-war years. The pre-1914 Girton and Newnham twelve from the years up to 1914 had mostly done Natural Sciences courses at Cambridge and then pursued pre-clinical and clinical studies elsewhere, usually in London.

The route to a medical qualification was thus long and arduous; it was also exceedingly expensive. This demanding combination meant that women medical students and the handful of women doctors in general came from significantly more affluent social backgrounds than did university women students and graduates as a whole;[14] and the subsequent careers of those who stayed the course appear to reflect a combination of determination, family support and secure and financially assured social position. Three of these women were among the tiny minority of the Cambridge sample who continued professional work after marriage. The career of the first Girtonian in the Cambridge sample to go on to medical school demonstrates this dramatically. Nolini Bonnerjee was the daughter of a wealthy Indian barrister and politician, a passionate enthusiast for education – three younger sisters would be sent to Newnham. Nolini was despatched to school in England when she was only three years old and arrived at Girton to read Natural Sciences in 1889. From there she went on to the London School of Medicine and the Royal Free. Marrying a Scots lawyer apparently based in Liverpool, she practised in Liverpool from 1899 until 1922, when she returned to India to work for the Indian Famine Fund.[15]

Louisa Martindale, sister of Hilda, the factory inspector, became a doctor; but as we have seen, there was substantial family money and both Hilda and Louisa had the warm support of their widowed mother in constructing their career paths.[16] The struggle of Octavia Wilberforce, protégé of Louisa's friend the actress and writer Elizabeth Robins, represents the exception that proves the rule. Octavia's parents had never

Education in Britain 1900–1939', unpublished paper delivered to the conference, 'The Transformation of an Elite? Women and Higher Education since 1900', Cambridge, 24 September 1998 (held to mark the fiftieth anniversary of the admission of women to the University).

[14] For the social background of medical students, see Dyhouse, *No Distinction of Sex?*, pp. 25–6; for the costs of the training, see Morley, ed., *Women Workers*, pp. 138, 151–6.

[15] Where no other reference is cited, information comes from the Girton and Newnham biographical *Registers*.

[16] Hilda Martindale, *One Generation to Another*, pp. 46, 65–7.

allowed her to go to school; so it took her eight attempts to achieve matriculation. Nor would her parents provide any financial help or support. Elizabeth and a wider group of friends and kin stepped into the breach; and Octavia at last completed her pre-clinical qualifications in 1915, at the age of 33. Clinical qualifications took another five years.[17]

Once qualified, what did – what could – they do? Setting up in private practice required initial capital. Octavia Wilberforce begged and borrowed the sum necessary to buy a house at which she could 'put up her plate' in Brighton; and while she waited for her reputation to spread among patients, eked out a living with a part-time clinical post at the local hospital. Eventually she would become Virginia Woolf's doctor.[18] The presence of those women telegraph operators and clerks in the GPO meant that in 1883 a woman Medical Officer was appointed to look after their health and slowly other women Medical Officers were recruited to inspectorates elsewhere in government service, in the Education Department in particular. Equally slowly local government followed suit, gradually recruiting women doctors for public health work particularly in paediatric and maternity services. As far as salaries and conditions of service in the public sector were concerned, the male members of the medical establishment were impaled on the horns of a dilemma; if they allowed the recruitment of women doctors at lower stipends, they undercut their own position. Medicine was the one area in the public service where there was a formal commitment to equal pay – although a variety of dodges were tried to get round this.[19]

Overall, however, the opportunities for women doctors up to 1914 were few and limited and grew only slowly. A significant proportion of the women who qualified went to Britain's colonies to work, recognising that both need and scope were far greater there. Zenana missions were specifically from women to women.[20] From that perspective Nolini Bonnerjee's return to India in 1922 is again significant. Marian Mayfield (GC 1899) was working as Medical Officer to the Zenana Hospital in Peshawar when she married another doctor, and they

---

[17] Angela John, *Elizabeth Robins: Staging a Life* (Stroud 1993, pbk edition 2007), p. 266; Pat Jalland, ed., *Octavia Wilberforce: The Autobiography of a Pioneer Woman Doctor* (London 1989), chs. 4–7.

[18] *Ibid*. chs. 11 and 12; cf. Morley, ed., *Women Workers*, pp. 167–70.

[19] E. Moberley Bell, *Storming the Citadel: The Rise of the Woman Doctor* (London 1953), pp. 178–9; Morley, ed., *Women Workers*, pp. 139, 246, 254.

[20] Bell, *Storming the Citadel*, ch. 7; Geddes, 'Doctors' Dilemma', pp. 205–6.

subsequently both worked in mission hospitals in India. After completing her medical qualifications in Edinburgh in 1905, Norah Lenwood (NC 1894) went to work as a medical missionary in the north of China, subsequently marrying a fellow missionary, continuing in practice and eventually surviving internment by the Japanese from 1943 to 1945.

While women doctors were undoubtedly ladies, nurses uneasily straddled the divide between lady and woman throughout the period. Florence Nightingale was unequivocally a lady, with an unassailable social position. But part, at least, of her family's resistance to her wish to work in nursing stemmed from their awareness that English society in the first half of the nineteenth century regarded nurses as servants. The better ones might be upper servants, but that put them on a par with housekeepers. In Catholic Europe ladies might join nursing sisterhoods; but the movement to create Protestant sisterhoods in England was regarded with suspicion.[21] The parties taken to the Crimea in 1854–5 included both ladies and women, the ladies not prepared to undertake the heaviest physical work in the wards and even in some cases expecting the women to wait upon them in their quarters. Some of the women arriving in Smyrna went on strike, commenting that 'they came out as nurses, not to do housework'.[22]

The subsequent development of army nursing as an occupation for women was profoundly complicated by efforts to professionalise the army itself and then to integrate within it a medical service, doctors as well as nurses, whose initial formation was civilian. This has been admirably explored by Anne Summers. Moreover, even by the end of the century, army nurses were a tiny group – in 1890 there were only sixty Army nursing sisters, many of them officers' daughters.[23] Larger numbers were affected by the post-Crimea push to train civilian nurses; yet here too the social divide was only slowly bridged. When the Nightingale School, eventually to become part of St Thomas's Hospital, first opened its doors, their preferred candidates for admission were the daughters of small farmers; and in 1862 the Nightingale Fund Committee set out their views on candidates for nursing with candour:

---

[21] Anne Summers, *Angels and Citizens: British Women as Military Nurses 1854–1914* (London 1988), ch. 1; Mark Bostridge, *Florence Nightingale. The Woman and her Legend* (London 2008), pp. 146–7.

[22] Summers, *Angels and Citizens*, ch. 2, direct quotation from p. 55.

[23] Summers, *Angels and Citizens*, pp. 97–8 and parts II and III.

Ladies in fact are not as a rule the best qualified, but rather women of some-what more than average intelligence emanating from those classes in which women are habitually employed in earning their own livelihood. Ladies, however, are not excluded; on the contrary, where sufficient evidence is shown that they intend to pursue the calling as a business, and have those qualifications which will fit them to become superintendents, their admission would be considered an advantage.

From 1867 the position was systematised and two modes of entry to the School were established, one for ladies and one for women. Women probationers received their keep while training; lady proba-tioners paid the School for their training. Ladies, however, could expect to move into more highly paid supervisory roles at the end of their training; and the Nightingale School gradually emerged as a training ground for matrons rather than for ordinary nurses. By the end of the century the distinctions were beginning to blur; in 1900 the Guy's Hospital lady probationers petitioned to be able to wear the same uniforms as the women probationers; but the lady probationers were still expected to pay for their training. The Census of 1901 showed approximately 63,500 women calling themselves nurses in the population as a whole; but since compulsory registration would not be enacted until 1919, the majority of these were probably untrained. Abel-Smith has estimated the numbers with training, ladies and women altogether, as in the region of 5,000.[24] The social divide and the absence of registration were fully reflected in the salaries paid. On the eve of the First World War the average salary of a staff nurse was between £24 and £30 a year; a ward sister might command £30–40 a year in the provinces, more in London. For matrons, a cottage hospital salary might be as low as £40–50 a year, while the matrons of the biggest London hospitals might be paid between £200 and £300 a year.[25] Nursing as an occupation did not attract women with higher education in the years up to 1914. As a white-collar occupation, as we shall see, it ranked in status and rewards above work as a shop assistant but below many clerical posts.

[24] Brian Abel-Smith, *A History of Nursing* (London 1960), pp. 21–4 (direct quotation from p. 22), 30–2, 57, 257.

[25] Morley, ed., *Women Workers*, pp. 175–84; cf. Summers, *Angels and Citizens*, pp. 109–10, 225, Table 8.2. Cf. teaching salaries in Chapter 2 above, pp. 29–30.

In 1895, considering whether higher education had opened up any new opportunities for women, Mrs J. E. H. Gordon had commented that, 'In former days marriage, teaching, and philanthropy were the principal professions that were open to women.'[26] Given the expansion and formalisation of secondary school teaching, the precursors of professionalisation, it seems not unreasonable to look for the same processes at work in philanthropy, to expect to find the beginnings of its transformation into professional social work. The beginnings can be found; but overall the processes of change proceeded much more slowly than in teaching. The explanation for this is almost certainly rooted in the sheer acceptability of philanthropy as an activity for ladies, and one moreover which could be pursued part-time and after marriage. As Clara Rackham, née Tabor (NC 1895), trying to persuade her peers to stand for election as Poor Law Guardians, put it, 'To a woman who has a certain amount of leisure there is, as a rule, no work so well within her reach and at the same time offering so much interest and responsibility.'[27]

Ladies had not been without a public role and presence in philanthropic work, even when the rhetoric of 'separate spheres' was at its loudest.[28] For exactly this reason it was the area of activity in which voluntary and part-time engagement was slowest to disappear. Frances Power Cobbe had challenged the underlying assumptions as early as 1867, when she told ladies that to work in a hospital without pay was '*not* an heroic act of public charity but a serious social mistake'; it took paid work away from women who needed it 'and also degraded the profession by making it appear it had no monetary value'.[29] Yet many did not – or chose not to – hear, among them the housing reformer, stalwart of the Charity Organisation Society and co-founder of the

---

[26] Gordon, 'After-Careers', p. 959 (note her classification of marriage).

[27] NCCL, 1913, pp. 26–31, 'The Need of Women as Poor Law Guardians', p. 29. Married to the Cambridge classicist Harris Rackham, Clara was then serving on the Board of Guardians. She would do war service as a factory inspector and go on to serve as a Labour County Councillor – see *Register*. Cf. also *Girton Review* (henceforward *GR*), August 1897, pp. 2–6, anon., 'Women as Poor Law Guardians'.

[28] Anne Summers, 'A Home from Home – Women's Philanthropic Work in the Nineteenth Century', in Sandra Burman, ed., *Fit Work for Women* (London 1979), pp. 33–64; F. K. Prochaska, *Women and Philanthropy in Nineteenth Century England* (Oxford 1980); Morgan, *Victorian Woman's Place.*

[29] 'The American Sanitary Commission and Its Lesson', *Fraser's Magazine* 75 (March 1867), quoted by Sally Mitchell, *Frances Power Cobbe: Victorian Feminist, Journalist, Reformer* (Charlottesville, VA 2004), p. 169, FPC's emphasis.

National Trust, Octavia Hill.[30] For decades the assumption prevailed that 'nothing but willingness is needed on the part of a worker among the Poor', as Alice Gruner (NC 1883), one of the founders of the Women's University Settlement, put it. She added a further point about the effectiveness of the help provided by ladies: 'when at last a worker *is* brought to recognise that more than willingness is needed, he or she have [*sic*] bought their experience at the expense of those whom they wished to serve'.[31] When in 1913–14 Edith Morley and her Fabian Women's group surveyed the economic conditions and prospects of what they grandly called *Women Workers in Seven Professions*, they did not consider professional social work as one of the seven, even though they did try to look at the ways in which women might find jobs as sanitary inspectors and health visitors for local authorities.[32]

To mark the boundary between paid and unpaid charitable work is not to suggest there was little paid employment for women in the field. In 1893 Louisa Hubbard estimated there were about 20,000 paid women officers employed by charitable enterprises directed or part-directed by some 50,000 ladies.[33] And economic circumstances could propel a lady across that boundary. Olive Garnett, who intermittently helped out on a voluntary basis at a Charity Organisation Society (COS) branch, observed the beginnings of such a crossing in 1892:

Went to the C.O.S. office at 11 o'clock. There was a young lady already there waiting to be set to work. She has lately lost her money & her cousin who is member of the Highbury Committee asked that she might come to the office & get an idea of the work in case there might be a vacancy & a salary anywhere in the C.O.S. which she could have.[34]

Fresh from higher education, some of the women, like Alice Gruner, involved in the Women's University Settlement, founded in Southwark

---

[30] Summers, 'Home from Home', pp. 55–6.

[31] Quoted in Sybil Oldfield, *Spinsters of this Parish: The Life and Times of F. M. Mayor and Mary Sheepshanks* (London 1984), p. 51 (AG's emphasis).

[32] Morley, ed., *Women Workers*, s. IV, pp. 221–34; on the remarkable stability of the assumptions underpinning 'women's work', see also Anne Summers, 'Public Functions, Private Premises: Female Professional Identity and the Domestic Service Paradigm in Britain 1850–1930', in Billie Melman, ed., *Borderlines: Genders and Identities in War and Peace 1870–1930* (London 1998), pp. 353–76.

[33] Prochaska, *Women and Philanthropy*, p. 224.

[34] *Diary of Olive Garnett 1890–93*, ed. Johnson, p. 103, entry for 10 August 1892.

in 1887, perceived the uses of training and also began to demonstrate an awareness that those with an aptitude for the work might not have private means, or enough private means. Not everyone had either the resources or the contacts to wait and prepare for the right post, as Hilda Martindale had done.[35] In conjunction with the COS in 1896 the WUS launched a 'Training Course for Women Workers' which would by 1912 evolve into the School of Sociology at the London School of Economics (LSE). In 1896 too they raised an appeal fund to support women in training to undertake social work.[36]

In the years up to 1914 the newsletters of the Cambridge women's colleges, the *Newnham College Club Letter* and the *Girton Review*, reported regularly on the work of the WUS in Southwark and the Manchester Settlement which soon followed it, both sustained by a mix of paid and voluntary labour.[37] Yet this earnest and assiduous reporting embodied no commitment to, let alone campaign for, the development of a fully professionalised paid workforce. There is an absence here, or at least a profound ambivalence, which needs further decoding. Nineteenth-century notions of philanthropic endeavour were still powerful among many members of their audience. At the same time the circumstances of many of these individuals' lives could push them back and forth across boundaries between paid and voluntary work. Alice Stronach's 1901 novel, *A Newnham Friendship*, charts the lives of a group of young women who go on from Newnham to settlement work. One of its sub-texts, although it is uncertain whether the author herself recognised it, is the replication of the powerful female friendships of college years at the settlement. The overt primary text of the novel is that the highest fulfilment for women comes from marriage and family life and this is offered to Carol. Her friend Eppie urges her,

[35] Above, p. 43.

[36] Seth Koven, *Slumming: Sexual and Social Politics in Victorian London* (Princeton, NJ 2004), p. 224; Oldfield, *Spinsters of this Parish*, pp. 50–1.

[37] NCCL, published annually, carried a report each year and the WUS had its own College Society – see regular accounts in *Thersites*, the students' own magazine. The *Girton Review* (GR), published three times a year, often carried a piece in one of the year's issues – see e.g. *GR* July 1887, pp. 5–7, 'The Women's University Association for Work in the Poorer Districts of London'; December 1887, pp. 7–8, '44 Nelson Square'; July 1888, pp. 7–8; April 1890, pp. 2–7, Mrs F. Elder, 'The Women's University Settlement, Southwark'; August 1900, pp. 1–3, 'A Day at the Southwark Settlement'; Lent 1914, pp. 11–14, 'Report of the Annual General Meeting of the Women's University Settlement'.

'Marry, have children, know the highest happiness that life can give a woman. Your work – you need not give that up', apparently envisaging Carol playing the local Lady Bountiful in the interstices of family life. Eppie herself, a figure whose trajectory resembled Stronach's own, settles for second best as she sees it, accepting that the poverty of her background and its consequent limitation on her university work point to a single life, earning her own living teaching in an elementary school for working-class children and living in the settlement house.[38]

As a whole, the novel conveys deeply complex feelings towards both work in general and social work in particular, a complexity by no means fully acknowledged by the women graduates themselves. Another way of reading these uncertainties would be to see a co-existence in the women's attitudes, sometimes an uneasy co-existence, between a view of higher education as instrumental, a means to economic survival and independence, and a view which emphasised its wider cultural possibilities and riches. In her novel Stronach made Carol, the economically secure of her two heroines, the exponent of this second view:

Yes, it was all an enchanted world that she had lived in these three years, a garden where she had had only to put forth her hand to gather what flowers she would – knowledge and friendship, sympathy and quiet time for thought ... She who had had these three glorious years must go forth strong to help those on the other side, those who had never had even a glimpse of the enchanted world inside those high hedges. She would help to break down these hedges, to get for other women and girls the privileges that she herself had had.[39]

Essentially the same point had been made four years earlier by an anonymous contributor to the *Girton Review*, moved to take up the cudgels on behalf of higher education for women by a recent spate of attacks in the *Fortnightly Review*. Education, she argued, was a civilising force for the whole society: 'If the men of England are what their mothers make them, is not this a heavy responsibility that the mothers

---

[38] Alice Stronach, *A Newnham Friendship*, originally published London 1901, reprinted in the series, *Victorian Novels of Oxbridge Life* ed. Christopher Stray, Bristol 2004; the direct quotation comes from p. 285 of this reprint. On Stronach, see Stray's introductory essay in vol. I of the reprint. On elementary school teaching, see also below, Chapter 6.

[39] Stronach, *Newnham Friendship*, ed. Stray, pp. 204–5.

of the majority are in a great measure what we allow them to be, ignorant, wasteful, vicious, degraded by grinding poverty and uncheered toil into machines or worse?' She concluded somewhat lamely with a plea for settlement work to reclaim these mothers.[40] Successive editors of these college newsletters recognised that their readership was diverse; not all their readers worked, or had to work, for their living; not all were inclined to, or felt they had to behave like any version of a New Woman. The ideas of the editors and readers of both newsletters about ways of using higher education were as varied as those of the families and strata of society from which the women came; and their priorities might change. The trajectory of Ada Wallas's life again comes to mind. These seem statements of the obvious – yet ones that need to be made. The newsletters faithfully reflected diversity back both to their own constituents and to other readers, a range of ambitions, ideals and expectations, including ambivalence, uncertainty and tension.

Ambivalence about the nature and requirements of social work in particular was slow to fade. When the distinguished sociologist Barbara Wootton (GC 1915) began lecturing to Social Science students at Westfield College, London, in the early 1920s, she remarked of her students:

Few of them were training to become professional social workers: mostly they were young women of means and leisure who wished to engage in various charitable activities. Thanks largely to the influence of what was then the Charity Organization Society (now imperfectly disguised as the Family Welfare Association), they had grasped that if you want to make a success of 'slumming', or to set the poor to rights, it is better to know something about the lives of the people into whose business you propose to interfere. So they came in their cars and their pearls and their elegant clothes to hear what I and others had to say.[41]

Even growing recognition that good welfare provision for a workforce could have economic benefits did not do much to accelerate the process of professionalisation in social work, as the slow evolution of welfare provision in manufacturing and commercial enterprises into personnel management demonstrated. Quaker manufacturers were among the

[40] *GR* December 1886, pp. 3–5, direct quotation p. 4.
[41] Barbara Wootton, *In a World I Never Made* (London 1967), p. 56.

pioneers. In 1896 Seebohm Rowntree made a first paid appointment, Mary Wood, who had previously been a teacher at the Mount School in York. By 1904 Rowntree's were employing seven welfare workers, four women and three men. In 1906 F. N. Hepworth, a director of Hudson Scott's tin box manufacturers in Carlisle, turned for help in finding a welfare worker to E. J. Urwick of the LSE and Urwick recommended Eleanor Kelly, whom he had been coaching for a diploma in social studies. When she took the post, she was reported as encountering social ostracism in some quarters because she had moved from voluntary to paid work. By June 1913 there were enough such welfare workers to hold a national conference – forty-eight representatives from twenty-nine firms, students from Bristol and observers from the Home Office's Factory Inspectorate and the Board of Education; and the first Register of Members of the Welfare Workers' Association, with sixty-eight names, was created. However, it took the manpower demands of the First World War to achieve any real breakthrough and the Institute of Personnel Management was finally incorporated in 1924. Even so, there were many battles over agreed and accredited training left to fight.[42]

The conviction that philanthropy was a distinctively feminine and frequently voluntary activity had two very different consequences, in perpetual tension with each other. First it is plain that the heavy involvement of ladies delayed the systematisation of training and the improvement of the status of the women employees, making a significant contribution to the continuing low status of professional social work in the wider society. Yet it also meant that able and energetic women with limited outlets elsewhere made a huge contribution to voluntary organisations, local government and the associational life of that society in the first half of the twentieth century. This is not the place to explore the first process in any more detail; it must await the historian of the professionalisation of social work. However, some illustrations of the second process should be offered here.

Mention has already been made of Lettice Fisher née Ilbert;[43] and it is worth saying a little more here about her activities. In 1899 the

---

[42] Mary M. Niven, *Personnel Management 1913–1963* (London 1967), ch. 2, esp. pp. 21–2, 25; ch. 3, pp. 33–6; chs. 4 and 5 *et seq*. I am indebted to Jane Snowden for this reference. Would that there were comparably detailed studies of the growth of other areas of professional social work.

[43] Above, p. 38.

Somerville lecturer Lettice Ilbert (1894) married the academic historian H. A. L. Fisher, later to become a government minister and then Warden of New College, Oxford. Gradually thereafter she ran down her academic teaching in Oxford, replacing it with voluntary work. First starting the Oxford Health and Housing Association, she went on in 1918 to found the National Council for the Unmarried Mother and Her Child and to publish extensively on these and related matters.[44] The life of Florence Ada Brown of Newnham (1878) exhibited a similar pattern. In 1882 marrying the future Registrary of the University, John Neville Keynes, then becoming mother of Maynard, Geoffrey and Margaret, she became a power in Cambridge local government, charitable and social work, the first woman town councillor, later Mayor, JP, before moving on to the national scene as president of the National Council of Women and member of the Athlone Commission on the training of nurses.[45] Likewise Shena Potter (1904), daughter of a shipowner, went on from reading Economics at Newnham in 1907 to the LSE, to study social sciences. Marrying Ernest Simon in 1912, she went on to serve on the National Council of Women, on the Manchester City Council, on the WEA, on the Board of Education Consultative Committee and assorted government inquiries, being better known as Lady Simon of Wythenshawe.

These are among the big names. But there were a multiplicity of other women graduates who followed a similar, if humbler or less well-known, trajectory. The *Newnham College Club Letter* noted in 1903 that sixteen old students had immediately been coopted to serve on the newly constituted Education Committees of County and County Borough Councils.[46] Ada Wallas's work first with schools for mothers and then on the Council of Bedford College fits comfortably here.[47] There are a multiplicity of illustrations which can be found in the *Registers* of the two Colleges to illustrate the persistence of this pattern, of which a handful must suffice. Katherine McClure had entered Girton in 1909, reading for the Historical Tripos. Subsequently she combined secondary school history teaching with training to teach music, then adding music teaching to her portfolio. She gave up paid employment on her marriage in 1924 but worked during the inter-war years with

---

[44] *Somerville Register* 1879–1971, entry for Lettice Ilbert, 1894; Howarth, 'In Oxford but ... not of Oxford', p. 299.
[45] *NC Register; NCCL* 1914, p. 58.   [46] *NCCL* 1903, p. 61.   [47] Above, p. 9.

school and amateur choirs and orchestras in the North London area and with the local Boy Scouts. Frances Katherine Rolland had entered Newnham in 1909, reading first Mathematics and then Natural Sciences. Working initially at the Geological Museum in London and then in what was becoming the Women's Royal Air Force during the war years, she left paid work when she married a doctor in 1919. Then she became a Governor of Cirencester Grammar School, and a power in the Women's section of the British Legion, first in Cirencester and then in Gloucestershire as a whole. Muriel Gregory Read entered Girton in 1914 to read History. She resigned her teaching post at Brighton, Hove and Sussex Grammar School on her marriage in 1920; but from 1933 to 1949 she served as a coopted member of Brighton Education Committee and on the Committee of Management of the school where she had taught, now a GPDST school; from 1940 to 1945 she was a member of the Ministry of Labour Women's Advisory Panel in Brighton and after the War served on the Women's Sub-Committee of the Brighton, Hove and Mid-Sussex Local Employment Committee. Olive Millar, who entered Newnham in 1914, married Admiral Sir Algernon Willis in 1916, only a year after completing Part I of the Mathematics Tripos. She threw herself immediately into welfare work for naval families during the war. Between the wars and after the second war she was active in the Hampshire Girl Guides and Girls' Nautical Training Corps, while from 1940 until 1945 she was to be found in South Africa, driving an ambulance and organising war work for the non-European population.

As such examples suggest, another project for a future historian might be to consider the impact on local government and associational life in Britain in the second half of the twentieth century of the expansion during those years of women's paid employment. For the purposes of the current enquiry, however, the route leading from philanthropic and charitable activities to professional social work for able and energetic women was at least as slow and complex to negotiate, although for very different reasons, as the route into medicine. Neither can be seen to offer significantly expanding employment opportunities for women at the end of the nineteenth century and the first half of the twentieth century. Some opportunities could be found; but often they could be grasped only if economic security was already assured in other ways.

4 | *'impossible for a lady to remain a lady':*
art, literature and the theatre

The evidence from the Cambridge sample makes it plain that higher education was not an obvious route to creative achievement in art, literature or the theatre.[1] Only two out of the whole, one from each college, could be described in any sense as artists. The theatre barely figured at all, although two Newnhamites have been found who did do some acting; and both artists and actors will be discussed below. Although fifty-three Girtonians and eighty-seven Newnhamites had publications to their names, only a handful made any sort of a living from writing. Most typically their publications were either spin-offs from another occupation, research, teaching or missionary work, or occasional fiction or poetry. The questions then reshape themselves: why was higher education perceived as of negligible use here? What other ways were there of launching oneself into these worlds?

The route to serious drawing and painting for women as well as for men involved some formal training. Apprenticeship with a private teacher or teachers usually came first; and some artists, like Ford Madox Brown, were assiduous in fulfilling their responsibilities.[2] From 1860 onwards a handful of women began to enrol in the Royal Academy Schools. The Slade, founded in 1871, aimed to train women on the same terms as men; but the families of women varied in their attitudes to mixed classes and further study. Some needed convincing, as the experiences of both Vanessa Bell and Gwen Raverat attested. Other parents, like the editor of the *Athenaeum* William Hepworth Dixon and his wife, were more relaxed and Ella was allowed to study in Paris.[3] Whatever the route chosen, family agreement and financial support

---

[1] See Tables 2.1 and 2.2 above, pp. 24–5.

[2] Angela Thirlwell, *Into the Frame: The Four Loves of Ford Madox Brown* (London 2010) pp. 111–14.

[3] Frances Spalding, *Vanessa Bell* (London 1983), chs. 2 and 3; Spalding, *Gwen Raverat: Friends, Family and Affections* (London 2001), pp. 115–20, 155–60; for

were essential and higher education must have looked like either a luxury or a distraction. The lives of the two women in the Cambridge sample who could conceivably be described as 'artists' tend to confirm this. Isabella Townshend, one of the original Girton pioneers of 1869, was an enthusiast for the Pre-Raphaelites and settled in Rome as 'a student of painting' until her early death from typhoid in 1882. She did not appear to depend on her art to earn her living. The Newnham 'artist' was Leila Beatrice Legg, who arrived at the college in 1894. From 1897 to 1914 she is described as a 'Profl. [professional] worker in gold, silver, jewels and enamelling', continuing to work through her brief marriage in 1902 to Captain Philip Henry Flower, who died within six months. She was evidently a woman of many talents, however, for she spent most of the War as the supervisor of the catalogue of Controlled Establishments in the Ministry of Munitions, joining the prime minister's Secretariat in 1917 and serving as secretary to Philip Kerr (later Lord Lothian) at the Paris Peace Conference. Subsequently she ran the Information Department of the *Christian Science Monitor*, contributing occasional articles and book reviews herself.

The simplest route into an acting career was to belong to an acting family, one of the real-life equivalents of the immortal Crummles family in Dickens' *Nicholas Nickleby*, such as the Terrys, Ellen's family, the Moores, the family of Henry Irving's first love Nellie, or the Ternans, the family of Dickens' secret love Ellen.[4] Yet even for members of a family network the theatre hardly yielded a reliable living. Ellen Terry might get paid £40 a week at the height of her career, but the individual woman member of a provincial touring repertory company might expect to start at £1 a week – and have to find her own costumes. Even if she managed to rise to £2 a week, she would be lucky to find employment for forty weeks in the year. Cicely Hamilton, hating teaching and finding that lack of any higher education was becoming an increasing barrier, turned to acting and spent a year in a touring

Ella Hepworth Dixon, see Margaret D. Stetz, *Facing the Late Victorians: Portraits of Writers and Artists from the Mark Samuels Lasner Collection* (Newark, NJ 2007), pp. 9–10, the entries for Ella Hepworth Dixon in *ODNB* and Sutherland, *Longman Companion to Victorian Fiction*.

4 Michael Holroyd, *A Strange Eventful History: The Dramatic Lives of Ellen Terry, Henry Irving and their Remarkable Families* (London 2008), pp. 8–15, 100–2; Claire Tomalin, *Charles Dickens. A Life* (London and New York 2011), esp. pp. 187, 285, 289, 294, 322.

company run by Edmund Tearle. She 'got two pounds a week and found all my own clothes, and tried to save something for the time when I was "out".' It was the more difficult because she was not a good needlewoman; and twice she was thrown out of work 'to make room for a manager's mistress'.[5] A sanitised version of this kind of networking would be offered in 1910 by one Gwladys Wynne, commanded to write an article, 'How I Became an Actress', for the magazine of her old school. Apart from stressing the sheer physical hard grind involved, she wrote that the central drawback was the 'absolute lack of a business basis'; everything depended on who you knew.[6]

Gwladys Wynne had been reasonably fortunate or exceptionally talented. She secured work with Frank Benson's company and then that run by Henry Irving's son. When it became plain to Cicely Hamilton, however, that touring with Edmund Tearle's company was never going to lead to a London engagement, she began to turn her attention to writing, beginning with sensation serials for cheap periodicals catering to the young, before moving on to plays, more serious journalism and novels.[7] Elizabeth Robins (Octavia Wilberforce's friend), the American actress who, with Janet Achurch, pioneered performances of Ibsen on the English stage, estimated that she needed to earn £280 a year to be comfortable and to be able to give some help to her family. Like Cicely Hamilton she began to develop her writing as a way of supplementing her theatrical earnings and eventually succeeded in completing the transition to a career as writer and playwright.[8]

In addition the social status of the actress remained problematic, as it had been through the eighteenth and nineteenth centuries – and as displacement by the manager's mistress indicates.[9] Although the creation of

[5] Cicely Hamilton, *Life Errant* (London 1932), pp. 43–4, 47.
[6] OC May 1910; cf. also the brief experience in a touring company of one of the characters in Emilia Cox's novel *Courtship and Chemicals* (London 1898).
[7] Hamilton, *Life Errant*, pp. 30–57; Whitelaw, *Cicely Hamilton*, pp. 18–19, 32. See also Diane F. Gillespie and Doryjane Birrer, 'Introduction' to their edition of Cicely Hamilton's play *Diana of Dobson's* [opened 1908, acting edition 1925] (Peterborough, Ontario 2003), pp. 13–18.
[8] John, *Elizabeth Robins*, pp. 78, 140, 162; Edith Morley confirms the figures in *Women Workers*, pp. 300–4.
[9] The material on eighteenth-century actresses provided by Kimberley Crouch, 'The Public Life of Actresses: Prostitutes or Ladies?', in Hannah Barker and Elaine Chalus, eds., *Gender in Eighteenth Century England: Roles, Representations and Responsibilities* (London 1997), pp. 58–78, suggests that the

the first training courses at the very end of the nineteenth century, at the Central School and at Beerbohm Tree's Academy, which would turn into RADA, carried the seeds of enhanced status, too often men, whether colleagues or members of the audience, still assumed the actress could be treated as a *fille de joie*, a superior prostitute. W. S. Gilbert was the exception, stoutly protecting the actresses at the Savoy;[10] but among other actor-managers Beerbohm Tree himself offered to set Elizabeth Robins up in a flat of her own; while Charles Wyndham was notorious 'for his ways with women & his disposition to turn the Theatre into a Harem'. Strangers recognised and propositioned Robins in the street, while some of the male boarders in her first lodgings would lurk on the stairs in attempts to waylay her. She learned that she could not take an omnibus back after a late-night performance; it had to be a cab. Eventually she solved the lodgings problem by persuading her younger brother to join her in London to pursue his medical training; together they could afford a tiny flat. And she responded with fierce hauteur to any man – including George Bernard Shaw – who attempted to become familiar.[11] The situation in the theatre remained one in which Clement Scott, theatre critic of the *Daily Telegraph*, could assert in 1897 that it was 'impossible for a lady to remain a lady'.

Sos Eltis has pointed out that the furore which greeted this claim eventually brought Scott's resignation; and she argues more generally that the efforts of actresses like Helen Faucit, Fanny Kemble and Madge Kendal to lay claim to the status of a lady were having some impact. A handful of the superstars, Sarah Bernhardt, Mrs Patrick Campbell, Lillie Langtry, Eleanora Duse and Helena Modjeska, demonstrated a different kind of strength in being able to set up their own production companies. Yet Elizabeth Robins had to fight to assert and then fiercely to protect her status. Moreover such was the tendency of audiences to

label 'prostitute' could be made to stick much more easily than the label 'aristocrat'; see also Christopher Kent, 'Image and Reality: The Actress and Society', in Martha Vicinus, ed., *A Widening Sphere: Changing Roles of Victorian Women* (Indiana 1977), p. 95; Tracy C. Davies, 'The Actress in Victorian Pornography', in K. O. Garrigan, ed., *Victorian Scandals: Representations of Gender and Class* (Athens, OH 1992), pp. 99–133; Claire Tomalin, *The Invisible Woman: The Story of Nelly Ternan and Charles Dickens* (London 1990), p. 61; and Tomalin, *Charles Dickens*, esp. pp. 291–5.

[10] Kent, 'Image and Reality', p. 110; Michael Sanderson, *From Irving to Olivier: A Social History of the Acting Profession 1880–1983* (London 1984), pp. 40–1, 47.

[11] John, *Elizabeth Robins*, pp. 109–11, 116–18.

identify actresses with the roles they played that Madge Kendal was driven to avoid scandalous roles, while Robins and Achurch, so firmly associated with Ibsen's heroines, had to eschew fashionable comedies. As Eltis herself acknowledges, the growing contrast between the power, authority – and scandal – of Bernhardt's well-publicised life and the tragic and pathetic roles she played began to produce performances which verged 'on camp spectacles'.[12] The writer A. J. Symons was a passionate enthusiast for theatre in all its forms. Yet in 1891 he did his best to dissuade his young friend Katherine Willard, like him the child of a clergyman, from attempting to make a career in musical comedy. Theatre people, he wrote, '*are*, as a class, more uniformly immoral than any other class of people'.[13]

The uncertain and contested social status of actresses helps to explain why the authorities of the two women's colleges in Cambridge were initially hostile to all student drama.[14] They continued to set their faces against outsiders joining audiences, but gradually gave up trying to stop amateur dramatics among the students themselves. Performing in a dead language also helped. In 1883 Girton presented its first Greek play, Sophocles' *Elektra*, with Janet Case in the starring role; and in 1885, immediately after completing her Tripos examinations, she took the role of Athena in the University production of Aeschylus' *Eumenides*.[15] Aside from the regular performances of the dramatic society in Girton, it rapidly became an annual tradition that the second-year students wrote and performed an entertainment for the rest of the college.[16] In Newnham in 1906 a group calling themselves the Minor Poets wrote, acted, produced – and had printed – *Every Tripper*, a parody of *Everyman*;[17] and in July 1908 Newnham students were

---

[12] Sos Eltis, *Acts of Desire: Women and Sex on Stage 1800–1930* (Oxford 2013), pp. 153–9, direct quotation from p. 156. Cf. the reproduction of a photograph of Bernhardt in the coffin in which she reportedly slept, in Margaret D. Stetz, *Gender and the London Theatre 1880–1920* (High Wycombe 2004), p. 91.

[13] Stetz, *Gender and the London Theatre*, p.14, his emphasis.

[14] Barbara Stephen, *Emily Davies and Girton College* (London 1927), pp. 241–4; *A Newnham Anthology*, ed. Ann Philips (Cambridge 1979), p. 38.

[15] *GR* December 1883, pp. 3–5; December 1885, pp. 10–12; July 1899, pp. 5–6 (performance in Greek of Aristophanes' *The Birds*); see also the entry for Janet Case in the *GC Register*, 1881.

[16] *GR passim*, see e.g. March 1897, pp. 7–8 (Second Year Entertainment); January 1898, pp. 7–8 (two short plays performed by the College's Dramatic Society).

[17] A 'Tripper' was a student taking a full set of Tripos examinations. A copy survives in the College Library and there is an extract in *A Newnham Anthology*, ed.

allowed to participate in the University performance of *Comus*, part of the celebrations of the tercentenary of Milton's birth. Jane Harrison, Fellow in Classics, advised on the production in rehearsal and chaperoned from the stalls.[18]

As all this suggests, the lure of the footlights proved irresistible to a few. Blanche Annette Smith, who read Natural Sciences at Newnham 1874–7, is not recorded as an actress on the database because, in the course of a long and adventurous life, she did so many things, too many to fit tidily into any categories of analysis. She taught, she travelled, doing a spell as a headmistress in Thailand 1892–6; she was Steward of Newnham for a year 1897–8; while the end of the War found her working as a *Manchester Guardian* journalist. But she also acted with Frank Benson's Shakespearean Company for a short spell, would write a suffrage propaganda play and provided warm encouragement and support for another stage-struck Newnham student, Flora Macdonald Mayor. F. M. Mayor was the daughter of the distinguished classicist J. B. Mayor and Alexandrina Grote, and read History at Newnham 1892–5. After overcoming considerable parental opposition she secured walk-on parts with Benson's company. But she did not have either the stamina or the robust health which plainly sustained Blanche and eventually had to abandon any hope of a theatrical career. She did not need to earn her living; but gradually she began to write a little; and her 1924 novel *The Rector's Daughter* has achieved the status of a minor classic.[19]

F. M. Mayor, Elizabeth Robins, Cicely Hamilton – and Blanche Smith when she turned to journalism – all saw writing as an alternative creative option; and one in which the three of them who had to earn a living, might manage so to do. From the beginning of the nineteenth century writing had ranked with teaching as one of the two things a lady could do for money and not lose caste. The market for writers, like the market for teachers, had changed radically in the course of the century;

Phillips, pp. 69–71; for an account of the Minor Poets who met regularly to read and criticise each other's poetry, see *ibid.* pp. 56–7.

[18] *NCCL* 1908 Cambridge Letter, p. 7.

[19] Oldfield, *Spinsters of this Parish*, chs. 3 and 4; for Blanche Smith, see *NC Register*. Blanche's elder sister, Jane Macleod Smith (NC 1872), seems to have been the family anchor, remaining in Cambridge, running a small private school, playing chess regularly with Benjamin Hall Kennedy and reading to the blind Henry Fawcett.

and some of these changes offered new opportunities. Writing, like teaching, was an expanding occupation. In the 1861 Census just over 1,500 authors, editors and writers were recorded. By 1881 there were over 6,000 'authors, editors, journalists and publicists' recorded, and in 1911 just under 14,000.[20] Unlike teaching, however, the organisation and modes of entry to the occupation did not change. It remained a ruthlessly competitive open, free-for-all market-place – the *New Grub Street* of George Gissing's 1891 novel would have been immediately recognisable to the denizens of late eighteenth-century Grub Street. What did change were the commodities trafficked in that market. The end of the nineteenth century saw the demise of the three-volume novel and the increasing dominance of the single volume; over the century the market for poetry shrank; and in the last quarter of the century period- ical publication exploded: between 1875 and 1903 the number of weekly, monthly and quarterly magazines quadrupled. Not all of these were very long-lived and there was a widening gap between the popular and the highbrow, a gap noticeable also among novels.[21] All of these developments would have an impact on women which differed from that which they had on men.

As the most recent historians of the profession of authorship remark, all the evidence suggests that 'writers who depended primarily on their literary earnings always made up a small proportion of those who were active in the literary world'. George Henry Lewes had summed up the situation in a celebrated survey in *Fraser's Magazine* in 1847: the rest were 'barristers with scarce briefs, physicians with few patients, clergy- men on small livings, idle women, rich men, and a large crop of aspiring noodles'.[22] Women faced a particular handicap here because so few other supplementary earning opportunities were open to them. Family connections might help and provide a kind of informal apprenticeship. In the provincial press some editor-daughters succeeded editor-fathers; and when in 1885 the husband of Emily Crawford, Paris correspondent

---

[20] Patrick Leary and Andrew Nash, 'Authorship', in David McKitterick, ed., *The Cambridge History of the Book in Britain*, vol. VI, *1830–1914* (Cambridge 2009), ch. 4, at p. 173.

[21] *Ibid.* p. 195; Linda H. Peterson, *Becoming a Woman of Letters: Myths of Authorship and Facts of the Victorian Market* (Princeton NJ, 2009), pp. 107, 208, 219, 222–3; Nigel Cross, *The Common Writer: Life in Nineteenth-Century Grub Street* (Cambridge 1985).

[22] Leary and Nash, 'Authorship', p. 174.

of the *Daily News*, died, she simply took over his work, writing for the paper until 1907.[23] For those without such connections and entrées, teaching was usually the occupation pursued side-by-side with writing. At the time of her marriage in 1848 Camilla Toulmin was working as a governess and making jewellery, besides writing. The writing earned her about £50 a year and the other activities £60. Mary Elizabeth Braddon tried supporting herself and her mother by working as an actress before turning to write penny dreadfuls and finally hitting the big time with *Lady Audley's Secret* in 1862.[24] Evelyn Sharp would launch her career in London in 1894 by combining teaching – at one point every morning and two afternoons a week – with book reviewing, writing 'middles', short essays on topical subjects, and children's verse, and reading manuscripts for The Bodley Head.[25] Ella Hepworth Dixon, who did shape a successful career as a journalist, building on her late father's connections, nevertheless wrote one New Woman novel, *The Story of a Modern Woman* (1894), in which her heroine, having failed as an artist, then scrapes a bare living as a journalist.[26] Edna Smallwood, an old girl writing for her school magazine in 1912 on 'Literary Work', noted that there was work available editing and writing introductions and suggested that two possible routes in were either to take a clerical post in a publishing house or to signal one's availability for hackwork at the British Museum, looking up and preparing material for popular encyclopaedia entries. A few years later, Hilda Hochfeld, another old girl of the school given the same brief, was altogether blunter: 'She must not depend on this work but have another source of income.'[27]

Even so, the expanding field of journalism, whether highbrow, trash or hack, proved a lifeline here, as Sharp found, and as Elizabeth Robins and Cicely Hamilton found as they began the transition out of acting into writing. By 1890 there were sixteen women members of the Institute of

---

[23] Barbara Onslow, *Women of the Press in Nineteenth-Century Britain* (London 2000), pp. 41, 51–2.

[24] Leary and Nash, 'Authorship', p. 192; Sutherland, *Companion to Victorian Fiction*, entry for Braddon.

[25] Angela V. John, *Evelyn Sharp: Rebel Woman, 1868–1955* (Manchester 2009) pp. 15–19.

[26] See note 3 above.

[27] OC January 1912; *ibid*. September 1917, 'To the Prospective Journalist'. For a more detailed picture of women's journalism in the nineteenth century, but one which might have gained from sharper periodization, see Onslow, *Women of the Press*.

Journalists and the 1891 Census listed 600 women journalists;[28] in 1898, encouraged by Evelyn Sharp, John Lane of The Bodley Head deemed it worth publishing the young Arnold Bennett's *Journalism for Women: A Practical Guide*.[29] Initially the Women Writers' Club, founded in 1892, and the Society for Women Journalists, formed the next year, were vagrant, meeting in a variety of places. But in 1904 they gained their own clubhouse, the Lyceum, until 1909 bank-rolled by Constance Smedley, the writer and playwright, and her chartered accountant and company director father.[30] The Jewish heiress Rachel Beer, catapulted into journalism by her family's ownership of both *Sunday Times* and *Observer*, was also a staunch supporter, becoming Vice-President of the Society in 1900 and creating a holiday fund for women journalists.[31]

An important use of a club was the exchange of information and contacts; networks led to work and work reinforced networks. For male writers clubland had long played this role and in the late nineteenth century it was gradually reinforced by the rise of the professional literary agent.[32] Earlier in the century Richard Garnett, father of the diarist Olive and father-in-law of Constance, seems to have fulfilled a role as quasi-agent for women, proffering advice, help and guidance to a number of young hopefuls. Assistant Keeper of Printed Books at the British Museum, Superintendent of the Reading Room, from 1890 Keeper of Printed Books, and a prolific author and editor, Garnett was generous with his advice to many.[33] He had a particularly complex and intense relationship with the German writer Mathilde Blind. Mathilde, born in Mannheim in 1841, had been brought to London by her mother and step-father Karl Blind, in the wake of the crack-down on radical and subversive figures following the failed revolutions of 1848. Fluent in

---

[28] John, *Evelyn Sharp*, p. 20; Koven, *Slumming*, p. 334, n.33 to p. 151.

[29] Arnold Bennett, *The Journals* (Penguin Classics edition London 1971), pp. 45–6.

[30] Philip Waller, *Writers, Readers, & Reputations: Literary Life in Britain 1870–1918* (Oxford 2006), pp. 501–6.

[31] Eilat Negev and Yehuda Koren, *First Lady of Fleet Street: The Life, Fortune and Tragedy of Rachel Beer* (London 2011), esp. pp. 14, 16, 17, 61, 228.

[32] Waller, *Writers, Readers*, chs.13 and 17.

[33] See Barbara McCrimmon, *Richard Garnett: The Scholar as Librarian* (Chicago 1989) and the two selections from Olive Garnett's diaries so far published, ed. Johnson, *Diary of Olive Garnett 1890–93* and *Diary of Olive Garnett 1893–95*; also Bernstein, *Roomscape*, pp. 65, 74–6, 83–4, 92–109.

German, French and Italian as well as English, she determined to make a name for herself as a writer in English, publishing her first book of poems under the pseudonym 'Claude Lake', in 1867. She and her mother had both had readers' tickets for the British Museum Reading Room since 1859; but her relationship with Richard Garnett seems to have begun to flower towards the end of the 1860s, that is to say, the correspondence between them in the three volumes of her letters which survive, begins in May 1869.[34]

The letters are consistently heavy with literary comment, criticism and exchange, but also marked by an increasing intimacy. One suspects Garnett would have liked to carry the relationship further; but by the summer of 1871 Mathilde was in retreat and had begun the process of transferring the emotional centre of her life to Ford Madox Brown's household at 37 Fitzroy Square.[35] However, the literary exchanges continued. Garnett gave help in placing articles, encouraged and criticised her translations, corrected drafts and proofs, and advised on contractual matters. In 1873, with his help, Mathilde secured a contract for an authorised translation of D. F. Strauss's *The Old Faith and the New* and he then began to advise on her early drafts of this: '*Mind your tenses. Avoid ambiguity. Don't substitute feeble words for strong ones.*'[36] Fifteen years later, in October 1889, with the assistance of his son Edward, now working as a publisher's reader, he was giving advice on the form of contract to be negotiated for a translation of one of her own books and the choice of translator.[37] In 1891 he gave initial advice about arrangements with the magazine *Black and White*, although subsequent negotiations were carried out for her by the Society of Authors.[38] In their exchanges Mathilde reflected wryly on the time it

[34] British Library Additional Manuscripts (henceforward BL Add Mss) 61927, 61928 and 61929, at 61927 ff. 21–2.

[35] For a fuller account, see Thirlwell, *Into the Frame*, pp. 187–95, 197. Part IV of this study is the best and the fullest account of Mathilde's life and work available.

[36] BL Add Mss 61927 ff. 173–4, Richard Garnett to Mathilde Blind 21 January 1873, his emphases; see also *ibid.* ff. 168–9, Richard Garnett to Mathilde Blind 17 January 1873; ff. 170–1 Mathilde Blind to Richard Garnett, letter undated, envelope post-marked JA 20 1873.

[37] BL Add Mss 61929 ff. 41–2, Richard Garnett to Mathilde Blind 31 October 1889.

[38] BL Add Mss 61929 ff. 55–7, Mathilde Blind to Richard Garnett 29 January 1891; ff. 58–60, Richard Garnett to Mathilde Blind 30 January 1891; ff. 66–7, Sec., Society of Authors to Mathilde Blind 29 July 1891; ff. 68–9 same to same 3 August 1891.

had taken her to secure recognition. Some eighteen years earlier she had offered the *Fortnightly Review* an article on Mazzini, which they had turned down; now they were pursuing her for two.[39]

One of the elements in this lengthy interval may have been the time it took for Mathilde to master English idioms. In speech she never lost her heavy German accent and this prevented her becoming a successful lecturer.[40] Another element may have been her determination to write what she chose, regardless of the demands of the market. This included a substantial amount of poetry, which did not sell. Money was perpetually short, especially after she moved out of her mother and stepfather's house, although a small inheritance from her father, Jacob Cohen, was a lifeline. Comfort and some affluence came only in the last four years of her life from 1892 to 1896, after she inherited the fortune of her banker half-brother, Max.[41]

Careful observation of the market was all, particularly as the young writer struggled to get known. In this context it is instructive to look at the hard work put in by Alice Meynell to establish herself. When she married the journalist Wilfred Meynell in 1877 her father allowed them £150 a year; but this was insufficient to support them in a middle-class lifestyle, especially as, good Catholics both, they went on to have seven children. Both sought and took on every sort of journalism, which provided not only income but an apprenticeship in the craft. Gradually Alice began to establish a specialism in artistic, literary and cultural criticism, allowing her increasingly to pick and choose the subjects about which she wrote and what she reviewed. When in 1893 John Lane at The Bodley Head re-published her collected essays as a book, and in the very next year John Singer Sargent drew her, it was plain she had arrived not simply as a serious working journalist but also as a woman of letters. As Linda Peterson has put it, the trajectory of Meynell's career demonstrated that there need not be a fundamental opposition between 'symbolic credit' and 'economic credit'.[42]

---

[39] BL Add Mss 61929 ff. 55–7, Mathilde Blind to Richard Garnett 29 January 1891; ff. 61–2 Richard Garnett to Mathilde Blind 7 May 1891; ff. 63–4, Mathilde Blind to Richard Garnett 17 May [1891].

[40] Richard Garnett, *Memoir,* prefacing Mathilde Blind, *Poetical Works*, ed. Arthur Symons (London 1900), p. 23.

[41] Thirlwell, *Into the Frame*, pp. 188, 249.

[42] Peterson, *Woman of Letters*, p. 185; her illuminating discussion of Alice Meynell is ch. 6 of the book.

Mathilde Blind found it hard to accept that there need be no such an opposition. Alice Meynell had, moreover, skilfully placed herself to take advantage of the divide beginning to open up in the 1890s between the highbrow and the popular sections of the market, a divide which widened in the next decade. Peterson sketches this divide as having several elements: the increasing characterisation of the single-volume high-culture novel as distinctively masculine, the demise of long-running periodicals and the short life of new ones, especially the more innovative ones. She suggests that this divide seriously wrong-footed the more popular 'New Woman' novelists of the 1890s, using the career of Mary Cholmondeley to explore the hypothesis. *Red Pottage*, published in 1899, a feminist celebration of sisterhood, was a considerable success; but none of Cholmondeley's subsequent work came close to matching it, in either reviews or sales.[43]

It is true that those who had made their names as New Woman writers disappear from view in the course of the Edwardian decade, not only Mary Cholmondeley but also others like Sarah Grand and Mona Caird. However, to those factors to which Peterson attributes a general shift of market opportunities for women writers should surely in this case be added the displacement of the New Woman caricature by a far more potent image, grounded in an obvious and increasingly noisy social and political reality, the woman suffrage campaigner. The woman writer intent on earning a living had to engage with this, whether for – or, like Mrs Humphry Ward, against.[44] Modern critics seem agreed that the suffrage campaign produced more effective plays than novels and a number of women writers deliberately targeted the stage.[45] Changing contexts and issues apart, however, Peterson's central proposition is an important one: to survive, the woman of letters, like the man of letters, had to work with and respond to the market in which she found herself.

One more caveat is needed here. To become a woman of letters was to be recognised and financially comfortable; it was not to make one's fortune. In her last years Frances Power Cobbe reflected bitterly that the £5,000 she had earned in a lifetime of journalism was less than her elder

---

[43] *Ibid.* ch. 7.

[44] See John Sutherland, *Mrs Humphry Ward* (Oxford 1990), ch. 25, and Bush, *Women against the Vote*, ch. 4.

[45] See the extended discussion in Eltis, *Acts of Desire*, ch. 5, pp. 160–200, esp. pp. 164–8.

brother's annual return from the family estate.[46] The world of the best-
sellers seems marked by an almost terrifying randomness, with neither
writers nor publishers being very sure what would sell in large quanti-
ties – until it did. Some of its denizens, like Charles Garvice and Florence
Barclay, are now totally unknown, while the primary audience for Hall
Caine and Marie Corelli consists of students of the period. Of the two
women, Corelli was the illegitimate daughter of a journalist and Barclay
was a vicar's wife, who took to writing during convalescence from
serious illness. Neither had much in the way of formal education,
what they had coming mostly from governesses.[47]

  This brings us back to the apparent irrelevance of higher education to
any kind of literary success. Yet when Mathilde Blind died, she left the
money inherited from Max to Newnham College, Cambridge. She had
had a relatively small amount of formal schooling herself, although
seeking out private teachers in Latin and Old German when staying
with family in Zurich, and throughout her life engaging in a formidable
programme of self-education and reading in several languages. These
experiences nourished in her a conviction that the way forward culturally for women as a group could only come through access to the best
education available.[48]

  At the time a link between higher education and literary achievement,
however measured, was not perceived by many. Fourteen of the
Newnhamites and six of the Girtonians published enough for 'writer'
to figure as one of their major occupations; but only three of the
Newnhamites and one or perhaps two or three of the Girtonians earned
significant income, a living if they needed it, from the work. In addition,
determining which of the Cambridge women lived by their pens, or
could have lived by their pens, proves not to be straightforward. It
would, for example, have been pleasing to include among the Girton
writers Rachel Susan Cook, daughter of the Professor of Ecclesiastical
History at St Andrews, one of the 'pioneers' of 1869, who contributed
reviews to the *Manchester Guardian* and became involved with
its editorial policy. But as in 1874 she married its celebrated editor

---

[46] Caine, *Victorian Feminists*, p. 110; see also Mitchell, *Frances Power Cobbe*,
    pp. 83, 144, 156, 177, 301, 335; and as John Sutherland has shown, as fast as
    Mrs Humphry Ward made money, her family succeeded in spending it.
[47] For a more extended survey see Part III of Waller, *Writers, Readers*.
[48] Thirlwell, *Into the Frame*, pp. 176–7, 226–7.

C. P. Scott, it is difficult to disentangle her contribution to the paper from her husband's.[49]

Of the three Girtonians with substantial lists of publications in the sample, two, both coming up in 1889, came from outside the UK. Anna De Wit was the daughter of a judge in the Dutch East Indies and a French mother. Fluent in Dutch, English, German and Italian, she acted as a correspondent and reviewer for Dutch and German papers on Dutch, English and Scandinavian literature and published extensively in Dutch and English. She never married and is described firmly as 'Linguist, author and journalist'; but it seems likely that there was a cushion of family money as well. Alexandra Von Herder, daughter of German aristocrats, was twice married, her second husband, General Munthe, being a Norwegian employed by the Chinese government. She published extensively in English, plays, poetry and accounts of Chinese history and culture. Again it seems plausible to expect a firm foundation of family money here. Perhaps for the third, the Englishwoman Kathleen Coates, who came to the College in 1909, literary earnings were a very useful top-up. Daughter of the Assistant Bursar of Queens' College, and married in 1917 to an Army major, she had four sons. Described as 'Novelist and journalist', she published steadily through the inter-war period and the Second World War, both light fiction and contributions to all the major women's magazines.

Some of the fourteen Newnhamites who published extensively have similar profiles, family money, either inherited or via a husband, as a base, with the likelihood of some additional intermittent income from publication. Ellen Crofts came up to Newnham in 1874 and stayed on as College Lecturer in English, until she married Francis Darwin in 1883. Thereafter she published occasional pieces on literature and ethics. Madeleine Dodds and Shena Potter, who both came up in 1904, published in their respective fields of history and government; but there was family money in both cases, especially that of Shena Potter, later Lady Simon of Wythenshawe.[50]

However there are also differences between the Newnham and the Girton writers in the sample. Six of the Newnhamites have lists of publications which are clearly by-products of serious academic and

[49] See the description of their combined operations in Onslow, *Women of the Press*, pp. 153–4.
[50] See also above p. 56 for her career in voluntary work.

scientific careers – plenty of symbolic credit but little if any financial credit. Five of these came up in 1914, Elen Elaine Austen, Frances Bradfield, Margaret Green, Isaline Horner and Alice Ikin; and one, the celebrated classical scholar Jane Harrison, had come up to Newnham in 1874. Both Isaline Horner – Squizzy, as she was always known – and Jane Harrison had family money as well. Another of Jane Harrison's contemporaries from 1874, Katherine Harris Bradley, fits in no category whatever. Bradley and her niece Edith Cooper formed a celebrated lesbian pair, who as 'Michael Field' published twenty-three books of plays and poetry. Yet again, however, there was a cushion of family money here.[51]

Three, perhaps four, from the sample undoubtedly earned their living at one point or another by their pens. Two of them, the adventurous Blanche Annette Smith and the multi-talented Leila Beatrice Legg, have already figured in these pages.[52] Constance Garnett, née Black, half belongs here. As we have already seen, she and her husband Edward found it hard to make ends meet on his salary as a publisher's reader; and the earnings from her distinguished Russian translations were intermittent. The Civil List pension from 1910 made a significant difference.[53]

Exactly contemporary with Constance and with Ada Radford was Amy Levy, who passionately wanted to write. Initially her family were well-off; but as their finances became increasingly straitened, Amy had to rely more and more on her own efforts.[54] Like so many others, she turned to journalism, for example writing several articles for *The Woman's World*, then edited and being ambitiously reshaped by Oscar Wilde.[55] Levy was well aware of the potential for tension between literary ambition and the need to eat; and her first novel, *The Romance of a Shop*, in 1888 has one of its young characters, an

---

[51] See Emma Donoghue, *We Are Michael Field* (Bath 1998). On the dominance of academic work in the publications of Newnham College's old students, see also the lists of publications in the Old Students' Club Letter, first included in 1908, *NCCL* pp. 44–63 and annually thereafter.

[52] Above, pp. 59, 63.   [53] Above, p. 27.

[54] Linda Hunt Beckman, *Amy Levy: Her Life and Letters* (Athens, OH 2000), pp. 75–6; for an image of Amy as a student, see p. 73.

[55] See Appendix B to Levy, *The Romance of a Shop*, ed. Bernstein, which reprints some of her journalism. She also contributed to the *Jewish Chronicle* and the *Gentleman's Magazine*.

4 Amy Levy as a student, 1880

artist, exclaim about a pedestrian piece of work, 'We all have to get down off our high horse ... if we want to live. I had ten guineas this morning for that thing.'[56] The overall theme of the novel is the struggle of a group of sisters, the Lorimers, left penniless, to make a living out of photography, slowly establishing itself as a serious art form – and remain ladies.

Levy's second novel, *Reuben Sachs*, a powerful if bleak evocation of the world of the more affluent sections of London Jewry in the 1880s, followed hard on the heels of the first, appearing in 1889.[57] We shall never know, however, whether she would have succeeded in negotiating the tension between literary ambition and sheer survival, following the

[56] Levy, *The Romance of a Shop*, ed. Bernstein, p. 157; cf. also Beckman, *Amy Levy*, pp. 243–4, Amy Levy to Dolly Radford (Ada's sister-in-law) 1884.
[57] Reprinted by Persephone Books (London 2001), with an introduction by Julia Neuberger.

example of Alice Meynell rather than that of Mathilde Blind. Early in
the morning of 10 September 1889 Amy Levy ended her own life,
profoundly shocking and distressing all those who knew her and
knew and admired her talent and her work.[58]

In the decades immediately before 1914 it was not obvious to women,
or to men for that matter, that the route to a creative life and artistic and
literary success lay through higher education. It undoubtedly helped to
have a cushion of family money, even if not enough to live on, as it had
helped George Eliot, Olive Schreiner, Frances Power Cobbe and Alice
Meynell.[59] The next key step was some form of training, whether in a
studio, at the Slade, a provincial repertory company, or journalism;
learning the craft, making contacts, getting known, gradually building
up a reputation, becoming visible. Linda Peterson has used the career of
Charlotte Riddell and her 1888 novel *A Struggle for Fame* to go further,
arguing that to become a modern professional author entailed becoming a public presence, London-based, and having some encounters with
the social life of Bohemia.[60]

There are several elements within this proposition, all important and
worth disentangling and considering separately. The first element is the
importance of a London base and contacts. Harriet Martineau had
recognised this as far back as the beginning of the 1830s; and although
Frances Power Cobbe's partner Mary Lloyd came increasingly to detest
London, Frances could not do without a London base.[61] The second
element is a preparedness to engage with and largely accept the conventions of celebrity. By the 1890s these would include a willingness to
allow the use of one's physical image in advertising and the active
management of associated publicity. As we have seen, one measure of
Alice Meynell's achievement was to be drawn by John Singer Sargent in
1894; then in 1897 she was also drawn by William Rothenstein for
inclusion in his series of lithographed drawings, *English Portraits*

---

[58] Beckman, *Amy Levy*, pp. 200–10.
[59] Gordon S. Haight, *George Eliot: A Biography* (Oxford 1968), p. 70; Ruth First
and Ann Scott, *Olive Schreiner: A Biography* (London 1989), p. 111; Caine,
Victorian Feminists, p. 119, and Mitchell, *Frances Power Cobbe*; for Meynell, see
above, p. 68.
[60] Peterson, *Woman of Letters*, ch. 5, esp. pp. 166–7.
[61] *Ibid.* pp. 75–6; Caine, *Victorian Feminists*, p. 128; Mitchell, *Frances Power
Cobbe*, pp. 153, 168, 186–7, 216, 271.

(1898).[62] Mary Chavelita Dunne, writing as George Egerton, published a volume of short stories, *Keynotes*, in 1893 with The Bodley Head, which stirred up controversy with its bold descriptions of middle-class women's erotic desires and occasional conduct. She was encouraged by the publisher John Lane to be photographed and then painted for publicity purposes. But her short hair and pince-nez provided caricaturists with too good an opportunity to miss. On 28 April 1894 *Punch* presented her as *Donna Quixote*; while in the same year Albert Morrow used her profile for the playbill for Sydney Grundy's *The New Woman*, adding to the wall beside her head the symbolic key which had been used to advertise the original short stories. She found it all too much to take.[63]

Others coped – or managed – better. Sarah Grand, in reality Mrs Frances McFall, used a profile photograph of her head and shoulders for her *carte-de-visite* and in 1897 provided a photograph of herself standing at her desk for *Notables of Britain: An Album of Portraits and Autographs of the Most Eminent Subjects of Her Majesty in the 60th Year of Her Reign*. A rosary was prominently displayed on the wall behind her, even though she was not a Catholic. In 1894 she had dutifully filled in a questionnaire, 'A Page of Confessions' – favourite flower, novelist etc. etc. – which was a regular feature of the magazine *The Woman at Home*. In 1896 the bicycling magazine *The Hub* included 'A Chat with Sarah Grand' in its series 'Women of Note in the Cycling World'.[64] Grand defended her use of a pseudonym, explaining only after the death of her estranged husband that her reasons included a wish to protect his privacy.[65] In not dissimilar fashion the prolific 'Mrs' L. T. Meade (actually the wife of a solicitor, Alfred Toulmin Smith) presented herself to interviewers and to the public at large as above all a womanly woman, attaching primacy to the domestic sphere. In reality she employed two, sometimes three, secretaries,

[62] For the Sargent, see above, p. 68; for Rothenstein, see the reproduction in Stetz, *Facing the Late Victorians*, p. 79.

[63] *Ibid*. p. 48; Stetz, *Gender and the London Theatre*, p. 62 and plate 11; the *Punch* cartoon is reproduced in Richardson and Willis, eds., *New Woman in Fiction and in Fact*, 'Introduction', p. 21; for the playbill image, see jacket and p. 6.

[64] Sarah Wintle, 'Horses, Bikes and Automobiles: New Woman on the Move', in Richardson and Willis eds., *New Woman in Fiction and in Fact*, pp. 66–78 at p. 66.

[65] Stetz, *Facing the Late Victorians*, pp. 52–3; Mangum, *Sarah Grand*, pp. 3–4, 22, 24.

worked in her office in the city until seven each evening and then read proofs at home after dinner.[66]

Part and parcel of visibility in London, public presence and celebrity, often entailing some engagement with the social life of Bohemia, was the even larger issue of freedom of movement for women. In 1892 the male star of investigative journalism in London in these years, W. T. Stead, grumbled 'if a girl means to be a journalist she ought to be a journalist out and out and not try to be a journalist up to nine o'clock and Miss Nancy after nine'.[67] Acting this out, however, was less than straightforward. As Charlotte O'Connor Eccles commented in 1893, 'One is horribly handicapped in being a woman. A man meets other men at his club; he can be out and about at all hours; he can insist without being thought bold and forward.'[68]

In the last decades of the nineteenth century it was becoming easier for women to come and go, either individually, or in pairs or groups, greatly aided by a steadily expanding public transport system. The Reading Room of the British Museum provided one such meeting place. Ladies had been allowed to become readers since the beginning of the century. The new building which opened in 1857 included a ladies' cloakroom, complete with woman attendant, and the new Reading Room included two tables reserved for lady readers – even though, to the irritation of some male readers, they did not always choose to sit at them.[69] Clubs for women only and clubs admitting women members as well as men began to appear in London in the course of the 1880s, their existence publicised by Amy Levy in an article in *The Women's World*.[70] The Women Writers' Club and the development of a club sub-culture to support the networking of women writers had antecedents, parallels and reinforcements.

Levy herself, however, would have been the first to admit that navigating round London was not always straightforward for the woman alone. The Lorimer sisters, the heroines of her first novel, *The Romance of a Shop* (1888), set out to make a career out of photography. Knowing

---

[66] Koven, *Slumming*, p. 215.   [67] Quoted in Koven, *Slumming*, p. 154.

[68] Quoted in Onslow, *Women of the Press*, p. 37.

[69] P. R. Harris, *A History of the British Museum Library 1753–1973* (London 1998), pp. 189, 282, 766–8; Beckman, *Amy Levy*, pp. 81–2; Bernstein, *Roomscape*, pp. 5–10.

[70] Amy Levy, 'Women and Club Life', *The Women's World* 1 (June 1888), pp. 364–7, reprinted in Appendix B to *The Romance of a Shop*, ed. Bernstein.

her city well, she makes them choose the location of their studio and plan their travel with care. This did not simply entail being central and going the cheapest way. There were some routes a woman could travel by omnibus on her own; there were others where it was necessary, however expensive, to take a cab and/or be accompanied. In the 1880s and 1890s, in spite of the relative freedom some of the women with teaching posts considered that London offered,[71] ladies had still to be self-conscious about their behaviour in public places and to know where one could and could not go – and at what times – unaccompanied, without being molested. As we have seen, the actress Elizabeth Robins had learned that she could not take an omnibus back to her lodgings after a late-night performance: it had to be a cab.[72] Clubs admitting women might be opening their doors, but Robins, C. S. Peel and Helena Swanwick all had to deal with unpleasant experiences of being accosted in the street on the borders of London's male clubland; and *The Girl's Own Paper* provided guidance for its readers on how to cope in such situations. As Judith Walkowitz has commented, the streets and public places of the late Victorian metropolis remained 'a contested terrain'.[73]

Location, dress, demeanour and company or its lack all seem to have played their part in shaping such situations; and these are themes to which we shall return in Chapter 7 below. Boundaries were drawn in subtle and complex ways and are sometimes hard for the historian fully to grasp. Sometimes they were so part of the framework of assumptions about appropriate behaviour that they pass almost without comment. In trying to uncover the contours of such behaviour more fully Olive Garnett's detailed and extensive diaries are a major resource. Olive's diaries appear to show her moving about London and beyond with considerable freedom. In July 1893, for example, she went alone to the Lyric Theatre in Shaftesbury Avenue to see Eleanora Duse in *La Dame aux Camélias*. On her way out, 'it was raining & I fell flat on my back, indeed, measured my entire length on the asphalt. Fortunately no hansoms were near, & no crowd to assist me up, & I was not hurt, but it was nasty.' Yet in September 1895, attending a performance of *Romeo and Juliet* at the Lyceum, in which her brother Oliver was taking

[71] See above, pp. 32–3.   [72] John, *Elizabeth Robins*, pp. 109–10; above p. 61.
[73] Judith Walkowitz, *City of Dreadful Delight: Narratives of Sexual Danger in Late Victorian London* (London 1992), pp. 51–2, 10.

part, she was pleased to find herself sitting next to an acquaintance, Mabel Robinson; and at the end of the play, 'Mabel offered to chaperon me if I would go to the supper on the stage. I thanked her & declined.'[74]

Olive often took the train to go to the Stepniaks' regular Saturday night At Homes in Bedford Park on her own. But as her comments about her fall above suggest, she remained careful about her deportment in public places, anxious about who might be watching. On her way to Bedford Park one evening with her sister Lucy, 'Lucy gave me a violent nudge & said that someone was looking at me very hard as if I ought to know him, whereupon I looked up & saw the Belgian gentleman, M. Sarolea [met at the Stepniaks on a previous occasion] & shook hands.' M. Sarolea was also part of the group returning by train to the centre of the city at the end of the evening and escorted the two Garnett sisters to the gates of the British Museum, telling them 'how surprised he was at English political & social freedom; how strange we girls seemed to him, how independent, how unlike girls on the continent etc. Indeed I think we astonished him very much, & that he thoroughly enjoyed the new experience of free talk alone with two young & at the same time highly respectable ladies.'[75] M. Sarolea might think them liberated; but plainly on the train they had been mindful of the convention that women travelling never initiated conversations with strangers. As Elizabeth Robins put it, one had to be 'too well behaved to do more than steal covert glances'.[76]

In assessing the extent of Olive's freedoms it is important to remember also that they may tell us most about what was acceptable on the Bohemian fringe of the metropolitan middle class. Deborah Epstein Nord has argued that London was unique in the freedoms it offered.[77] The situations of middle-class provincial girls were likely to have been both different and more constrained. In the Edwardian years, three decades later, the constraints imposed on Vera Brittain growing up in Buxton in Derbyshire seem to have been considerable.[78]

---

[74] *Diary of Olive Garnett 1890–93*, ed. Johnson, p. 208; *Diary of Olive Garnett 1893–5*, ed. Johnson, p. 201.

[75] *Diary of Olive Garnett 1890–93*, ed. Johnson, pp. 237–8.

[76] John, *Elizabeth Robins*, p. 159.

[77] Nord, *Walking the Victorian Streets*, ch. 6, '"Neither Pairs nor Odd": Women, Urban Community and Writing in the 1880s'.

[78] Paul Berry and Mark Bostridge, *Vera Brittain: A Life* (1995, 2nd edition London 2008), pp. 38–46, 72; see also the experience of Mary Hutton, below, p. 135.

Even in London the boundaries of respectable behaviour could be dramatised from the other side, as it were. In 1887 Elizabeth Cass, a milliner, was arrested for streetwalking in Regent Street. Contesting the allegation, she was acquitted in the Magistrates' Court, but not before the magistrate had delivered himself of the observation that no respectable woman was likely to be found there at nine o'clock at night.[79] The novelist Olive Schreiner, who was London-based in the 1880s, had also collided with these boundaries. She was described by Edward Carpenter as a 'pretty woman of apparently lady-like origin who did not wear a veil and seldom wore gloves, and who talked and laughed even in the streets quite naturally'.[80] In successive sets of lodgings she had trouble with landladies about her frequent male visitors; and once while she was walking around late at night with one visitor outside her lodgings in Portsea Place, a policeman attempted to take her in charge as a prostitute. Subsequently the landlady gave her notice.[81] By 1891, however, she had emerged from behind the pseudonym Ralph Iron, under which *The Story of an African Farm* had first been published, and allowed her publisher Fisher Unwin to include an impeccably bourgeois studio portrait as a frontispiece to the volume of socialist allegories, *Dreams*.[82]

Living alone in lodgings in London was beginning to be acceptable; but here too there were boundaries to be observed. When in October 1895 Olive Garnett was visiting her friend Matty Roscoe, now a student at Newnham, she reported, 'Discussion on New Woman. She is not to be found at Newnham, the girls think she is living in lodgings in London, supporting herself.'[83] Yet a couple of years earlier in 1892 Olive had written tartly about a Miss Emily Hughes who,

accompanied by her mother came to look for a Bloomsbury boarding house. Permission for her to try London for a while & live alone here has at last been granted her & the mother who appears to be a sensible woman, had an interview with May [one of Olive's sisters] & said that she and the father had certainly hoped that their only daughter would stay contentedly at home

---

[79] Walkowitz, *City of Dreadful Night*, pp. 127–8 and 128–30 for the newspaper correspondence generated.

[80] First and Scott, *Olive Schreiner*, p. 161.

[81] *Ibid.* pp. 144, 157; cf. also Walkowitz, *City of Dreadful Night*, p. 127 – it is not clear whether this is the same or a separate episode.

[82] Stetz, *Facing the Late Victorians*, p. 104.

[83] *Diary of Olive Garnett 1893–5*, ed. Johnson, p. 214

where she would have every luxury etc. etc. but since she wouldn't well she was to have her own way & would the Garnett family befriend her.

Miss Hughes, however, did not like the other people in her boarding house and initially took fright at the absence of a lock on her bedroom door. Clementina Black, union organiser and sister of Constance Garnett, did her best to help out by arranging a meeting with someone 'who might give her something to do on a ladies paper'; but although Miss Hughes thought she had 'to find what I am fitted for', she had no ideas of her own. 'Everyone hopes', concluded Olive, 'that she will get disgusted with failure in London, since it seems impossible she should succeed & that she will then return, sadder and wiser to her proper sphere.'[84] Ada Radford too lived on her own in lodgings in London in the 1880s and 1890s. However, her relations with her landlady were good enough to enable her to give at least one large and successful evening party in February 1895;[85] and she had at least some ideas about what she wanted to do and was prepared to try. The freedoms in finding accommodation and moving about in which Margaret Tew, the London teacher, would rejoice in 1912,[86] had been hard won.

Since one of the major themes in New Woman writing was the re-assessing and reshaping of boundaries in human relationships, one might expect some of the women writing in the genre to practise what they preached. Some, like George Egerton, and Menie Muriel Dowie, appear to have done so; however, following her third marriage in 1901, George Egerton's life and relationships seem to have followed a more conven-tional pattern, as did the lives of Emma Frances Brooke (*NC* 1872), Mona Caird and Sarah Grand.[87] Olive Schreiner, whose 1883 novel *The Story of an African Farm* had been the trail-blazer for the New Woman genre, did not seem to have been entirely sure, at least initially, whether she wanted to be considered a lady or not. More generally,

---

[84] *Diary of Olive Garnett 1890–3*, ed. Johnson, p. 79
[85] *Diary of Olive Garnett 1893–5*, ed. Johnson, pp. 150–1.
[86] See above, Chapter 2, p. 32.
[87] For individual biographical details, see John Sutherland, *Companion to Victorian Fiction*; Stetz, *Gender and the London Theatre*, p. 62. On Emma Frances Brooke, see also Kay Daniels, 'Emma Brooke: Fabian, Feminist and Writer', *Women's History Review* 12:2 (2003), pp. 153–68, which sets out not only her Fabian contacts but also those with the Men and Women's Club, see below. Sadly Dr Daniels' article was published posthumously, without footnotes. On Sarah Grand, see also Mangum, *Sarah Grand*, pp. 3–4.

despite media excitement about rethinking marriage and other human relationships, such boundaries appeared remarkably resilient.

In the wake of the Criminal Law Amendment Act of 1885 and Oscar Wilde's trial in 1895, friendships between males were becoming more circumscribed, and, if they had a sexual dimension, more discreet.[88] Strong female friendships still attracted less attention and were less likely to be labelled deviant – provided they too were discreet. Flamboyance and promiscuity were always a hazard. In the early 1860s the supporters of the *Englishwoman's Journal* had ended up giving the assertively lesbian Matilda – 'Max' – Hayes a wide berth.[89] While her sister was alive, Katherine Bradley and her niece Edith Cooper, who wrote as 'Michael Field', took pains to be discreet in the family circle and to present their relationship as one of shared intellectual pursuits and friendship; however, their joint *carte-de-visite* in the second half of the 1880s sent some clear signals – heads and shoulders touch, they might almost be joined at the waist.[90] J. A. Symonds was eager to suggest that the relationship between Violet Paget (the writer Vernon Lee) and Mary Robinson was a lesbian one; but Mary's parents were quite comfortable with what they saw as the older woman's intellectual friendship with and patronage of their daughter, more comfortable than they would be with Mary's eventual choice of a husband, the physically handicapped Jewish scholar James Darmesteter.[91]

What New Englanders knew as 'Boston marriages', long-term relationships between two women, often otherwise unattached and quite likely to be pioneers in professional work, were not uncommon and excited little censure in the years up to 1914. Frances Power Cobbe, writing at the beginning of the 1860s, had celebrated the freedom of the old maid to 'make true and tender friendships, such as not one man's heart in a hundred can imagine'. She herself would set up house with Mary Lloyd in 1864.[92] Such households were a common pattern among

[88] Rowbotham, *Edward Carpenter*, ch. 10.

[89] Pam Hirsch, *Barbara Leigh Smith Bodichon: Feminist, Artist and Rebel* (London 1998), pp. 196–200.

[90] Donoghue, *Michael Field*, pp. 29–33, 43, 46; Stetz, *Facing the Late Victorians*, p. 50.

[91] Vineta Colby, *Vernon Lee: A Literary Biography* (Charlottesville, VA 2003), pp. 51, 123–4.

[92] Mitchell, *Frances Power Cobbe*; see p. 126 for the quotation from her 1862 article 'Celibacy v. Marriage'.

the women teachers discussed above – the support Hannah Osborn provided for Kate Harding Street is one example. The relationship between Octavia Wilberforce and Elizabeth Robins gradually evolved in this way. Likewise Louisa Martindale's staunch companion was Ismay Fitzgerald; and for many years the MP and social campaigner Eleanor Rathbone and Elizabeth Macadam would share activities and eventually a household.[93]

Octavia Wilberforce remarked to another friend that 'a lasting and deeply loving relationship was entirely possible without sex'[94] and there is no reason to disbelieve her, despite the ways in which the advent of Freud seriously impoverished notions of friendship. And in Elizabeth Robins' case at least, her life had room not only for important female friendships – Florence Bell as well as Octavia Wilberforce – but also for major heterosexual relationships. She had been briefly married to a fellow actor in the United States and his suicide, in the depths of depression, was traumatic. A decade later she and the drama critic William Archer, who was already married, may have had a full-blown affair in the course of their collaboration in translating Ibsen and they remained close until the end of Archer's life. Both went to great lengths to conceal the extent of the relationship. Robins had no intention of jeopardising either her social status or her independence; and neither wanted to hurt Archer's wife, who preferred to live in the country.[95]

There were powerful taboos here which were slow to lose their power. In Florence in 1860 Frances Power Cobbe had declined to meet George Eliot, now living with the already married G. H. Lewes as his wife – 'What infinite pity it was that her real genius allied itself in such base fashion!'[96] In 1869 the Harvard critic and art historian Charles Eliot Norton described to an American correspondent the complexities and ambivalence of George Eliot's status:

She is an object of great interest and great curiosity to society here. She is not received in general society, and the women who visit her are either so *emancipée* as not to mind what the world says about them or have no social position to maintain. Lewes dines out a good deal, and some of the men with

---

[93] Above, pp. 46–7; John, *Elizabeth Robins*, p. 270; Susan Pedersen, *Eleanor Rathbone and the Politics of Conscience* (New Haven and London 2004), ch. 9.
[94] John, *Elizabeth Robins*, p. 271.   [95] *Ibid. passim* but esp. pp. 110–22.
[96] Mitchell, *Frances Power Cobbe*, p. 111; see also Cobbe's ostracism of Anna Kingsford in 1882 – *ibid.* p. 285.

whom he dines go without their wives to his house on Sundays. No one whom I have heard speak, speaks in other than terms of respect of Mrs Lewes, but the common feeling is that it will not do for society to condone so flagrant a breach as hers of a convention and a sentiment (to use no stronger terms) on which morality greatly relies for support. I suspect society is right in this.

Yet such 'suspicions' did not stop Norton and his wife from accepting invitations to lunch at the Lewes house.[97] And in June 1877 a woman student, Mary Hutton, who was not allowed to travel unaccompanied between Cambridge and Dublin wrote excitedly to her sister, 'I have seen George Eliot and Mr Lewes !!!!!' Eliot and Lewes were staying in Cambridge with the recently married Henry Sidgwick and his wife and visited Newnham, its students and its library one afternoon.[98] Even so, a quarter of a century later the twenty-four-year-old Susan Lushington could be found vehemently asserting to a Sussex house-party that George Eliot 'having lived in that way detracts immensely from the moral influence of her books upon a very large class of people'.[99] The lower-middle-class Lavinia Orton, mother of the writer Richard Church, was kin to George Eliot but collectively Lavinia's family disapproved of Eliot's 'brazen unconventionality over her domestic affairs'.[100]

A few years earlier, in the mid 1880s, the Men and Women's Club had been established, intended to explore unflinchingly 'the status of moral judgement, moral change, fact and truth, in the face of received opinion about the sexes'. Olive Schreiner was an active member, although, as we have seen, her efforts to act out her belief in free and unfettered friendships between the sexes were not problem-free. Eleanor Marx, who had recently set up house with Edward Aveling, declined membership of the Club, remarking, 'it is a very different matter to advocate certain things in theory and to have the courage to put one's theories into practice ... probably many of the good ladies in the Club would be much shocked at the idea of my becoming a member of it'.[101]

---

[97] Haight, *George Eliot*, p. 409.
[98] NCA, Hutton Papers, Mary Hutton to sister, 3 June 1877, see below, p. 135.
[99] Susan Lushington's ms diary, entry for Friday 13 April 1894 [actually 14 April]. I am indebted to Dr David Taylor for this reference and quote with his permission. Susan was the daughter of the Positivist lawyer Vernon Lushington.
[100] Richard Church, *Over the Bridge: An Essay in Autobiography* (London 1955, reprinted 1956), p. 53.
[101] First and Scott, *Olive Schreiner*, pp. 146–7.

Eleanor's liminal social position, as the daughter of a political exile, might have provided her with more leeway, a leeway which in this situation she chose not to exploit. The growing disjunction between Sarah Bernhardt's life and the roles she played was doubtless the more easily tolerated because she was French. Certainly Mathilde Blind, step-daughter of another émigré, the journalist Karl Blind, seems to have made the most of the difficulties people had in placing her within the English social system. She lived for spells in or in close proximity to the household of Ford Madox Brown; and for part of the time the relationship may have had a sexual dimension.[102] As we have seen, Mathilde was also close to Richard Garnett.[103] Her foreign origins may have combined with the self-consciously bohemian style of the Garnett circle to make it easier for Mathilde to bend conventions; and in her last years the bequest from her banker brother meant that she was a comparatively wealthy woman – money always helped.

More generally Eleanor Marx's and Elizabeth Robins' assessment of the enduring power of conventional assumptions is likely to be nearer the mark. Eleanor Marx certainly did not care about being seen as a lady; but as her comments make plain, she was under no illusion about majority attitudes. Assessing the reactions of her close friends to her relationship with Aveling is, however, difficult. He was not simply married and separated from his wife, he was also a dishonest trouble-maker; and many of Eleanor's friends, including Ernest and Dollie Radford, chose to make much of the latter as a ground for refusing to meet him.[104] Elizabeth Robins was quite clear that exposure of the full extent of her relationship with William Archer would do her serious damage socially. She might pioneer the presentation of Ibsen's controversial heroines upon the English stage;[105] but her own private life was kept firmly private.

---

[102] ODNB; Angela Thirlwell, 'Tender Human Tie. The Unconventional Intimacy of Ford Madox Brown and Mathilde Blind', *Times Literary Supplement* 10 October 2008, pp. 14–15.

[103] See above, pp. 66–8.

[104] Yvonne Kapp, *Eleanor Marx II: The Crowded Years 1884–1898* (London 1976, pbk 1979), p. 203.

[105] Sally Ledger, 'Ibsen, the New Woman and the Actress', in Richardson and Willis, eds., *New Woman in Fiction and in Fact*, pp. 79–93.

George Bernard Shaw had already made one of his most direct challenges to prevailing attitudes towards marriage in *Mrs Warren's Profession*, completed in 1894 but not allowed public performance by the Lord Chamberlain until 1925, although Shaw regularly re-submitted it, declaring himself content to pay the annual reader's fee because, as he informed the Lord Chamberlain, the play 'should be read carefully through each year by your whole staff'.[106] He was, however, under no illusions as to the length of time the process of re-education might take. In 1908 St John Hankin's play, *The Last of the De Mullins*, which asserted the freedom single parenthood might offer to a woman, was produced for two matinees at the Court Theatre by Granville Barker. The heroine was played by his wife, Lillah McCarthy; and Shaw commented afterwards to Barker that even the Court's audience, generally considered as one of the more advanced in London, were taken aback. He wrote:

In the 3rd Act Lillah appealed with extraordinary gusto to every unmarried woman of twenty-eight in the house to go straight out and procure a baby at once without the slightest regard to law or convention. As Lillah regards this as a most obvious and reasonable doctrine, she had no idea of the effect she was producing in the audience. At the end of the Act the majority were simply afraid to applaud: the thing had gone quite beyond mere play-acting for them, and although they were interested, they felt – quite rightly – that to clap such sentiments would be to vote for them.[107]

The dominant conventions were likewise acknowledged by Amy Levy: one of the sub-plots in her *Romance of a Shop* is a familiar and traditional one, the attempted seduction of one of the Lorimer sisters by the already-married society painter for whom she is sitting. The attempt is foiled at the last minute by the eldest sister; and the reader is left in no doubt that right and moral strength lie with her.[108] From 1901 onwards, Evelyn Sharp would be involved with fellow writer and journalist Henry Nevinson, already married and in the midst of a tempestuous affair with a third woman, Nannie Dryhurst. Eventually in 1933 Evelyn and Henry would be free to marry; but in the intervening period Evelyn lived alone and preserved an iron discretion. Both wanted

[106] Quoted Eltis, *Acts of Desire*, p. 162; see also below, p. 138, for a fuller account of the play.
[107] Quoted in *ibid*. p. 180; see also below, pp. 137–8, 140.
[108] Levy, *Romance of a Shop*, chs. xviii–xx.

to protect their families; and as some of Evelyn's writing was for children, she had to be extra watchful for her reputation.[109]

Late Victorian women writers – and actors and artists – had to be publicly visible in ways in which women teachers in secondary schools and universities did not. Indeed, women in the latter occupations risked endangering their livelihoods if they were publicly visible. For writers, actors and artists behaviour which breached dominant social conventions might bring a loss of social status but a gain in notoriety/publicity; women working in the creative arts might act as New Women, without necessarily sacrificing their livelihoods. However, to acknowledge this possibility is not to pretend there were no social and reputational costs in so behaving, costs of which many of them showed themselves aware.

[109] John, *Evelyn Sharp*, ch. 3.

5 | 'The real social divide existed between those who ... dirtied hands and face and those who did not': women white-collar workers (I)

New Women, then, are hard to find among those small numbers of women who went into independent secondary school and university teaching, into the higher ranks of government service, or into medicine. The professional advancement, survival even, of the first two groups depended upon impeccably lady-like and conventional behaviour. The women doctors had had to be bolstered from the beginning by the financial resources of family and/or friends to survive at all. Once qualified, these resources might allow a degree of eccentricity and/or non-conformity. In the creative arts and the media, the situation was different: a public profile and high visibility were increasingly necessary for success; they brought commissions and audiences. As we have seen, some enhanced visibility through notoriety. So were the real New Women the handful of the notorious? They seem painfully few to bear the whole burden of responsibility for the media feeding frenzy at the end of the 1880s and through the 1890s. Far more observed the prevailing conventions and kept their private lives, regular or irregular, firmly private.

Notoriety is not the only measure of visibility available; mass presence may offer an alternative. Yet, as we have seen, there were not that many women graduates, doctors, senior civil servants, writers or artists. If we really want to find large numbers of women moving into public or semi-public spaces, it is time to turn our attention to the much larger numbers of women who aimed for respectability rather than ladyhood: the women who were to be found in white-collar work, as rank and file nurses, as clerks in commercial enterprises and in the lower grades of government service, as librarians, as teachers in maintained schools and as shop assistants. It is time to look at the working women of the emerging lower middle class.

In the UK the middle class in general and the emergent lower middle class in particular have attracted less attention in the historiography than elsewhere in Europe, although Geoffrey Crossick has done much to remedy this.[1] Part of the explanation is that, as Crossick remarked in his first study, the British lower middle class at the end of the nineteenth century appeared an amorphous and several-stranded group. They included not only the 'classic petty bourgeoisie of shopkeepers and small business men', but also 'the new white collar salaried occupations, most notably clerks, but also managers, commercial travellers, school teachers and certain shop assistants'; possibly also 'lesser solicitors and the like [,] a range of small operators acting on the margins of their professions'.[2] A further part of the explanation for relative neglect, which bears directly on our enquiry, may lie in the conceptual demands made on historians and social scientists in locating and describing women in social class terms. It was and still is common to label women, working and non-working, on the basis of the occupations of the menfolk in their families, fathers or husbands.[3] If the men are difficult to classify, it is even harder to classify the women.

Yet young, self-supporting, mostly unmarried women were to be found in increasing numbers in the middle strand of the group, the new, white-collar salaried occupations. Moreover, according to that shrewd observer from Salford, Robert Roberts, they were more likely to achieve upward mobility from the working class than their male peers. He described his grandmother's careful positioning of his three aunts, so that each married 'above her station', one a journalist, a second a traveller in sugar and a third a police inspector; while their brother, Robert's father, stayed working class. It was, he concluded, 'always harder for a man to break into the higher

---

[1] See Geoffrey Crossick, ed., *The Lower Middle Class in Britain* (London 1977); Crossick and H.-G. Haupt, eds., *Shopkeepers and Master Artisans in Europe 1780–1914* (London 1984); Crossick, 'From Gentleman to the Residuum: Languages of Social Description in Victorian Britain', in Penelope J. Corfield, ed., *Language, History and Class* (Oxford 1991), pp. 150–78; Crossick, 'Metaphors of the Middle: The Discovery of the Petite Bourgeoisie 1880–1914', *Transactions of the Royal Historical Society*, 6th ser., 4 (1994), pp. 251–79; Crossick and Haupt, eds., *The Petite Bourgeoisie in Europe 1780–1914* (London 1995); Crossick and Serge Jaumain, eds., *Cathedrals of Consumption: The European Department Store 1850–1939* (London 1999).

[2] Crossick, *Lower Middle Class*, p. 12.

[3] Cf. Crossick, 'From Gentleman to the Residuum', p. 176. On twentieth-century sociologists' difficulties with this problem, see my comments in the survey article 'Setting the Scene', in the special issue on Cognitive Capital, edited by Marcus Richards and Ingrid Schoon, of the *Journal of Longitudinal and Life-course Studies* 1:3 (2010).

echelons'.[4] Later he mused more generally on the ways in which the aspirations of labour aristocrat and the more economically secure shop- and pub-keeping families were likely to be expressed:

Publicans' and shopkeepers' daughters, for instance, set the fashion in clothes for a district. Some went to private commercial colleges in the city, took music lessons or perhaps studied elocution – that short cut, it was felt, to 'culture' – at two shillings an hour, their new 'twang' tried out later over the bar and counter, earning them a deal of covert ridicule. Top families generally stood ever on the look-out for any activity or 'nice' connection which might edge them, or at least their children, into a higher social ambience.

'The real social divide', he concluded, 'existed between those who in earning daily bread, dirtied hands and face and those who did not.'[5]

That divide was beginning to widen in the second half of the long nineteenth century; and the process whereby, by the early 1950s, non-manual employment had become a realistic aspiration for many young women, including women from the working class, was under way before the outbreak of the First World War.[6] The main contours of these shifts can be discerned, albeit imperfectly, from census data 1861–1911. The fullest analysis is offered by Lee Holcombe in the Appendix to her 1973 study *Victorian Ladies at Work*.[7] The imperfections of the data make it possible to qualify and challenge parts of her detailed discussion; but the overall direction of her conclusions has not been challenged and it is an important one. In 1861 slightly under 200,000 women had been employed in teaching, nursing, shop and clerical work, both commercial and civil service, in England and Wales; by 1911 there were almost 800,000 of them – visibility indeed.

Such grand totals need to be qualified in various ways. These white-collar occupations grew much faster than other types of employment for both men and women in the period. In 1861 they had represented 7.6% of the total working population; by 1911 they represented 14.1%. In teaching, the census figures do not disaggregate totals for different kinds

---

[4] Robert Roberts, *The Classic Slum: Salford Life in the First Quarter of the Century* (first published Manchester 1971, Pelican pbk 1973), pp. 14–15.

[5] *Ibid.* p. 19.

[6] Selina Todd, *Young Women, Work, and Family in England 1918–1950* (Oxford 2005), p. 25.

[7] Lee Holcombe, *Victorian Ladies at Work: Middle-Class Working Women in England and Wales 1850–1914* (Hamden, CT 1973), pp. 203–17, on which the remainder of the paragraph is based.

of teaching – elementary school, endowed secondary school, maintained secondary school etc. – and as we shall see below, this obscures some crucial differences and developments. Nursing was an almost entirely feminised occupation. Even so, the overall shift is a dramatic one.

Within white-collar work for women there was a clear status hierarchy in the years before 1914. At the bottom of the heap were shop assistants, whose pay and conditions of service could resemble indentured servitude, especially if they were required to live in. Next came nurses. Their status would improve only after the First World War and professional registration. An extensive middle ground was occupied by clerks. Commercial clerks might do better – or worse – than those within the security of government employment. Librarianship, just beginning to take shape as a career path for men, but also one on which some women embarked, fits here. At the top of the heap were teachers in maintained schools, numerous, able to contemplate the possibility of professional status and the transmogrification of respectability into ladyhood, should they wish it.

It makes sense to start at the bottom of the heap, looking at the lives of women shop assistants. There are no English equivalents of Zola's great department store novel, *Au Bonheur des Dames*, in the *Rougon-Macquart* sequence (1883), although this novel was translated into English straightway and interestingly was the first of the sequence to be translated.[8] But women shop assistants are beginning to feature in the fiction of the period. Although neither H. G. Wells nor Arnold Bennett puts ordinary women shop assistants centre stage in *Kipps* (1905) or *The Old Wives' Tale* (1908), they are present in the supporting casts and Wells describes the life and working conditions of a young male shop assistant, from which his hero flees. Henry James characteristically constructs a complex imaginative and emotional life for a young woman telegraph clerk, employed among the staff of a post office counter within a grocer's shop, in his story *In the Cage* (1898).

In *The Odd Women* (1893), George Gissing takes the basic plot line which Amy Levy had used in *The Romance of a Shop* and develops it in

---

[8] The Cambridge University Library Catalogue lists a first translation from 1883 and a second from 1886. Zola liaised with the first translator, even before the French text was published – Robin Buss, editor's and translator's introduction to Penguin Classics translation (London 2001), p. xxxi.

far bleaker fashion.[9] The Madden sisters, like the Lorimer sisters, are left destitute on the death of a parent and have received neither an education nor a training which would fit them to earn their living. Alice, thinking she might have some aptitude for teaching, seeks positions as a governess, while recognising that 'there is so little choice for people like myself. Certificates and even degrees are asked for on every hand. With nothing but references to past employers, what can one expect? I know it will end in my taking a place without salary.' As indeed it does. Monica, aged 15, is apprenticed to a draper. 'She had no aptitude whatever for giving instruction, indeed had no aptitude for anything but being a pretty, cheerful, engaging girl, much dependent on the love and gentleness of those about her.'[10] Working first in Weston-super-Mare and then in Walworth, she finds the working hours and conditions, and the life of the hostel in which she is required to live, exhausting, deadening, and occasionally frightening. Eventually she escapes into marriage to a much older man; but as one might expect from Gissing, that proves disastrous in a different way.

Although there was no department store or shop-girl novel in English, English playwrights seized upon both phenomena with avidity. The subject of Harley Granville Barker's *The Madras House*, first performed in 1910, revived in 1925 with an entirely re-written last scene and performed again as recently as 1977 and 1992, was a department store of that name and its impact on all involved with it, from employees to owners. The subtleties and complexities of the play, however, puzzled both early audiences and critics.[11] Much more immediately accessible were the series of musical comedies performed at the Gaiety Theatre, including *The Shop Girl* (1894), *The Girl from Kays* (1902) and *The Girl Behind the Counter* (1906). The flavour is conveyed by a snatch of one of Bessie Brent's songs from *The Shop Girl*:

> But I soon learnt with a customer's aid
> How men make up to a sweet little maid,
> And another lesson I've learnt since then
> How a dear little girl 'makes up' for men.[12]

[9] For Levy's novel, see above, pp. 72–3, 76–7, 85.
[10] Penguin Classics edition 1993, pp. 15, 12.
[11] For text and performance history, see Harley Granville Barker, *Plays: Two*, edited with an introduction by Margery Morgan (London 1994); for initial reception, see Eltis, *Acts of Desire*, pp. 188–90.
[12] Eltis, *Acts of Desire*, pp. 182, 195–6.

One of Cicely Hamilton's earliest successes as a playwright was *Diana of Dobson's*, first performed in 1908. Her grim opening act, set in the women assistants' dormitory of Dobson's, the drapery store where the heroine is employed, was a deliberate challenge to the frothy fantasies of the musical comedies.[13] Hamilton in her turn was parodied by the Melville brothers in the dormitory scene of *The Bad Girl of the Family* in 1909, one of their hugely successful series of 'bad girl' melodramas, which also included *The Shop-Soiled Girl* of 1910, made into a film in 1915. The Melvilles' wicked but feisty heroines were often shop-girls; and the melodramas were strikingly successful in attracting cross-class audiences.[14]

Cicely Hamilton herself had never worked as a shop assistant; but she had guidance on the detail of conditions from the Labour politician Margaret Bondfield, who had.[15] The tenth of eleven children of a foreman lace-maker, autodidact, radical and ardent Congregationalist, Margaret, born in 1873, had tried being a pupil-teacher and hated it, so became an apprentice shop assistant in Brighton, earning £25 per annum, working a 75-hour week, and required, as the majority were, to live in accommodation provided by the employer. Spiritual and intellectual stimulus came only from the At Homes held every other Sunday for shop-girls, by Louisa Martindale, who lived in Brighton, the widowed mother of Hilda the factory inspector and Louisa the doctor.[16] Moving to London in 1894, Bondfield found working conditions which were no better; but through her printer brother she joined the Ideal Club, a debating and recreational centre in Tottenham Court Road. Next she joined the National Union of Shop Assistants, Warehousemen and Clerks; and making political contacts, she moved through the SDF to the ILP and then to the Fabians. From 1896–8 she went undercover, funded by the Women's Industrial Council, to investigate working conditions in as wide a range of shops as would employ her. Her 1898 report fleshed out what was already known, detailing the prevalence of long hours, unhealthy working conditions and even more unhealthy living conditions, low pay, reduced further by fines for trivialities, and a host of restrictions and petty tyrannies. It provided ample

---

[13] See Hamilton, *Diana of Dobson's*, Act 1.
[14] Eltis, *Acts of Desire*, pp. 196–200.
[15] Margaret Bondfield, *A Life's Work* (London 1949), p. 72.
[16] *Ibid.* p. 26; Martindale, *One Generation to Another*, pp. 33–4.

ammunition for Sir John Lubbock, now Lord Avebury, who had been campaigning for twenty years to try to regulate shop opening hours, and he secured a Select Committee in the Lords.[17]

Effective legislation to limit hours was not, however, achieved until 1911. Smaller shopkeepers, with narrower profit margins, long resisted such efforts. Staying open that extra hour could, they reckoned, make all the difference to the bottom line.

The union was weak, the supply of desperate candidates for jobs appearing always to exceed demand. The census data are least satisfactory in terms of these occupations, beginning to distinguish 'dealers' from 'workers' only in 1901.[18] Hosgood, however, has guessed that women shop assistants numbered some half-million by 1914.[19] Although some more enlightened employers began to develop their own training schemes, personability and relevant experience still counted for far more in securing a job than any 'skill'; and both men and women assistants were crucially dependent on references from previous employers.

Personability, the foundation equally of musical comedy fantasies and the early successes of the 'bad girls' of melodrama, led directly into considerations of class and status. As Hugh McLeod explained: 'Clerks and shop assistants had to behave in ways that many manual workers would have regarded as demeaning: they not only had to work for their employers, but they had to dress and speak in ways acceptable, and often to make some show of deference towards employers or [and?] customers.' They could resent this or embrace it as respectability.[20] Women shop assistants were peculiarly exploitable on this score. As Bill Lancaster put it, the 'quest for respectability, particularly among women, presented employers with an abundance of potentially deferential and, because of their sex, cheap labour'.[21] An 1892 Select

---

[17] For the early stages of Bondfield's career, see the first four chapters of *A Life's Work*; see also the informative entry on Bondfield by Marion Miliband in John Saville and Joyce Bellamy, *Dictionary of Labour Biography*, vol. II (London 1974).

[18] Holcombe, *Victorian Ladies at Work*, Appendix, s. 3, pp. 205–9.

[19] Christopher Hosgood, '"Mercantile Monasteries": Shops, Shop Assistants and Shop Life in Late Victorian and Edwardian Britain', *Journal of British Studies* 38:3 (1999), pp. 322–52, at pp. 335–6.

[20] Hugh McLeod, 'White Collar Values and the Role of Religion', in Crossick, ed., *Lower Middle Class*, pp. 61–88, at p. 72.

[21] Bill Lancaster, *The Department Store: A Social History* (London 1995), p. 141.

Committee estimated that women shop assistants were paid a third less than men;[22] and they were invariably required to give up work on marriage. Living-in was a less prevalent feature in the North than in the South; but it did not disappear entirely until the inter-war years.[23]

McLeod lumped clerks together with shop assistants in having to behave deferentially towards employers and customers. This is to over-state the degree of deference competent clerks needed to show, partic-ularly as the skills of shorthand and typing gained currency and importance. It is also to understate, indeed to ignore, the extent to which nurses were still regarded as domestic servants. It will not do to claim, as Chris Willis does, that nursing 'was a highly acceptable middle class profession' by the late 1890s.[24] The icon that Florence Nightingale had become was insufficient on its own to raise the status of the occupation, the more so as she herself was ambivalent on the subject of compulsory registration. A rise in status would come only with the 1919 legislation compelling registration of all those claiming to be nurses. Thenceforward training to secure registration became the order of the day. In the years up to 1914, however, the majority of those describing themselves as nurses had had no training: Brian Abel-Smith has estimated that 90% (57,500 out of 63,500) of those returned as nurses in the 1901 Census were untrained.[25] The achievements of the Crimea may have put paid to grosser caricatures like Sairey Gamp in Charles Dickens' *Martin Chuzzlewit* but the majority of 'nurses', espe-cially those working in private employ, were still regarded as servants and effectively functioned as such. The 1912 comments of Hannah Floretta Cohen, much involved in schemes to encourage women with some education to emigrate to Canada, underline the low status of English nurses, even those with training. 'The demand for nurses [in Canada],' she wrote,

22 Hosgood, 'Mercantile Monasteries', p. 329.
23 For more detail about conditions see in particular Hosgood, 'Mercantile Monasteries' and Lancaster, *Department Store*, ch. 8; for attempts to legislate on the subject, see the patchy accounts in W. B. Whitaker, *Victorian and Edwardian Shopworkers: The Struggle to Obtain Better Conditions and a Half Holiday* (Newton Abbot 1973) and Lancaster, *Department Store*.
24 Chris Willis, '"Heaven defend me from political or highly educated women!": Packaging the New Woman for Mass Consumption', in Willis and Richardson, eds., *New Woman in Fiction and in Fact*, pp. 53–65 at p. 63.
25 See above, p. 49.

is even greater than the demand for teachers. There is a certain amount of prejudice against English trained nurses, due in part to the lack of any definite and recognised standard of training, and in part to the differences of method. But the remuneration is excellent, and the conditions of training, at any rate in the Winnipeg Hospital ... are infinitely more agreeable than those which obtain in most hospitals in England.[26]

The scant coverage of nursing in the news of old girls in *Our Chronicle*, the magazine of the Skinners' Company School for Girls, makes the same point by omission. The one article, 'Lady Nurses – An Opening for Girls', in 1906 is about training to become a Norland Nanny. A list of the known occupations of old girls in 1913 includes some nurses – but that is all. By contrast the successes most frequently and regularly celebrated were in examinations for government clerkships and in the commercial world.[27]

The case for treating the fortunes of the old girls of this one school as a significant pointer – a weather-cock – is twofold. First, situated as the school and its catchment area were at the top of Stamford Hill, they were highly sensitive to the massive demographic and employment shifts which affected London in this period; the area was briefly buoyant as the tides of migration and economic innovation lapped its edges and then went into decline as these moved on.[28] Second, the school recruited its pupils from exactly the constituency in which we are interested: the lower middle and respectable working classes. For in the years up to 1914 the Skinners' Company Girls' School was not in the front rank of girls' independent schools. Although founded and governed by a livery company, the school's funding was never lavish: the capital set aside as a quasi-endowment had all been used up by 1908 and the school had availed itself of the earliest opportunities to seek financial support from the Local Education Authority (LEA), first the London School Board

---

[26] *NCCL* 1912, pp. 70–5, 'Openings in Canada for Educated Women'. She makes it plain that her target audience is not graduates but girls with a secondary schooling. See also her earlier article, 'The Colonial Intelligence League', *NCCL* 1911, pp. 59–60.

[27] *OC* May 1906 and May 1913; *OC* 1891–1914 *passim*. See e.g. Old Girls' News, June 1895, March and June 1896, March and June 1897; February 1898 list of occupations of the members of the Old Girls' Association; June 1897 article, 'Shorthand and Typing as a Career for Girls'; May 1908 article, 'Life as a Post Office Clerk'.

[28] Gillian Sutherland, *The Education of Girls: The Contribution of the Skinners' Company 1890–2010* (London 2010), pp. 10–13.

and then its successor, the London County Council.[29] The normal leaving age for Skinners' girls was 16 rather than 18; and although a trickle of old girls went on to higher education, they usually managed it by means of a couple of extra years in the sixth form at the North London Collegiate School, or St Paul's Girls' School, or through evening classes.[30]

At the same time the Skinners' Company Girls' School did not lack ambition. Staff celebrated their academic successes whenever they had them – their first graduate, Etta Taylor in 1899, and one of their earliest medical students, Eva White in 1910 – and *Our Chronicle* carried periodic articles about life at the Cambridge, Oxford and London colleges for women.[31] There were the usual poems and stories from current pupils. In addition the articles from old students – presumably invited – not only described life in higher education, they also represented a steady drip-feed of information about other occupations, on the work of deaconesses, on elementary school teaching, on careers in domestic science teaching, horticulture, gymnastics and sport, fashion illustration and running an employment bureau. There is every sign that there was a strong, almost missionary, editorial policy, using the magazine to disseminate information about occupational opportunities and raise aspirations.[32] All of this makes the absence of mention of nursing, other than nursery nursing, whether in hospitals or private employment, the more striking. It is hard to escape the conclusion that it simply did not rate.

---

[29] Sutherland, *Skinners'*, pp. 16 n.29, 20 n.35.

[30] E.g. OC Old Girls' News, March 1897, reports a girl holding a leaving exhibition at the North London Collegiate School (henceforward NLCS); October 1900 report of Louise Davey now at Somerville College, Oxford via NLCS; March 1904 leaving exhibition held at St Paul's Girls' School; January 1908 leaving exhibition at NLCS. *Skinners' Academy Archives*, Programme for prizegiving 1906 reports leaving exhibitions being held at NLCS, at Bedford College, London, at Newnham College, Cambridge and at the Domestic Economy Training College of the Northern Polytechnic.

[31] OC February 1899 (Etta Taylor), September 1910 (Eva M. White, 'Life in a Medical School'); regular reporting of all academic successes, e.g. as in September 1909, but see also articles June 1892 (Girton), May 1907 (Bedford), January 1910 (Newnham).

[32] OC June 1894 (deaconesses), October 1894 (elementary school teaching), February 1899 (cookery, needlework and laundry work), October 1905 (horticulture), February 1907 (gymnastics), January 1911 (employment bureau), May 1913 (fashion illustration).

The distinctiveness of *Our Chronicle* and an editorial policy which was quite clear and unashamed about the instrumental value of the education the school offered, whatever else it also brought, is underlined by a comparison with *The Persean*, the magazine of the Perse School for Girls in Cambridge. This school considered itself a first-rate one and a proportion of its pupils did indeed go straight on to higher education, often to Newnham and Girton. Its style and aspirations are perfectly conveyed by the following paragraph from news of old girls in March 1911: 'Miss Olive Clarkson is at home and does parish work, she is also assistant secretary to the Girls' Friendly Society. Her sister is in her third year at Newnham and is taking Mathematics.'[33] Lorina Clarkson would go on to teach Mathematics. These were ladies rather than women and the content and style of *The Persean* more closely resembled the *Girton Review* and the *Newnham College Club Letter* than it did *Our Chronicle*, with literary contributions from old girls as well as current pupils, accounts of charitable work, local government involvement, occasional travelogues and cultural experiences.[34] In December 1910 an enterprising new editor attempted to launch a regular series, 'Where We Live and What We Do' but this folded after a few contributions; and the semi-serious, carefully self-advertising

[33] *Persean*, 6, p. 263.

[34] *Persean*, October 1894, pp. 18–22, Mary Burn, 'Among the Water Babies' (mission and charitable work with barge people); October 1894, pp. 25–31, M.E.F., 'The Oxford Movement'; February 1895, pp. 129–33, H. Kempthorne, 'A School Board Election'; June 1895, pp. 141–4, M.E.F., 'School's Aftermath' ('no girl now aspires to be "finished" at seventeen or eighteen'); October 1895, pp. 157–61, R.R., 'The Keswick School of Industrial Arts' (Ruskin and the Rawnsleys); February 1896, pp. 253–6, anon., 'The Royal Holloway College'; February 1897, pp. 371–4, A.M. Tebbutt, 'Our Exam' (on practical and theoretical tests in butter and cheese-making); October 1898, pp. 8–13, C. Bradbury, 'Dispensing as an Occupation for Women'; 1899-1902 (a single undifferentiated bound volume), pp. 238–4, anon. 'St Leonard's'; 1899-1902, pp. 296–301, R. A. S. M., 'An Excavator's Day on an Archaeological Site in Palestine'; March 1905, pp. 240–3, Anne Gross, 'A Peep into an Indian Frontier Medical Mission'; November 1909, pp. 25–33, D. F. Conybeare, 'The Children's Country Holiday Fund'; March 1910, pp. 62–5, E. M. Spearing, 'A London College' (Bedford); December 1911, pp. 329–32, C. L. Digby, 'Social Service' (a call for voluntary work); December 1912, pp. 12–14, M. A Gaskell, 'Girl Guides in Cambridge'; March 1914, pp. 151–5, Caroline Grosvenor, 'The Colonial Intelligence League for Educated Women' (focus on opportunities in Canada, cf. the article by H. F. Cohen in *NCCL* cited above, p. 95, note 26).

efforts of Frances Beales, living in Chelsea, who described herself cheerfully as 'a literary hack', stand out in their difference.[35]

A handful of old girls did go into nursing and one contributed 'A Short Account of the Work of a Nurse at St George's Hospital' to the short-lived series.[36] Yet the information that the training took four years, that one could not be accepted for training before the age of 23 and that at the end of all this a sister's post might bring £35 p.a. did not make the work appear attractive or competitive with other occupations. It is possible, although nowhere stated, that the stipend was to be augmented by free or subsidised board and lodging and possibly by the provision of uniform. Even so, the article, based on the experience of the author's sister, reads as if it were designed to explain there could be some financial reward for what was essentially charitable work, undertaken by a lady who had given up all hope of marriage. A number of women who had begun teaching in elementary schools in London between 1900 and 1914, interviewed by Frances Widdowson at the end of the 1970s, stressed the disincentives represented by the late age at which any nursing training began and the necessity of living in hospital accommodation; and two, whose mothers had worked as nurses, strongly discouraged their daughters from following in their footsteps.[37]

The extensive coverage of Skinners' old girls' employment in commercial and government clerical posts underlines the importance of this developing field of work. While there might have been little to choose

[35] The first of the series in *Persean*, December 1910, pp. 214–15, Barbara Beck, 'Training as a Children's Nurse', the last the article on nursing cited below in note 36. In between came dispensing and a domestic training college. It is not clear whether Frances Beales' contributions had initially been intended to be included in the sequence. She had described herself as a 'literary hack' in the news she sent in to the regular column of old girls' news, December 1910, pp. 215–16, but then went on to contribute two articles, 'Discursive Digressions of a Working Woman', March 1911, pp. 225–30, and June 1911, pp. 279–84.

[36] *Persean*, October 1911, pp. 309–11, A. M. Nicholls. An article later in the year, Lucilla S. Lincoln, 'Kindergarten Work', is explicit that after three years' training the head of a kindergarten could expect either £40 p.a. + full board or £100 p.a. if non-resident, December 1911, pp. 361–3.

[37] Frances Widdowson, '"Educating Teacher": Women and Elementary Teaching in London 1900–1914', in Leonore Davidoff and Belinda Westover, eds., *Our Work, Our Lives, Our Words: Women's History and Women's Work* (Basingstoke 1986), pp. 99–123, at pp. 108–9, 118.

between the pay and working conditions of the lowest grade of women commercial clerks and that of shop assistants – always excepting the requirement to live in – at the other end of the scale, the possibilities of reasonable pay and interesting work could be significantly greater. Those who have attempted to analyse census data – Holcombe, Anderson and Zimmeck – have produced differing totals for the national situation in 1911, ranging from about 125,000 to 180,000; but all are agreed on the trend: clerical work was a rapidly expanding area of employment in the economy in general in the second half of the century and the employment of women as clerks grew faster than that of men.[38]

It has been a convention of the historiography, reinforced by Anderson, to portray the overall expansion in the market for clerical labour as leading to over-supply, the deterioration of terms and conditions and the development of fierce hostility on the part of male clerks to the entry of women workers. However Michael Heller's study, *London Clerical Workers, 1880–1914*,[39] convincingly challenges this narrative of decline and conflict. Heller's primary focus is the work and life of male clerks;[40] but a crucial part of his argument for buoyancy is to show the development of a dual clerical labour market, women clerks gradually displacing boys as secondary labour. A high turnover in their numbers was ensured by the operation of a near-universal marriage bar, which meant they offered no threat to men in the primary labour market, intent on working their way up within organisations. Of the 32,893 female clerical workers recorded in London in the 1911 Census, 31,939 were single.[41]

Although, *pace* McLeod, personability continued to play a part in clerical work, there was also a skill element which grew steadily in

---

[38] Holcombe, *Victorian Ladies at Work*, Appendix, s. 4, pp. 209–11 (about 125,000); Gregory Anderson, *Victorian Clerks* (Manchester 1976), p. 56 (177,000); Meta Zimmeck, 'Jobs for the Girls: The Expansion of Clerical Work for Women, 1850–1914', in Angela John, ed., *Unequal Opportunities: Women's Employment in England 1800–1918* (Oxford 1986), pp. 153–77, at p. 154 (166,000). And all have problems with estimating the clerical grades of the civil service, since census returns did not adequately differentiate between clerical and other posts.

[39] London 2011. I am indebted to Jonathan Wild for this reference.

[40] *Ibid.* pp. 3, 15.

[41] *Ibid.* p. 113; see also ch. 5, 'The Mechanization and Feminization of the Office 1870–1914: Threats or Opportunities?', pp. 111–31.

importance for both men and women. Even from mid-century good penmanship and some acquaintance with a foreign language could give a girl a distinct 'edge'. In 1863–4 that devoted student of Victorian womanhood A. J. Munby was fascinated to meet

A bona fide female 'city clerk'; a copying clerk, in fact, at a mercantile house in Old Broad Street. It was interesting to know the details & results of such a phenomenon. One of these results was, that she had none of the frippery and giggling frivolity of other girls of her class. She had spoken to me frankly at first, and now she talked soberly and gravely, just as a young man might have done, about her affairs. She was twentytwo [*sic*], and had been three years a clerk under her present employers ... There were only three or four other firms that she knew of, who have any female clerks. In the office where she is, there are several other girls; & their work is the same as the men's. 'We are instead of gentlemen', she said.

The girls however are all mere copying clerks, and have nothing to do with the accounts. She knew nothing of accounts: but 'it requires you to have a good plain education', she said, 'to do our work'. There is one German girl in the office, who copies the German letters; and she herself is able to copy French ones tolerably.

She worked an eight-hour day for a salary of £1 per week. Two years later he would himself employ a woman clerk from a law stationer's to copy his own manuscript.[42]

Language skills continued to be important; but the advent of shorthand and typing soon displaced good penmanship. By the end of the century there were popular novels about girl typists, such as Olive P. Rayner's *The Typewriter Girl* of 1897 and Tom Gallon's *The Girl Behind the Keys* in 1903. Besides the unqualified governess Alice, and the equally unqualified shop-girl Monica, Gissing's *Odd Women* also offered a portrait of Rhoda Nunn, who had used a tiny legacy to lever herself out of teaching and learn shorthand, book-keeping and commercial correspondence; soon she realised she needed typewriting as well. Subsequently she joined forces with her typewriting teacher to open their own school to teach women these skills.[43] In the novel a plan is hatched to teach these skills to Monica and rescue her from the draper's shop, but it fails – she simply does not apply herself. The playwrights climbed on

---

[42] Derek Hudson, *Munby: Man of Two Worlds. The Life and Diaries of Arthur J. Munby 1828–1910* (London 1972), pp. 156, 209.

[43] Gissing, *Odd Women*, pp. 23–4.

this band-wagon too, although women clerks offered less scope for visual spectacle than women shop assistants. Netta Syrett's portrayal of a woman clerk's life in *The Finding of Nancy* (1902) was a bleak one. J. M. Barrie went to the other extreme, however, in *The Twelve-Pound Look* in 1910; his heroine was a woman who divorced her husband in order to achieve economic independence as a shorthand typist.[44]

As Jonathan Wild has pointed out, Gissing was the foremost chronicler of late Victorian clerks, both women and men, in British fiction. Yet while Wild himself has explored literary representations of male clerks in the period 1880–1939, a study which complements Heller's study of their life and work, the lives and literary portrayals of female clerks in either life or literatures have yet to be examined.[45] For the time being, we have to make do with clues and fragments. For example, in challenging the argument that hostility to women clerks was widespread among men clerks, Heller makes the telling point that many fathers who were clerks encouraged their daughters as well as their sons into such work. In the competitions for female clerical posts in the GPO in April 1911, for example, over a third of the applicants had fathers employed in clerical and civil service work.[46] The background and experience of Florence Johnson, born in 1892, seems typical. Her father was a correspondence clerk with the Southern Railways and her mother had been a Post Office telegraphist before marriage. When Florence left school at 16 she went to a private secretarial college, where she learned shorthand and typing. At 18, in 1910, she joined the secretarial staff of the Metropolitan Water Board, where she remained for over thirty-eight years, never marrying. One of two women clerks interviewed at the beginning of the 1970s for the Essex University project, 'Family Life and Work Experience before 1918', she was asked how she might place her family in the social structure of the day and responded, 'we were middle class'. Her parents 'didn't have a lot of money but – there was no evidence of struggling I would say'.[47] Her two brothers became respectively an accountant and a solicitor.

[44] Eltis, *Acts of Desire*, pp. 176, 182–3.

[45] Jonathan Wild, *The Rise of the Office Clerk in Literary Culture 1880–1939* (Basingstoke 2006), pp. 5, 33 *et seq.* I am indebted to Chris Stray for this reference.

[46] Heller, *London Clerical Workers*, pp. 127, 129.

[47] British Library Sound Archives (henceforward BLSA), C707/300. Information about Florence's life comes entirely from this interview. For more about the original study, see Paul Thompson, *The Edwardians: The Remaking of British*

Florence remembered a household where there were books, news-papers and magazines. Although their visitors were mostly family members living nearby, they also went out, to the theatre, opera, music hall and concerts. Work at the Water Board provided access to a whole range of clubs and their social activities, 'dances and whist drives and concerts and – all sorts of things you see. Football would give a dance – and the rifle club would give a dance and the tennis club and the golf club ... A lot of social life.' Tennis was the game she learned there and most enjoyed playing, but she was plainly a good organiser, since she also found herself on a number of the other committees. Following a stroke, Florence's mother was bedridden for the last fifteen years of her life. Florence continued to work – 'two doctors said don't give up your job' – and probably helped with the medical bills but she felt unable to bring friends home. The family situation set narrow limits on her social and cultural life.

Florence Johnson was unadventurous politically, taking her political views 'over from father', a staunch Conservative. Elsie Barralet, born in 1891 and interviewed at the same time, developed somewhat wider horizons: 'I had a friend who was a suffragette and she did open my eyes to the poor deal that women were getting and I began to think in her direction although I never had any activities, but she did.'[48] Elsie's route to white-collar employment was less typical than that taken by Florence but nevertheless one which underlines the importance of the general expansion of educational opportunities from the end of the 1880s onwards, an expansion which is mapped in greater detail below. Elsie's father had started as a clerk in the offices of the Great Eastern Railway but then became the secretary and subsequently one of the directors of a builders' merchants. Her mother, his second wife, had been a seamstress before marriage. At the age of 12 Elsie's parents let her compete for a place at one of the new Technical Schools, which she secured: '"I was one of the superior ones" – laughs'. She was worked very hard there and by the age of 16 had had enough. She changed direction and became a milliner and seamstress. However the sudden deaths of both her father and her favourite brother meant she needed a better-paying job: 'It was a warehouse and they used to make clothes and they used to give material out to people in the East End of London,

Society (London 1975). All the interviews are available as both sound recordings and transcriptions.
[48]   BLSA, C707/216.

mostly Jews, and they wanted someone to do the booking and the checking of the work.' It was a situation in which her literacy, numeracy and hands-on experience of work in the garment trade all came together. She married in 1916 but continued working at the warehouse until the end of the War and the return of her husband from the Navy. He, having been a clerk in a piano factory, then moved to his father's and uncle's builders' merchants as a manager. During the Second World War, Elsie would work again, as an insurance agent, which she quite enjoyed, but eventually gave it up because both her husband and her daughter disapproved.

In their different contexts and ways both Florence Johnson and Elsie Barralet developed interests which began to push out the boundaries of home and work; and it seems plausible to suggest that clerical work for women could bring with it some real possibilities for social and cultural enhancement. In his discussion of the cultural lives of male clerks, a chapter called 'What Was Leonard Bast Really Like?', Jonathan Rose suggested that after 1900 there were beginning to be some 'female Basts as well'.[49] There were certainly 'female Basts'. Women's job opportunities may have been capped by a marriage bar, but there are ample signs that, like their male colleagues, they took advantage of the expansion of educational opportunities from the end of the 1880s on. These opportunities were most conspicuous in London but not absent elsewhere. A series of shifts in national policy made it much easier for localities to provide post-elementary teaching. From 1889 the windfall of the 'whisky money', the proceeds of the duty on spirits, was diverted to the new county and county borough councils, to be spent in the encouragement of technical education, an education which tended to be broadly interpreted, capable of embracing everything from French and history through book-keeping and typing to mechanical engineering. From 1893 a new Code of government grants for night schools was promulgated, untying them at last from the elementary curriculum. The expansion of night school provision thereby triggered made a particular contribution, allowing those already working to take further courses to enhance their skills and prospects. Then the Education Act of 1902 required the new Local Education Authorities, the county and county

---

[49] Jonathan Rose, *The Intellectual Life of the British Working Classes* (London 2001), ch. 12, see esp. pp. 412–13. Leonard Bast was the culturally and socially insecure clerk in *Howard's End*, E. M. Forster's novel of 1910.

borough councils, to provide maintained secondary schools. These were unlikely to teach book-keeping and typing but they certainly taught more mathematics and English than had been available in the elementary school – and French.[50] It would be good to know more about the responses of individual LEAs outside London to these new resources and responsibilities.

In London the London County Council had seized the opportunities offered by the whisky money from 1889; and in 1903 they succeeded the London School Board as the LEA for London at elementary and post-elementary level. They made the most of these growing resources and responsibilities. Besides the Technical School which Elsie Barralet attended, another illustration of this is provided by the LCC's relationship with the Skinners' Company School for Girls, developing steadily from the early 1890s and sketched above.[51] By 1910–11 those attending evening classes in London numbered 128,464 and three of the six most popular subjects were book-keeping, shorthand and French.[52] LEA evening class work was complemented by the efforts of the Polytechnics and by an explosion of private enterprises. The Polytechnic pace-maker was Regent Street. By 1910 it had developed two commercial departments; and between 1905 and 1913 almost 29% of the female students attending classes were estimated as being in white-collar occupations, a proportion not far off that among male students, estimated at 34%.[53] In *The Odd Women* Gissing had offered Rhoda Nunn's shorthand and typing school as emblematic of private enterprise. In real life Florence Johnson's school was one such. The great success story, however, was Pitman's. Their pitch to young women was clear and unambiguous, as their 1893 Prospectus put it, 'girls would do much better by learning Shorthand and Typewriting (by which, when proficient, they could earn a competency), than in acquiring mechanical dexterity on the piano, which only pays those who have great musical taste and ability, or in endeavouring to earn a living as governesses

[50] See Gillian Sutherland, 'Education', in Thompson, ed., *Cambridge Social History of Britain*, pp. 119–70, at pp. 151–2; also the discussion of the 1902 Act below, pp. 122–3, 125–7.

[51] See above, pp. 95–6 and note 29.

[52] Heller, *London Clerical Workers*, p. 166; cf. also Susan D. Pennybacker, *A Vision for London 1889–1914: Labour, Everyday Life and the LCC Experiment* (London 1995), p. 43.

[53] Heller, *London Clerical Workers*, p. 165.

without having been specially trained in the work'.[54] By 1904 Pitman's principal 'Metropolitan School' in Southampton Row had between 1,500 and 1,600 students, a mixture of part-time and full-time. The Pitman motto was 'Learning and Earning' and they endeavoured to spread the burden of their not inconsiderable fees by an instalment system. Like the Regent Street Polytechnic, Pitman's ran a Situations Bureau or employment agency to place their successful students.[55]

The Skinners' Company School girls give us some examples of the ways in which at the micro-level these expanded educational opportunities might work for women in the London area in these years. The experiences of Florence Johnson and Elsie Barralet offer two more. Yet others come from the correspondence and diaries of two close friends, Ruth Slate and Eva Slawson over the period 1897–1917. Ruth began with a warehouse job, then took a low grade clerical job, while going to night school to learn drawing, composition, arithmetic, book-keeping and mensuration. Although she had to give up the evening classes before completing the course, they had provided enough to secure her a more responsible clerical job in the grocery firm Kearley and Tonge, in which she stayed twelve years.[56] Her friend Eva had begun work in domestic service; but Eva's grandparents scrimped and saved to find the money for shorthand and typing classes, enabling her to secure a job as a secretary in a solicitor's office. She carried on with evening classes, now in grammar and literature, and began to learn French. By August 1908 her salary had been raised to £1.6s per week.[57]

---

[54] Quoted in Teresa Davy, '"A Cissy Job for Men; a Nice-Job for Girls": Women Shorthand Typists in London 1900–39', in Davidoff and Westover, eds., *Our Work*, pp. 124–44, at p. 125; for *The Odd Women*, see above, pp. 90–91, 100.

[55] Heller, *London Clerical Workers*, pp. 169–72.

[56] Tierl Thompson, ed., *Dear Girl: The Diaries and Letters of Two Working Women 1897–1917* (London 1987), pp. 25–39; cf. also pp. 102–3, 111, 132. The primary sources which lie behind this study have been deposited in The Women's Library (henceforward WL), in the group 7RSJ; where possible reference will be made to both. In no senses is this meant to imply criticism of Ms Thompson's work. She is owed a great debt of gratitude for rescuing the papers and making them available to a wider audience; and her commentary, dating and transcriptions (failing only to indicate editorial omissions) are models of scrupulous accuracy. The material is so rich, however, that other and different questions can also be asked of it; and my efforts should be seen as complementary to hers.

[57] Eva to Ruth 24 January 1905, WL, 7RSJ/B/01/04, Eva 13 July 1908, WL, 7RSJ/B/01/07, Thompson, ed., *Dear Girl*, pp. 43, 61, 124.

5 Ruth Slate, 1914

6 Eva Slawson, 1916

The expansion of commercial opportunities like these, at least in the metropolitan area, began to take its toll on recruitment to clerical posts for women in the civil service; and women clerks began to leave government service for posts elsewhere. In 1907 the Treasury commissioned Clara Collet to find out why. She reported that many business firms paid better salaries: the Bank of England, the Metropolitan Water Board, the Metropolitan Asylums Board and the London County Council paid at the same rate as the civil service and offered more attractive conditions. All these organisations offered women better prospects of promotion and more stimulating work.[58] Even so, Janet Hogarth, the first lady superintendent of the women clerks in the Bank of England from 1894, took a low view of the attractions of what was supposed to be an exalted position: she quit after only two years for the more precarious but infinitely more exciting world of journalism and its related activities. She would wholeheartedly agree with Collet's general conclusion, remarking that the work of women civil service clerks was 'deadly dull and not too handsomely rewarded'. Such views, however, had no impact in the years up to 1914; it would take the War to begin to stir things up.[59]

Yet as both Hogarth and Collet knew, from experience and investigation, many of these young women had lively minds and interests which stretched beyond a clean but orderly and routinised work environment. In the end both Florence Johnson and Elsie Barralet gave priority to the demands of family and home. The diaries and letters of Ruth Slate and Eva Slawson, on the other hand, show them gradually shaping for themselves – and encouraging each other to shape – trajectories as autodidacts. As noted above, both had used evening classes for commercial and other skills. Yet pressures of work and the demands of family could and did interrupt attendance; and after a depressing encounter with an arithmetic class at the City of London College in the autumn of 1914, Eva commented sadly that 'These schools and Colleges appear to me to be great temples of *facts* – the end in view

---

[58] Zimmeck, 'Jobs for the Girls', pp. 166–7.

[59] Janet Courtney (her married name), *Recollected in Tranquillity* (London 1926), direct quotation from p. 139; see also her chapters X, XI and XII, 'A Clerk's Life in London', 'The City Thirty Years Ago' and 'The Reading Public'. Like Collet, Hogarth had begun her government career working for the Royal Commission on Labour in 1892.

commercial.' She concluded, 'for one with my slow mind private tuition is the only satisfactory method'.[60]

More important in the initial stages of their development were regular and increasingly adventurous use of the public library and the organisations associated with the Methodist chapel in Manor Park, East London, where they had first met in 1903. Both read widely and with a fine eclecticism. Among nineteenth-century novelists George Eliot was a particular favourite, to whom they returned time and again. Ruskin's *Sesame and Lilies* was an important discovery. They also ranged extensively among more recent novels, from novels about the position of women, such as Olive Schreiner's *Story of an African Farm*, through Grant Allen's *The Woman Who Did* and Sarah Grand's *The Beth Book* to Hardy and Wells. Nor were they above sampling Marie Corelli; and in the autumn of 1914, when war news was consistently grim, Eva admitted to finding diversion and distraction in the romances of Baroness Orczy.[61] A few examples must suffice to illustrate their developing critical senses and discrimination. In 1904, having been lent Marie Corelli's *God's Good Man*, Ruth expressed her doubts to Eva: 'as a rule there is a very disturbing unhealthy exciting element in her books'.[62] In May 1908 Ruth recorded in her diary, 'Read *The Story of an African Farm* in lunch hour. Am I presumptuous in feeling that *much* of what I have been thinking and feeling so strongly is here expressed.'[63] Embarked on H. G. Wells's *The New Machiavelli* in 1913, Eva commented, 'a brilliant but shallow book. Wells remind me of sherbert [*sic*] which when shot into water causes it to effervesce – he is stimulating,

---

[60] WL, 7RSJ/G/01/09 ff. 31–2, Eva's diary 6 October 1914, her emphases. For the varieties of classes attempted and the interruptions, see Thompson, ed., *Dear Girl* and Eva's and Ruth's diaries, WL, 7RSJ.G/01/01 – 13 and 7RSJ/A/01/01 – 17 *passim*. For images of Ruth and Eva, see p. 106.

[61] E.g. Eva to Ruth 19 September 1913 (*The Beth Book*) WL, 7RSJ/B/01/12; Eva to Ruth 23 August 1904 (*Sesame and Lilies*) WL, 7RSJ/B/01/03; Eva's diary 16 August 1913, ff. 2–3 (*The Woman Who Did*) WL, 7RSJ/G/01/03, Thompson, ed., *Dear Girl*, p. 180; Eva's diary 16 December 1913 (Wells, *Ann Veronica*) WL, 7RSJ/G/01/04, f. 1; Eva's diary 19, 24 and 27 September 1914 (Baroness Orczy) WL, 7RSJ/G/01/08, f. 86, – /09, ff. 10 and 22; Ruth to Eva 3 March 1904 (*Life* of George Eliot), 10 April 1904 (*Sesame and Lilies*), 30 May 1904 (*Romola*) WL, 7RSJ/G/02/02.

[62] 20 October 1904 WL, 7RSJ/G/02/02.

[63] 28 May 1908, her emphasis, WL, 7RSJ/A/01//14, f. 31, Thomson, ed., *Dear Girl*, p. 117.

but, I think, transitory.'[64] In August 1915, when her half-sister Gertie, a militant suffragette, was expressing a wish to read Hardy's *Jude the Obscure*, she noted that such was the novel's power that it might do good or ill – 'Hardy is like a great organ, but he plays in the minor key.'[65]

Chapel structures and friends provided additional suggestions for reading and important other experiences. It seems plausible to suggest that one of the impulses towards keeping a diary was the Protestant emphasis on the need for a regular moral accounting. Keeping a diary also provided important and regular practice in writing, describing and summarising. It is easier to see this at work for Ruth, since the diaries that have survived run from 1897, when she was 13, to 1909; then, after a break, they resume in 1914.[66] What began as a childish record gained gradually in fluency, sophistication and power; and these gains are reflected also in her correspondence.[67] Only Eva's diaries from 1913–16 have survived; but a comparison of these with her letters to Ruth from 1903 to 1916 suggests a similar development.[68] Summaries of lengthy sermons and addresses also demanded concentration, the recapitulation of arguments and practice in the art of précis. In addition chapel organisations also provided some practice in public speaking. Both young women taught Sunday School classes and led week-night discussion groups.

Both women, however, came to find the patriarchal framework of Methodism constraining and began to explore other ways of living an ethical life. For Ruth, the opportunities for such exploration were easier of access; working in the City, she could and did use her lunch hours to sermon-taste and attend all sorts of lectures and meetings. Her family moved house to different areas of suburban London, with different chapels, several times. Then at the end of 1909 she moved out of the family home and into lodgings in central London. Among the contacts brought by this mobility were Quaker groups. Eva made only one move,

---

[64] Eva's diary, 28 June 1913, WL, 7RSJ/G/01/02, f. 15, Thomson, ed., *Dear Girl*, p. 175.

[65] 4 August 1915, WL, 7RSJ/G/01/12.   [66] WL, 7RSJ/A/01/01 – /17.

[67] WL, 7RSJ/G/02/01 – /15, Ruth's letters to Eva.

[68] WL, 7RSJ/G/01/01 – /13, Eva's diaries; WL, 7RSJ/B/01 – /14, Eva's letters to Ruth. The account in the paragraphs that follow is drawn from these sources, those named in notes 60 and 61 above, and from the editor's introduction and framing summaries for each chapter in Thompson, ed., *Dear Girl*.

from Manor Park to Walthamstow; and became increasingly involved in the work of the Congregational Chapel there, with its charismatic and radical minister Mr James, becoming Superintendent of its Girls' League and Women's Conference.

In counterpoint to this exploration of other Christian denominations' offerings, both women from 1906–7 onwards became involved not only with more heterodox organisations but also with overtly political ones. Ruth joined the Progressive Thought League, promoting the Congregationalist R. J. Campbell's 'New Theology', and both she and Eva taught at the Hoxton Adult School, which combined religious and social teaching. In the autumn of 1912 Ruth joined the radical feminist group The Freewoman Discussion Circle. In 1909 Eva joined the Independent Labour Party and the Women's Labour League, retaining her links with the latter when, for reasons which are not clear, she left the ILP in 1912. Both too joined the Women's Freedom League, which broke away from the Pankhursts' Women's Social and Political Union in 1908, being both less militant and more democratic in its structure. While active in the suffrage movement, neither was disposed towards militant or direct action; and on the outbreak of war both emerged as committed pacificists, joining the Fellowship of Reconciliation and later the No Conscription Fellowship.[69]

As the sheer range of these involvements indicates, Ruth and Eva had begun to scrutinise and to question everything, from religious faith and practices, through social purpose and the search for the just society, to human relationships, including their own. Ruth's first serious hetero-sexual relationship had been with a childhood friend, Ewart Johnson, but he died from tuberculosis in the summer of 1903. Subsequently she became engaged to Walter Randall – 'Wal'; but he emerged as a tricky, devious young man, and a firm opponent of women's suffrage. The relationship painfully unravelled during the autumn of 1908 and the first months of 1909. In the autumn of 1912 through the Freewoman Circle Ruth met Françoise Lafitte, whom she considered 'a second Olive Schreiner' and they went on to share a flat together, in which Ruth sustained Françoise through the birth of her baby, the product of a short-lived 'free union'.

---

[69] For further reading on these organisations and their context, see Delap, *Feminist Avant-Garde* and Rowbotham, *Dreamers of a New Day*.

Although Ruth remained supportive of Françoise and her subsequent relationships, she showed no disposition to follow her example. In the course of 1913 her Quaker connections brought her two new and important male friends, the somewhat older American, David Thomson and the Englishman Hugh Jones. David Thomson tried a number of times to persuade Ruth to become his wife and move to the United States with him but she always hesitated. Her feelings for Hugh were somewhat more complex. Initially he considered himself in search of a high ideal of friendship rather than love for a particular individual; and Ruth wrote to Eva in June 1913, 'through me he loves and interprets Woman. He loves Womanhood in me but he does not love *me*. Oh my dear, will that gift ever be mine?'[70] Subsequently Hugh was shaken to discover the depths of his personal feelings for Ruth; still hankering after his ideal, he then had bouts of wanting to break off the friendship. Eventually in 1917 they would marry.

Eva had no comparably close male friendships, although there are signs that her office colleague, Frost, would have liked more than a working relationship with her; and she was undoubtedly attracted by Mr James, the Walthamstow Congregationalist minister. Her closest relationship with a contemporary outside her family, apart from her friendship with Ruth, was with the married Minna Simmons, whom she met in the Walthamstow congregation. Minna's husband Will died of tuberculosis early in 1914, while she was still carrying their fourth child. Subsequently Eva and Minna became very close, both emotionally and physically. Eva often spent the night at Minna's house and was present at the birth of the baby, Joan. Eva was familiar with the writing of Edward Carpenter and his celebration of same-sex love and relationships in *Love's Coming of Age* (1896); but she seems never to have acknowledged that his teaching might be applied to her relationship with Minna. In other respects, however, their discussions ranged widely. Having been married, Minna was sceptical about the durability of romance, thinking that 'often the less romantic marriages, built upon kindly, friendly feeling and trust, were the happiest'. Eva, however, felt that 'one lowers one's standards unless one can feel in some degree a three-fold attraction – physical, mental, spiritual. I do not think I could marry unless I felt this!' Later on, discussing polygamous relationships, 'Minna felt she could share a man with me – neither of us felt we could

---

[70] Ruth to Eva 3 June 1913, her emphasis, WL, 7RSJ/G/02/11.

share a man with Lily or Ruth – I think because we recognise they are essentially lovers, and I suppose would in some way possess a decided advantage over us!'[71]

Although David Thomson eventually recognised that Ruth would not become his wife, he was still determined to help her and encourage her development. With his financial help and a scholarship, Ruth was able in 1914 to go to Woodbrooke, the Quaker college near Birmingham, where she flourished and secured a formal social science qualification. Urged on and helped with the practicalities by Ruth, Eva followed her to Woodbrooke in the autumn of 1915, also on a scholarship. She found it harder than Ruth had done to settle to a structured work pattern. In the spring of 1916 she was just beginning to get its measure, when tragically she collapsed and died from undetected diabetes.[72]

The sources for the lives of Ruth Slate and Eva Slawson and their exceptional richness bring hope that there are others like them, still undiscovered in cupboards or attics. Ruth and Eva are amongst the most plausible candidates for the label 'New Woman' encountered yet, although their voyages of intellectual and personal discovery occur a decade later than the media feeding frenzy over that label. And were they exceptional? Perhaps the experiences of Florence Johnson and Elsie Barralet were the more typical ones. It would be especially good to know what possibilities and opportunities beckoned to young women clerks outside London. Ruth, moving to York in 1916 to use her Woodbrooke qualifications and experience to do personnel work for Rowntree's, considered London unique in cultural and political if not in work terms. The work at Rowntree's at first seemed all too similar to that at Kearley and Tonge's, although being better paid and gradually giving her more autonomy.[73] In York as a whole she considered 'the air

---

[71] Eva's diary 19 June 1913, WL, 7RSJ/G/01/02, f. 11, Thomson, ed., *Dear Girl*, p. 174; Eva's diary 13 September 1914, WL, 7RSJ/G//01/08 ff. 68–9, Thompson, ed., *Dear Girl*, p. 247. Lily had come to look after Minna's children and home while she trained as a nurse.

[72] WL, 7RSJ/B/01/12–14, 7RSJ/ G/01/12–13, 7RSJ/G/02/12–15, 7RSJ/G/03/01–02 and Thompson, ed., *Dear Girl*, chs. 8–10 and Epilogue. On Rendel Harris, the first Director of Studies at Woodbrooke, see *ODNB* and Janet Soskice, *Sisters of Sinai: How Two Lady Adventurers Found the Hidden Gospels* (London 2009, pbk 2010), pp. 278, 288.

[73] Thomson, ed., *Dear Girl*, pp. 297–8; her salary began at £120 p.a., rising by increments to £150 p.a.

and people lack exhilaration and one meets with very little which touches the imagination – at least, such has been my fate hitherto! I suppose one never realises the extraordinary stimulation of London life until one misses it.' In 1918 she moved back to the London area, where the remainder of her long working and politically active life was spent.[74] The attractions of life in London for Ruth sound similar to the pulls felt by women graduates who sought teaching posts in the capital.[75]

Even if no more diaries and letters of the quality of those written by Eva and Ruth can be found, there is more work to be done in hunting out the records and school magazines of provincial girls' secondary schools, particularly those created by LEAs after 1902, and trying to discover how many of their old girls went on to employment and what they did. This might also give us some links to the employment of women in local government, a field of work so far barely explored.

The possibilities offered by local government employment are well – if tantalisingly – illustrated by the arrival of women in library work. Librarianship itself only emerged as an occupation, and one with some career possibilities, in the second half of the nineteenth century, the foundation stone being William Ewart's Act of 1850, 'for enabling Town Councils to establish Public Libraries and Museums'.[76] Manchester was one of those local authorities who seized the opportunity to open a Free Public Library. Initially their employees were boys and young men, but in 1871 they decided to advertise for some women library assistants as well. They found themselves overwhelmed with applicants, many of them well- if not over-qualified. By 1879 Alderman Thomas Baker could report to the Library Association of the UK that while

the librarians like to have one youth at their command: he is better for any rough work there may be, such as opening and shutting windows, going errands, also in reaching books from the higher shelves, and perhaps in case of disorder in the reading rooms, though this is of very infrequent occurrence;

---

[74] Direct quotation from Ruth's diary, 16 March 1916, WL, 7RSJ/A/01/17 f. 5, Thompson, ed., *Dear Girl*, p. 297; *ibid*. pp. 308–10.
[75] See above, p. 33.
[76] See Edward Miller, 'Public Libraries', in Gillian Sutherland, ed., *Government and Society in Nineteenth-Century Britain: Commentaries on British Parliamentary Papers: Education* (Dublin 1977), pp. 125–36.

but for attendance on readers and applicants, for books, they prefer the girls.[77]

Clerkenwell was the first London borough to copy Manchester and others soon followed suit, although the promotion possibilities for the women were limited and they were required to resign on marriage. However, women library assistants were sufficiently numerous for the journal *The Librarian and Book World* to carry a regular column by Margaret Reed, 'Women's Work in Libraries', from 1911 to 1913.[78] By 1915, 500 of the 3,500 library assistants in the country were women; although of the 566 who held Library Association Certificates, only 118 were women. In London the salary scales for junior assistants ranged from £29 to £52 per annum and for seniors £58 to £95 p.a.; in the provinces the parallel scales were £17.10s to £41.10s and £52 to £78 p.a. The handful of women Chief Librarians, none of whom were London-based, could expect to earn around £110 p.a.[79]

These are modest beginnings and temporary war-time gains would be eroded in the immediate post-war period. Yet the conditions of work and the salaries stand up well in comparison with nursing and with what little we know about pay and conditions of work for clerks. Moreover the development, side by side with free public libraries, of specialist academic libraries began to offer prospects for women graduates, especially those who could not face teaching. Constance Black's appointment as Librarian of the People's Palace Library in East London in 1887, on the recommendation of Charles Booth, was something of a precedent and in February 1889 Constance published an article in *The Queen, the Lady's Newspaper* entitled 'A New Career for Women:

---

[77] *Transactions of the Library Association of the United Kingdom*, September 1879, part of which is reprinted in Kathleen Weibel, Kathleen M. Heim with Dianne J. Ellsworth, eds., *The Role of Women in Librarianship 1876–1976: The Entry, Advancement, and Struggle for Equalization in One Profession* (Phoenix, AZ 1979), pp. 8–9, a most valuable source book for the UK and USA; also Julia Taylor McCain, 'Women and Libraries', in Alistair Black and Peter Hoare, eds., *The Cambridge History of Libraries in Britain and Ireland*, vol. III, *1850–1900* (Cambridge 2006), pp. 543–7.

[78] Evelyn Kerslake, 'The Feminisation of Librarianship: The Writings of Margaret Reed', in Black and Hoare, eds., *Libraries in Britain and Ireland*, pp. 548–55.

[79] Mizpah Gilbert, 'The Position of Women in Public Libraries', *Library World* October 1915, reprinted in Weibel *et al.*, eds., *Women in Librarianship*, pp. 67–71, esp. pp. 67–8.

Librarians'.[80] One of the contributors to the discussion of library work at the International Congress of Women in London in 1899 was Miss Toulmin Smith, the Librarian of Manchester College, Oxford;[81] and the new schools and colleges for women spreading over the country invariably employed women in their libraries. The addition of this rung, however notional, to the career path for women librarians enhanced their status, bringing respectable women and ladies closer together, increasing the experience and the ground that they shared. A similar process was beginning to take place in maintained school teaching. It is to maintained school teachers, a group much better-known and, relatively speaking, an elite group among white-collar women workers, that we must now turn our attention.

[80] Bernstein, *Roomscape*, pp. 55–9; for Constance, see also above, p. 27.
[81] *Women in the Professions*: vol. II of the *Proceedings of the International Congress of Women, London 1899*, extracts printed in Weibel *et al.*, eds., *Women in Librarianship*, pp. 26–37, p. 34.

6 'a beggarly makeshift, but for me it was wealth beyond price': women white-collar workers (II)

Ruth Slate had been deemed 'not strong enough for teaching'; Margaret Bondfield had hated her first employment as a pupil-teacher.[1] These illustrations serve to remind us, if reminder were necessary, how widely acceptable teaching, so easily portrayed as an extension of the domestic sphere, was considered for all women in the nineteenth century. The teaching contemplated by Ruth and tried by Margaret was not, however, the genteel governessing among middle- and upper-class families essayed by Gissing's Alice Madden, but the hard grind of teaching in schools for the working and lower middle classes, elementary schools as they were known. Gertrude Tuckwell, the niece of Emilia, second wife of Sir Charles Dilke, embarked on such work in London with an almost missionary fervour in the early 1880s and stuck it for six years. She found it exhausting, especially when the size of her class rose to seventy, and she eventually succumbed to scarlet fever. On recovery she chose a less gruelling field. With the support of the Dilkes, she began to work to help organise women's labour unions.[2]

Conventional assumptions about appropriate female roles were hardly enough on their own to make such demanding work attractive. Other factors were also in play to put maintained school teaching at the top of the status hierarchy in white-collar work for women. First and foremost it paid better than shop work, nursing and all but a handful of clerkships. It paid better in part because it was preceded by a recognised period of training. Within the occupation as a whole there was something approaching a career structure and the work was less sex- and gender-segregated than that in other occupations. All these factors

[1] Thompson ed., *Dear Girl*, pp. 20–2; above, p. 92.
[2] Dina Copelman, *London's Women Teachers: Gender, Class and Feminism 1870–1930* (London 1996), pp. 11–14.

interacted to enhance the status of the work and attract increasing numbers of young women into maintained school teaching.

First let us look at the most visible indicators of status: pay and allied considerations of security of tenure and pensions. When Etta Dan, née Chamberlain, began her first teaching job in Essex in 1913, she earned 30/- per week – good money. 'Not many working men were earning 30/- a week'.[3] By 1914 the average salary of the certificated woman teacher nationally was £96 per annum, higher in maintained secondary schools, and higher in both elementary and secondary schools in London, London teachers being the elite group within the elite throughout the period. Such earnings far outstripped pay for shop work and nursing, while only 3% of women clerks were earning over £100 per annum by 1914. Moreover while, in the majority of occupations employing both men and women, women's pay tended to be just over half that of men, in teaching women earned three-quarters of the salaries paid to men.[4] The continuing expansion of school provision over the century, outlined more fully below, brought teachers considerable security of tenure. Pensions were the subject of a separate and prolonged battle, eventually won by the teacher unions; from 1898 there was a national pension scheme open to women as well as men.[5]

Behind these visible markers of a status approaching the professional lay the untidy evolution of teacher training provision. Voluntary and charitable organisations were the first providers of elementary schools at the beginning of the nineteenth century. The first government grants in aid to such schools were made in 1833; and eventually, following legislation in 1870, there was commitment to a national network of such schools.[6] An early and obvious preoccupation was the provision of adequate teaching. From the 1840s financial support was given to the teacher training schools, initially called Normal Schools, later called Training Colleges, of the voluntary societies associated with the principal denominations; and a scheme of apprenticeships within the schools themselves was developed for abler adolescents within the schools themselves, these apprentices called pupil-teachers. They received modest payments to assist and to learn from more established teachers, while

---

[3] BLSA, C707/21, recording and transcript.
[4] Oram, *Women Teachers*, p. 25; Copelman, *London's Women Teachers*, pp. 76–9.
[5] Copelman, *London's Women Teachers*, pp. 78–9.
[6] See Sutherland, 'Education', in *Cambridge Social History of Britain*, ed. Thompson, pp. 127–8, 141–2.

also doing more advanced work themselves. The work of the pupil-teachers, both practical and intellectual, was inspected by Her Majesty's Inspectorate (HMI); and the best pupil-teachers could compete for scholarships and bursaries to attend the training schools and colleges.

Sometimes even with this help training courses proved beyond the means of some candidates and places were few anyway. For those who did not or could not go to Normal School or Training College, it was nevertheless possible to achieve certification on the basis of apprenticeship, HMI reports and examination performance. After 1870 when new local authorities, school boards, were created, a number of the larger boards began to develop pupil-teacher centres to deliver the more advanced work and these were in due course inherited by the county borough and county councils who superseded them as Local Education Authorities (LEAs) following legislation in 1902. This institutional provision was however gradually dismantled over the next decade.[7]

Positions as pupil-teachers and then as teachers offered new opportunities for steady, non-manual work to the daughters of the respectable working class, the labour aristocracy, and the emergent lower middle class. In 1859–60 Thomas Hardy's parents, he a small builder, she a former domestic servant, had somehow found the money for Hardy's sister Mary to go to the Anglican Normal School in Salisbury. Hardy drew on this experience thirty years later, in the writing of *Jude the Obscure*. Soon after their first meeting, Jude urges Sue Bridehead to become a trained teacher, describing the occupation as bringing an income sufficient to ensure freedom. Later Hardy describes her fellow students as 'a very mixed community, which included the daughters of mechanics, curates, surgeons, shopkeepers, farmers, dairymen, soldiers, sailors and villagers'.[8] Lavinia Orton, the mother of the writer Richard Church, was the daughter of a railway employee who became the goods manager at St Pancras Station – and a domestic tyrant – from whom

---

[7] For the early nineteenth-century provision, see Asher Tropp, *The School Teachers: The Growth of the Teaching Profession in England and Wales from 1800 to the Present Day* (London 1957), ch. 2; for the period 1870–1914, see Wendy Robinson, *Pupil Teachers and their Professional Training in Pupil Teacher Centres in England and Wales 1870–1914* (Lampeter 2003).

[8] Claire Tomalin, *Thomas Hardy: The Time-Torn Man* (London 2006), pp. 57–60; Thomas Hardy, *Jude the Obscure* (first published in book form London 1895, multiple printings thereafter) Part Second, 'At Christminster' chapter IV, the suggestion; Part Third, 'At Melchester', direct quotation.

Lavinia escaped into school teaching at the end of the 1870s. Of the four teachers interviewed for the Essex survey, 'Family Life and Work Experience before 1918', three came from a similar background, with fathers respectively a master cordwainer, a corn factor and provision merchant, and a naval carpenter. The odd one out was the daughter of a Welsh solicitor; however her mother, a farmer's daughter, had been an elementary school teacher and head. Daughters of the middle middle and upper middle class, like Gertrude Tuckwell, tended to be the exceptions rather than the rule among elementary school teachers.[9]

Already by 1859 46% of the pupil-teacher workforce was female. By the end of the century teachers in maintained schools included a small core of trained and certificated teachers surrounded by a much larger group of untrained certificated teachers, assistant teachers, and a curious group called additional women teachers, whose only qualifications were that they were over 18, had been vaccinated and 'satisfied' HMI, plus pupil-teachers still in training and probationers preparing to train. Altogether they numbered just under 150,000, 75% of whom, that is, over 100,000, were women, clustered disproportionately in the untrained and least trained categories.[10] Part of this clustering was attributable to the shortage of training college places for women, part to the lower priority attached by families to the education and employment of daughters. Even so, these numbers represented new opportunities for the young women concerned and offered the possibility of economic autonomy. Etta Dan, born in Essex in 1891, who was trained, reflected, 'That was the only thing that anybody with brains could do, really. 'Cos, I mean, there were no jobs for girl secretaries or even typists and shorthand people then.' Florence Dart, born in Chatham in 1895, expressed a similar view: 'There was nothing else – going – counter job if you like. But I – I was not going behind a shop counter, I'd made up my mind for that.' After her father's premature death, there was not the money for a training college, so she spent two years as a pupil-teacher – interestingly she called herself a monitor. Then in 1913, aged 18, she began teaching for Dorset County Council, continuing for the next

[9] Church, *Over the Bridge*, pp. 50–3; BLSA, C707/ 21, /143, /368 (Mary Rosser, the solicitor's daughter), /406; see also Copelman, *London's Women Teachers*, pp. 32–33.

[10] My summary calculations from the detailed figures given in Tropp, *School Teachers*, pp. 117–18. He in turn drew them from the Board of Education's report for 1899.

forty-five years, but seizing the opportunity, when it came, of some in-service training to specialise in the teaching of mentally handicapped children.[11] Women teachers were becoming a substantial presence in the workforce.

For the women who, like Etta Dan, managed to secure some training, there was also a career structure. They were less likely to secure head-ships than their male colleagues; yet there were some women heads. The London School Board's first Promotion List in 1886 named fifty men but also twenty-seven women.[12] Nor was a marriage bar universal. Again, London led the way: in 1901, 11.2% of women teachers there were married. In Manchester the proportion of married women teach-ers was just under 5% and in Birmingham 4%. The headmistress mother of Mary Rosser, the solicitor's daughter from Pontypridd, continued to work for several years after her marriage, as she and her husband were saving to buy a house.[13] Few concessions were made to married women with families, however. Between the 1870s and 1890s the expectation was that they would take no more than four weeks' maternity leave and for that time find and pay a substitute.[14] Richard Church described his mother's experience following his birth: 'within a few weeks Mother was back to her teaching in an elementary school in the Horseferry Road, Westminster. How she travelled to and fro at that time, I have no idea; but the fatigue of this journey four times a day (for she had to come home to feed me), plus the task of handling some sixty slum urchins from the wilderness of Pimlico, must have tasked her vitality.' Between feeds Richard was looked after by Harriet, the eldest daughter of a large working-class family nearby.[15]

The London School Board and its successor, the London County Council, became increasingly uneasy about the employment of married women teachers, especially after the LCC instituted a marriage bar for all its other women employees in 1906. However, neither breakdowns in health nor absences were more common among women teachers who were married than among London women teachers as a whole and the pressure to impose a marriage bar on London women teachers would be

---

[11] BLSA, C707/21 (Mrs Dan), /406 (Miss Dart).

[12] Copelman, *London's Women Teachers*, p. 50.

[13] *Ibid.* p. 179; see also the estimate of 10–12% nationally in Oram, *Women Teachers*, p. 26; BLSA, C707/368.

[14] Copelman, *London's Women Teachers*, p. 185.

[15] Church, *Over the Bridge*, p. 41.

successfully resisted until 1923.[16] Even then, there proved to be some flexibility. All of the retired London teachers interviewed by Frances Widdowson in the late 1970s emphasized the security offered by the knowledge that, if widowed, they would be accepted back into the workforce. And Mary Hatch, whose husband became an invalid, was allowed to return, although having to provide a medical certificate from her husband's doctor each year until the poor man died.[17]

Headships and some possibility of continuing work after marriage were not the only opportunities available to women elementary school teachers. The pupil-teacher centres, which the larger boards developed to deliver advanced work for pupil-teachers more effectively, required staff, and some of those recruited were women. Wendy Robinson has managed to discover enough about some of these individuals to compile a database of pupil-teacher centre staff, which includes eighty women and seventy-three men.[18] Increasingly these centres required evidence from candidates of further academic study; and 68% of the women and 73% of the men either had degrees, usually having been external students of the University of London, or were engaged in degree-level work. The status and pay of such posts began to attract middle-class women candidates, with higher education but without the classroom experience; and not all of them proved able to cope in the latter situation. An anonymous contributor to the *Newnham College Club Letter* on 'Some Aspects of Work in Board Schools' in 1898 warned of the hazards, stressing that the woman who did not establish her authority over her class within the first five minutes was lost.[19] These graduate women simply did not have four years of apprenticeship as a pupil-teacher behind them when they embarked on work with elementary school pupils. As Mary Hatch, née White, born in Dewsbury in 1886, put it, even 'before we went to college we knew how to handle a class 'cos we'd had to'.[20] One third of Robinson's sample moved around the country, to posts in other centres; but the women moved less often than the men and some of these moves appeared to be sideways moves rather than promotions. Robinson speculates that there

---

[16] Copelman, *London's Women Teachers*, pp. 184–5, 186, 190–2.
[17] Widdowson, 'Educating Teacher', p. 116; BLSA, C707/143 (Mrs Hatch).
[18] Robinson, *Pupil Teachers*, pp. 77–8.
[19] NCCL 1898, pp. 27–34; Robinson, *Pupil Teachers*, pp. 82–5; cf. obituary of Caroline Browne in NCCL 1900, p. 55.
[20] BLSA, C707/143.

may have been a status hierarchy among centres and suggests that the women attached particular importance to the wider cultural pro-grammes, including travel, associated with some of the centres.[21] However, a marriage bar did operate in pupil-teacher centre employ-ment, in London at least.[22]

There were also other posts representing career enhancement in local authority employment, in the so-called higher grade elementary schools. The first higher grade schools had been opened by the Bradford School Board in 1876 and combined some of the features of a pupil-teacher centre with the provision of more advanced work for the elementary school pupils themselves, as well as opportunities for pupils and pupil-teachers to take courses examined by other bodies, the Science and Art Department at South Kensington, the College of Preceptors, the lower grades of government service etc. Higher grade schools were of somewhat lower status than the pupil-teacher centres; but they recruited similarly and did not operate a marriage bar.[23]

The legislation of 1902 and the policy changes that followed it altered the situation further, offering some new opportunities and reshaping existing ones. The Education Act of 1902 abolished school boards, making county and county borough councils the new Local Education Authorities (LEAs). These not only became responsible for the elemen-tary schools in their area but for the first time were charged also with developing maintained secondary schools. Hitherto secondary school-ing – defined by class rather than age and so for the middle and upper classes – had been delivered by private schools and/or endowed schools. These were the models of boys' schools that Cheltenham Ladies' College, the North London Collegiate School and the schools of the Girls Public Day School Company/Trust had set out to copy and to which many of the women graduates discussed in Chapter 2 above went to teach. LEA secondary schools began to appear, to complement and possibly to compete with these.

Much of the work done in pupil-teacher centres and higher grade schools was comparable to that done in the smaller, less prestigious endowed schools and almost certainly pupil-teacher centres and higher grade schools offered better and more systematic science teaching than

---

[21] Robinson, *Pupil Teachers*, pp. 87–99.   [22] *Ibid.* p. 111, n.84.
[23] Meriel Vlaeminke, *The English Higher Grade Schools: A Lost Opportunity* (Woburn 2000), pp. 1–45.

existing secondary schools, whose curricula were still dominated by classics. It might have been possible after 1902 to develop an interestingly diverse maintained secondary provision with strong roots in local communities, foreshadowing attempts to do this later in the twentieth century, had any effort been directed to the articulation of these institutions into a new framework. However, the regulations promulgated by the Board of Education for new maintained secondary schools in 1904 showed the continuing ideological and social power of the traditional classically based curriculum; and this received further reinforcement from the decision to end the pupil-teacher system. Between 1904 and 1907 it was made plain that intending teachers would in future be required to attend secondary schools before going on to training college at 18 or 19. Some financial assistance was provided. This forced the closure of the remaining pupil-teacher centres and cut the ground from under the feet of the higher grade schools.[24]

We simply do not know what happened to the women employed in pupil-teacher centres and higher grade schools and whether some fraction of them, particularly those with external London degrees, managed to find posts in the new maintained secondary schools, or even in the expanding training college sector. Etta Dan remarked in passing that her pupil-teacher centre in Colchester turned into a girls' high school while she was there – which would date the change somewhere around 1909–11.[25] Did others undergo the same transmogrification? It does seem significant that the real growth in numbers and strength of the Association of Assistant Mistresses dates from this time. As we have seen, they hastened to open their membership to women teachers in the new maintained secondary schools, and by 1921, for the first time, over half the women teachers in secondary schools of all kinds would be members.[26] More generally, by the beginning of the twentieth century school teaching offered real employment and career opportunities to the daughters not only of the middle class but also of the labour aristocracy and lower middle class. In his classic of social commentary *The*

[24] For details of a fraught and contested process see Robinson, *Pupil Teachers*, pp. 40–2; and the discussion of her Bristol case-study 1903–10 by Vlaeminke. *Higher Grade Schools*, ch. 4.
[25] BLSA, C707/21. She began her first job in 1913 after four years as a pupil-teacher and two at the training college in Bishop's Stortford.
[26] Above, Chapter 2, p. 30.

Condition of England, first published in 1911, the MP Charles Masterman noted the emergence of

the new type of elementary teacher – a figure practically unknown forty years ago – drawn in part from the tradesmen and the more ambitious artisan population, and now, lately, in a second generation, from its own homes. It is exhibiting a continuous rise of standard, keen ambitions, a respect for intellectual things which is often absent in the population amongst which it resides. Its members are not only doing their own work efficiently but are everywhere taking the lead in public and *quasi*-public activities. They appear as the mainstay of the political machine in suburban districts, serving upon the municipal bodies, in work, clear-headed and efficient; the leaders in the churches and chapels, and their various social organisations. They are taking up the position in the urban districts which for many generations was occupied by the country clergy in the rural districts; providing centres with other standards than those of monetary success, and raising families who exhibit sometimes vigour of character, sometimes unusual intellectual talents. A quite remarkable proportion of the children of elementary schoolmasters is now knocking at the doors of the older Universities, clamouring for admittance; and those who effect entrance are often carrying off the highest honours.[27]

As the last sentence signals, Masterman's primary focus was the male teacher and his sons. In general it would take another generation before the daughters of elementary school teachers began to join the daughters of independent schoolmasters in applying to universities as 18-year-olds. In other respects, however, women elementary teachers were not slow to follow their male colleagues in taking a lead in community activities, particularly in voluntary organisations and those associated with the work of churches and chapels. Mary Rosser, born in 1890, the daughter of the Pontypridd solicitor, noted that her mother, the former headmistress of the junior school, was co-opted to the LEA; and she also took immense satisfaction in successfully challenging the revising barrister who attempted improperly to remove women's names from the electoral roll.[28] Mrs Rosser took pains as well to see that both her two daughters and the nephew she adopted were all equipped for a

[27] C. F. G. Masterman, *The Condition of England* (1911, 6th edition), pp. 75–6.
[28] BLSA, C707/368. My surmise is that Mrs Rosser's efforts related to the attempt of the revising barrister to prevent women exercising the local government franchise before 1914, rather than the parliamentary franchise after 1918; see Patricia Hollis, *Ladies Elect: Women in English Local Government 1865–1914* (Oxford 1987), pp. 31–2.

professional life. Mary had specialist Froebel training and initially worked with very young children; Gwladys became a secondary school domestic science teacher; and Ori (short for Origen) was articled and took over the solicitor's practice when his uncle died. Women teachers who married and had children were almost invariably ambitious for their families, a point to which we shall return.[29]

The self-confidence bred by extended education, recognised formal training, the incompleteness of marriage bars, the relatively small differentials between the salaries of men and women teachers, and the opportunities for career advancement offered by an expanding and evolving set of institutions also all point to larger issues about the segregation of work by sex and gender. The discussion of the employment of women shop assistants, nurses and clerks above suggested that in these occupations such segregation was marked. In shops women for the most part served women customers; the nursing force was almost entirely female; and women and men clerks were segregated at least in larger offices and undertook overlapping but distinct tasks.[30] In schools for the middle and upper classes, independent secondary schools and their associated preparatory schools, pupils were segregated by sex and so for the most part were staff: women taught girls and men taught boys.

However in maintained school teaching segregation by sex and gender was much less complete. Residential training colleges were single-sex; but in the majority of pupil-teacher centres staff and students were a mixed group, with women in the majority among the students.[31] In the schools themselves, the pupils of infant schools (to age 7) were a mixed group, taught almost entirely by women. Junior school pupils (7–11+) tended to be segregated but the teaching staff were mixed, again with a preponderance of women. Both Etta Dan and Mary Hatch spoke warmly of mixed staff rooms and the support received from their male colleagues in the first decades of the twentieth century.[32] In the 1890s the London School Board began to expand its mixed Junior Schools, increasing the number from forty in 1893 to ninety-seven in 1903; but the real growth of mixed schools for this age group would come after the First World War. Only in the new maintained secondary schools was the segregation of both pupils and staff in the independent sector

[29] See below, pp. 128–9.   [30] See above, pp. 99–100.
[31] Robinson, *Pupil Teachers*, p. 67.   [32] BLSA, C707/21, /143.

copied in the period up to the War. Again, this began to change in the inter-war period; by 1938 mixed secondary schools would represent 30% of total maintained provision.[33]

The relative weakness of sex segregation in their workplace was an important part of the context within which the increase of activism and indeed of militancy among women teachers at the turn of the century should be set. When the legal secretary Eva Slawson joined the ILP in 1908, her comments about a woman 'fellow comrade' are illuminating: 'Mrs Shimmins, however, has been a teacher and has passed through college. I am not sure yet whether I like her. She is young and very bright – talks with ease (which I do not) and has a decided manner.'[34] From the other side of the fence, as it were, both Etta Dan and Mary Hatch commented that if you had survived four years as a pupil-teacher, two years at a training college and a plethora of demonstration lessons with the Head, the college's Mistress of Method, HMI and fellow-students as audience besides the children you were actually teaching, you built up a certain strength and confidence.[35] Between 1900 and 1920 female membership of the National Union of Teachers, the elementary school teachers' union, grew faster than male membership; by 1914, 75% of certificated women teachers were members. Equal pay was already a live issue and from 1904 members of the NUT could join an Equal Pay League; in 1920 a group of women teachers would break away over this issue to form the National Union of Women Teachers.[36]

Alison Oram and Dina Copelman have argued that from the early 1900s onwards a developing sense of professional identity for women teachers at all levels converged with suffrage feminism.[37] In 1900 the President of the Association of Assistant Mistresses (AAM) was Katharine Wallas, the Girton-educated sister of Graham, Mathematics mistress at the GPDSC/T school in Notting Hill and increasingly a power in London government. During her presidency she focused particularly

[33] Copelman, *London's Women Teachers*, p. 211; Oram, *Women Teachers*, pp. 5–6.

[34] WL, 7RSJ/B/01/07 Eva to Ruth 13 July 1908, Thompson, ed., *Dear Girl*, p. 124.

[35] BLSA, C707/21, /143.   [36] Oram, *Women Teachers*, p. 3.

[37] Oram, *Women Teachers*, p. 104. See also Copelman, *London's Women Teachers*, pp. 202–5, 212–19, who argues that in London the process began in the 1890s. Nurses who were in favour of registration also tended to be suffragist – I am indebted to Anne Summers for this point.

on the role of women in local government, both generally and in education. After the War she would go on to have a national role in the work of
Burnham committees on teachers' pay and terms of service. To focus on
the role of women in local government in these prewar years was not to
deflect attention from the campaign for the parliamentary vote. From
1869 onwards women had expanded their access to local government
franchises and in using these had made the most of their 'caring' roles in
social welfare programmes like poor relief, sanitary reform and education, in the process learning political skills and demonstrating competence, as well as being 'caring'. In the course of the 1890s, pressure grew
for national strategies in these programmes, to the point where the
Liberal government of 1906 took office with a major programme of
social intervention. As Martin Pugh has commented, 'social reform
became the bridge between local and national politics across which
women could advance without posing a fundamental threat to conventional thinking about gender'.[38]

Formal involvement in national suffrage campaigns was trickier for
AAM members; too many of their employers were hostile, a problem
experienced also by women doctors.[39] However, the issues were
debated and individual teachers worked for the suffrage movement,
where they could. On Census Night 1911 a number of elementary and
secondary women teachers in London and elsewhere did as Margaret
Tew of St Hugh's had done and camped out in public places – and even
in caves – to avoid the enumerators. If, their argument ran, they were
non-citizens because of the refusal to grant them the vote, they would
dramatise their ghostly existence by absenting themselves from any
habitations in which they could be listed. This act of civil disobedience,
the brain-child of the Women's Freedom League, attracted support
particularly in the London area from members of the National Union
of Women's Suffrage Societies and of the Women's Social and Political
Union – and carried limited personal risk.[40] It has proved difficult to
assess the actual extent of evasion and/or refusal to complete a return in

---

[38] Martin Pugh, *The March of the Women: A Revisionist Analysis of the Campaign
for Women's Suffrage, 1866–1914* (Oxford 2000), p. 136; also pp. 72–7. On
Katharine Wallas, see Oram, *Women Teachers*, p. 111; *GC Register*,
matriculation year 1884.

[39] Geddes, 'The Doctors' Dilemma'.

[40] Pugh, *March of the Women*, pp. 197–8; for Margaret Tew, see above, p. 32.
Jill Liddington and Elizabeth Crawford, '"Women do not count, neither shall

1911 from the Census itself; however, the contemporary view was that
the vast majority of women teachers in both elementary and secondary
schools were committed to women's suffrage, feeling keenly the mis-
match between their self-image as professionals and the lack of the
vote.[41]

Reflecting on this self-image, on the political consciousness and
activity of women teachers, Copelman suggested that, 'While the New
Women have been located in the novels of the period, in the heterodox
salons of elites and the middle-class intelligentsia, in the ranks of feminists and the classrooms of New Women's high schools and colleges,
they were also to be found among the expanding white-collar and
service sector female labour force.'[42] 'Also' seems too weak. 'New
Women' were *more* likely to be found among white-collar workers,
especially maintained school teachers, than elsewhere. There were far
more of them and they were as a group less constrained by social
expectations of their behaviour. Those climbing the professional ladder
taking shape in maintained school teaching were expected to be respectable; they did not all have to aspire to be ladies.

Behind the more secure forms of white-collar work, superior clerkships and maintained school teaching might lie a considerable cultural,
social and political hinterland, access to it facilitated by the security and
status of their employment. Some of these women might pour all their
energies beyond school into the lives, material but also cultural, of their
families. Richard Church's mother Lavinia spent her courtship coaching her fiancé Tom to pass the Post Office examinations to become a
sorter in the office, an important step upwards from his current work as
a postman, making his rounds in all weathers. Her careful planning of
their combined finances to enable them to buy their own house left no
margin for buying books or music and she was disconcerted when
Richard at 16 spent 1/6 out of his first wages on Palgrave's *Golden
Treasury* of verse.[43] It is little wonder that in 1883 the Finsbury Park
Building Society was congratulating itself on the number of women
teachers among its investors.[44] Yet Lavinia Church was herself a good

they be counted": Suffrage, Citizenship and the Battle for the 1911 Census',
History Workshop Journal 71 (Spring 2011), pp. 1–30.
[41] *Ibid.*; Oram, *Women Teachers*, pp. 112–23.
[42] Copelman, *London's Women Teachers*, p. xvi.
[43] Church, *Over the Bridge*, pp. 55, 89–90.
[44] Copelman, *London's Women Teachers*, p. 170.

musician and painted in oils; and both boys were encouraged to make the most of the local lending library. They would become, respectively, a teacher and an established civil servant and writer.[45] Mary Hatch would return to work full-time when her husband became an invalid in 1922, and was a single parent from his death in 1930. She brought up not only her two stepsons but also her own three children, supporting these two daughters and a son through university.[46]

It was easier for the ambitions of women who married late or not at all to range further. The diaries and letters of Ruth Slate and Eva Slawson have already given us some glimpses of such a process. Dora Marsden and Mary Gawthorpe, founders and editors of the radical periodical *The Freewoman* and ardent suffrage campaigners, both began their careers as pupil-teachers in Yorkshire.[47] The better pupil-teacher centres developed wider cultural programmes, including travel opportunities, seized with alacrity by the women.[48] In London Canon Barnett, his wife Henrietta and Toynbee Hall played a key role in developing the cultural life of maintained school teachers. The first major expedition of the mixed Travellers' Club was to Florence in 1888. In 1887 Newnham College, Cambridge held the first summer course for women teachers from maintained schools; and from 1891 London women teachers joined their male colleagues at regular Summer Schools held in Oxford. However, the scheme organised by Canon Barnett to allow pupil-teachers to compete for scholarships at Oxbridge colleges was open only to the men.[49]

London offered most scope for such cultural exchanges and shared activities; but these were not a metropolitan monopoly. Two major novelists of the period, Thomas Hardy and D. H. Lawrence, knew and used the lives of women teachers in their work, although in very different ways. Mention has already been made of Hardy's use of his sister's experience of training to become an elementary school teacher at the Normal School in Salisbury in *Jude the Obscure*, eventually published in book form in 1895.[50] Hardy showed his awareness of the

---

[45] Church, *Over the Bridge*, pp. 94–7, ch. 19.   [46] BLSA, C707/143.
[47] Delap, *Feminist Avant-Garde*, pp. 22, 24, 209; see also chs. 1–3 of Les Garner, *A Brave and Beautiful Spirit: Dora Marsden 1882–1960* (Aldershot 1990).
[48] Robinson, *Pupil-Teachers*, p. 99.
[49] Copelman, *London's Women Teachers*, pp. 133, 171–5; NCCL 1887, 'College Letter', p. 16; Robinson, *Pupil-Teachers*, pp. 167–8.
[50] Above, p. 118.

aridity and narrowness of contemporary approaches to teacher training, describing his fictional Normal School in Melchester as 'a species of
nunnery' and Sue Bridehead in her early days there as having 'altogether
the air of a woman clipped and pruned by severe discipline'.[51] Yet he did
not follow this through to make tension between the range and intellectual reach of her own reading and the constraints of the daily grind of
classroom control and work a strand in her self-torment. Sue does well
in the time she spends in training and both before and after is portrayed
as a highly successful teacher. Her burdens appear to be not intellectual
frustrations but the crushing weight of social convention and expectation and the problems of controlling her own emotions. At one point
she bursts out to Jude, 'I should shock you by letting you know how I
give way to my impulses and how much I feel that I shouldn't have been
provided with attractiveness unless it were meant to be exercised! Some
women's love of being loved is insatiable'. Claire Tomalin's summary is
blunt but not unfair: 'a tease, wanting to be loved while sexually
unarousable, and emotionally a masochist'.[52]

By contrast, tensions between intellectual aspirations and means of
earning a living play substantial roles in the portrayals of Jude, the
stonemason, and the other principal male character of the novel,
Phillipson, who is an elementary school teacher. Hardy's preface to
the first edition of the book described his intention, 'to tell without a
mincing of words, of a deadly war waged between flesh and spirit; and
to point the tragedy of unfulfilled aims'. The 'tragedy of unfulfilled aims'
is altogether easier to identify in the lives of Jude and Phillipson than in
Sue's life. Each of these men has a life of the mind and we are told a little
of their reading and the ways in which they try – and fail – to sustain this
life. They both say, and we keep being told, that Sue has a life of the
mind, but we never see it in action.

The young women teachers among whom D. H. Lawrence moved in
Nottinghamshire and then in Croydon had intellectual and cultural as
well as emotional lives. It would be foolish to generalise from any aspect
of Lawrence's own career about the life of a maintained school teacher;
but his early women friends, all teachers, Jessie Chambers, Louie
Burrows, Agnes Mason and Helen Corke, although probably out of
the ordinary, were less extraordinary than Lawrence himself. Their

---

[51] *Jude the Obscure*, Part Third 'At Melchester', chapters I and III.
[52] *Ibid.*, Part Fourth, 'At Shaston', chapter I; Tomalin, *Thomas Hardy*, p. 254.

relationships with Lawrence and his ruthless use in his fiction of material from their lives, melded with material from his own, means that we know a great deal more about their experience than might otherwise be the case. This material must be used with great caution; but it would be foolish to ignore altogether what it suggests about what *might* be made of the teacher's life and the complex tangle of intellectual, practical, emotional and sexual concerns it might entail.[53]

All four women had begun as pupil-teachers; of them, only Louie Burrows had gone on to a university college. The others eventually secured certification as teachers by examination. In Helen Corke's case there was simply no money to go down this route. Lawrence himself had pursued it, securing an external London degree as a Nottingham University College student, sharing classes there with Louie Burrows. Yet he urged Jessie Chambers' farming family not to support her in doing the same, commenting, 'They grind them all through the same mill.' He may also have had an ulterior motive, as he told Jessie herself, 'You might so easily become a blue-stocking, you know.'[54]

All the women had had, however, some experience of the teaching at a pupil-teacher centre and Jessie Chambers remarked that although what was on offer was 'a beggarly makeshift, for me it was wealth beyond price'.[55] With friends and colleagues they supplemented their formal work with voracious and eclectic reading. Helen Corke's reading at this stage in her life included Carlyle and evolutionary theory, but also lightweight fiction, Wilkie Collins, Hall Caine, Sarah Grand and Mrs Henry Wood.[56] Jessie Chambers, urged on by Lawrence, was early on much more ambitious. She and Lawrence read French together,

---

[53] Lawrence sustains a whole academic industry. Relevant to this discussion are: Jessie Chambers, *D. H. Lawrence: A Personal Record* (3 editions, London 1935, 1965, 1981); Chambers, 'Letters' in consecutive numbers 1 and 2 of the *D. H. Lawrence Review* 12 (spring and summer 1979); Émile Delavénay, 'D. H. Lawrence and Jessie Chambers: The Traumatic Experiment', *D.H. Lawrence Review* 12:3 (fall 1979), pp. 305–25; Helen Corke, *D. H. Lawrence: The Croydon Years* (Austin, TX 1965); Corke, *In Our Infancy: An Autobiography* (London 1975); James T. Boulton, ed., *The Letters of D. H. Lawrence*, vol. I, *1901–1913* (Cambridge 1980); John Worthen, *D. H. Lawrence: The Early Years 1885–1912* (Cambridge 1991); D. H. Lawrence, *The Rainbow* (first published 1915, suppressed by court order, republished 1930, Cambridge edition ed. Mark Kinkead-Weekes in 2 parts, 1989).
[54] Corke, *In Our Infancy*, p. 132; Chambers, *Lawrence* (1935), pp. 81, 82–3.
[55] Chambers, *Lawrence* (1935), p. 45.   [56] Corke, *In Our Infancy*, p. 115.

Shakespeare and the poetry of Blake; he encouraged her to attend
Saturday morning lectures in Nottingham on the Metaphysical
Poets.[57] They sought out like-minded friends and in 1909 Lawrence
read his essay *Art and the Individual* 'to a little gathering of the
Eastwood intelligentsia at the house of a friend ... It was a member of
this little circle, a Socialist and a Suffragette, who first showed us A. R.
Orage's *New Age*.'[58] In correspondence with Émile Delavénay in
1933–5 Jessie Chambers noted that her 'copy of Schopenhauer is in
the Scott Library edition ... with the marginal notes that Lawrence
made at the time he read the essay on the "Metaphysics of Love"'; and
recorded that her present to Lawrence on his twenty-second birthday
was a copy of J. L. Motley's *Rise of the Dutch Republic*.[59]

Meanwhile Helen Corke had discovered Wagner and Nietzsche; and
in the autumn of 1908 she also met Lawrence, newly arrived to teach in
the Croydon elementary school where her friend Agnes Mason was his
colleague. Corke and Lawrence began to read together in both English
and German, and while she introduced him to Olive Schreiner's *Story of
an African Farm*, he introduced her to the fiction of H. G. Wells, Arnold
Bennett and E. M. Forster and to the poetry of Walter de la Mare.[60]

With literary exploration went exploration of personal and sexual
relationships. Helen Corke had been very close to Agnes Mason and the
relationship may well have included some physical intimacy. At the
same time her married violin teacher had been attempting to persuade
her to become his mistress. Failing, he committed suicide. Lawrence too
wanted to sleep with Helen, but was rebuffed. Later, reading Edward
Carpenter's *Love's Coming of Age*, she would conclude that she was
probably bisexual.[61] What Helen Corke did do, however, was to seek
out Lawrence's other current muse, Jessie Chambers, and establish a
firm friendship with her. They corresponded, exchanged visits and were
able to sustain each other in the face of the news that Lawrence had
become engaged to Louie Burrows. They were together too, travelling
down the Rhine in 1912, when Jessie told Helen of Lawrence's

[57] Chambers, *Lawrence* (1935), pp. 56–63, see also ch. 4, pp. 94–123.
[58] Chambers, *Lawrence* (1935), p. 120.
[59] JC to ED 1 November 1933; JC to ED 1 February 1935, in *D. H. Lawrence
Review* 12.
[60] Corke, *In Our Infancy*, pp. 157, 160, 184.
[61] Corke, *In Our Infancy*, pp. 155–6, 162–70, 173–4, 191, 210–11; Corke, *The
Croydon Years*, p. 13.

elopement with Frieda Weekley.[62] Neither ever saw him again; although both, with very mixed emotions, read what he wrote and subsequently published. The account of what the early reviewer Catherine Carswell was to call the 'bitter baptism' of Ursula Brangwen as a teacher in *The Rainbow*, first published in 1915, made ample use of their experiences at work as well as his own.[63] At the risk of a descent into bathos, such use could also be construed as illustrating how little sex-segregation there was in elementary school teaching.

Hardy's Sue Bridehead serves as poor advertisement for the woman elementary school teacher. Claire Tomalin has suggested that in the novel Hardy was working out some of the frustrations experienced in his relationship with Florence Henniker.[64] Insofar as this is the case, then Sue's occupation is an accident, of no real importance to Hardy's plot. However the lives of the young women in Lawrence's circle in the early years can be read to show that, despite an often brutal daily grind, young women teachers in maintained schools had the financial independence and in some cases the ambition, appetite and stamina to explore a larger cultural and political world and to experiment with relationships. As a group, they look stronger candidates for the label 'New Women' than many of their graduate sisters. Their formal training and occupation provided framework, confidence and opportunity to read and range more widely in their thinking, opportunities which a number of them took. Those opportunities apart, some of these individual voyages of intellectual, cultural and emotional discovery were not very different from those undertaken by those two autodidact clerks, Ruth Slate and Eva Slawson.

---

[62] Corke, *In Our Infancy*, pp. 187, 191–4, 198–200, 204, 219.
[63] Carswell quoted in Lawrence, *The Rainbow*, ed. Kinkead-Weekes, part I, p. lxxii; see especially ch. xiii, 'The Man's World' in part II.
[64] Tomalin, *Thomas Hardy*, ch. 17, 'The Terra-Cotta Dress'.

7 | Ladies and women

The growing presence in the society of women white-collar workers, clerks and teachers prominent among them, raises larger questions about the articulation of the class structure and the permeability of the boundaries between respectability and ladyhood.[1] These questions take us into complex interactions of class, status and gender which so often generate wholes which are greater than the sum of their parts. What distinguished a lady from a respectable woman and both from plain 'women'? Was respectability for women but a pale imitation of ladyhood? Or are we seeing among white-collar women workers the first emergence of distinctively feminine versions of respectability, which might be set beside the characterisations of respectability among male skilled workers from the 1840s and male white-collar workers from the 1870s?[2] To prosecute such an enquiry further now would take us far beyond the present study; but at least the question can be posed. At this stage we can ask where the most important boundaries for women were drawn and how were they drawn? How difficult might such boundaries be to cross? Birth and/or wealth could help in laying claim to the status of a lady but were not necessarily enough; they could be undermined by overt departure from the norms of conventional social and sexual behaviour – as the complicated and ambivalent reactions to George Eliot showed.[3] Dress, demeanour, social relations and public conduct all played their parts in signalling status – as Elizabeth Robins' careful construction of her public identity demonstrated.[4]

---

[1] The very existence of this chapter and some of the points in it owe much to discussion with Ben Griffin over several years.

[2] On male skilled workers, see Geoffrey Crossick, *An Artisan Elite in Victorian Society: Kentish London 1840–1880* (London 1978), esp. pp. 135–6, 138–9; on male workers of the lower middle class, see above, Chapter 5, especially the references in notes 1–3.

[3] See above, pp. 82–3.   [4] See above, p. 61.

Elizabeth Robins' care not to use public transport unaccompanied late at night, and her decision to take a flat with her brother rather than live in lodgings, launched a discussion in Chapter 4 above of behaviour in public and no-go areas in London. It is time now to try to take the themes raised in that discussion further and consider not simply the experience of women trying to make a career for themselves in creative occupations but also the experience of middle-class women more generally. We need to examine what constraints there were on freedom of movement for them; what roles were played by dress codes, demeanour and behaviour in a whole range of social situations and encounters. It is already plain that there were some things a lady did not do and some places where she went at her peril. Olive Garnett's diaries show even the Bohemian fringes of the middle class negotiating these boundaries; and considerations of this kind help explain the preoccupation, bordering on obsession, with chaperonage on the part of the Oxbridge women's colleges. Mary Hutton went up to Newnham from Dublin in 1875. At the end of her first term in December, she proposed travelling home on her own, telling her mother, not entirely accurately, 'Everyone here travels alone, unless there chance to be two going in the same direction at the same time.'[5] This precipitated a snowstorm of letters and telegrams between Mary, her mother and Miss Clough;[6] and at no point during her two years at Newnham did Mary make the journey back and forth from Cambridge to Dublin without a roster of companions for its various stages. The exchanges reinforce the suggestion made above that greater supervision was – and could be – exercised by parents living outside London.[7]

Rules about chaperonage remained at the Oxbridge women's colleges into the 1930s, although increasingly challenged by the students and more honoured in the breach than in the observance. Audrey Richards, later to become a distinguished anthropologist, went up to Newnham in 1918 and remembered:

The chaperon rules were of course resented, even by those who did not want to break them! It was impossible to go into a college room without a chaperon or to have a young man into one's own room if one was alone. It was necessary to have a chaperon in some part of the theatre if one went there.

---

[5] NCA, Hutton Papers, Mary Hutton to mother 5 December 1875.
[6] NCA, Hutton Papers, Mary Hutton to mother Wed. [December 1875], Thurs. [December 1875], 9 December 1875.
[7] NCA, Hutton Papers, *passim.*; above, p. 78.

When I asked Miss Clough [Blanche Athena Clough, niece of Anne Jemima Clough, fourth Principal] what help it would be to have a female don sitting in the stalls when we could only afford gallery or pit seats, she replied, 'There might be some unpleasantness, Miss Richards. I do not think I need say more!'

Yet as Audrey Richards concluded, 'It must be remembered too that Newnham did not invent the chaperon rules. One's own parents had very much the same ideas and behaved in the same way.'[8]

The parents of Newnham students also took a firm line on smoking, despite the cigarettes which adorned the many pictorial representations of the New Woman, including Albert Morrow's poster for Sydney Grundy's play of that name.[9] Before 1914 there was a total prohibition on smoking in college. Blanche Athena Clough, Vice-principal and then Principal 1920–3, was driven to rent a small garden nearby to which she could retreat to enjoy a quiet cigarette. In February 1915, however, the students petitioned the then Principal, Katharine Stephen, to be allowed to smoke at least in their own rooms, perhaps wishing to legitimate something already clandestinely happening. Cunningly, Katharine Stephen sent a questionnaire to all parents, seeking their views; 160 out of 165 replied and, of these, 123 were totally opposed to any relaxation of the rules.[10] Since this was well before any concern about the impact of smoking on health, one can only assume that smoking was not considered appropriate behaviour for a lady.

There is no indication that either Eva Slawson or Ruth Slate smoked – the cost may have been a disincentive. However, choosing routes and modes of transport and finding an appropriate companion or companions were certainly luxuries that white-collar women workers could not afford. They usually travelled to work on their own by the most direct and economical means. For a spell in 1907–9 Ruth Slate's family lived in Abbey Wood and she and her father commuted to their respective places of work in the City daily: 'Dad and I leave home at seven every morning in order to catch the last workmen's train for we could never pay full fare on this line.'[11] At least

---

[8] Phillips ed., *Newnham Anthology*, pp. 133–4; see also Sutherland, *Faith, Duty and the Power of Mind*, pp. 186–9 and Pauline Adams, *Somerville for Women: An Oxford College 1879–1993* (Oxford 1996), esp. pp. 33–4, 213–15. Adams chooses the spelling 'chaperone'.

[9] See jacket, p. 6 and Nelson's summary, p. 3, above.

[10] Sutherland, *Faith, Duty and the Power of Mind*, p. 189, n.24.

[11] Ruth's diary, summary notes 31 December 1907, WL, 7RSJ/A/01/14, f. 4, Thompson, ed., *Dear Girl*, p. 111.

she had her father's company in the mornings. But often Ruth returned on her own, sometimes quite late in the evening, if she had been to a meeting or a concert after work, or spent her precious free Saturday afternoon at a gallery or a theatre, either with a friend or on her own. On several occasions she had frightening encounters, feeling herself at risk of molestation. One such encounter drove her to hail a passing hansom cab; another made her wish she had had an umbrella with which to attack the offender, although perhaps it was as well she had not. On yet another occasion she found herself alone in a railway carriage with one man who went to sleep and another who proved to be drunk. The drunk however was maudlin rather than aggressive and his story was rather a pathetic one.[12] It appeared socially acceptable for Ruth to go on holiday for a week to a boarding house in Margate in July 1908 with her then fiancé Walter Randall.[13] But when that autumn she joined a ballroom dancing class, trying to improve her skills to match Wal's, she found her intentions were misconstrued by some of the young men attending the same class.[14] At one level therefore, respectable women had more freedom of movement than ladies. At another, its use had always to be carefully negotiated and managed and can seldom have been care-free.

Careful travel, a demeanour in mixed company and public places which endeavoured to avoid what Blanche Athena Clough had magnificently if vaguely described as 'some unpleasantness', what else was needed to construct an identity as a lady – or indeed as a respectable woman? Elizabeth Robins' efforts may have been aided by being American and arriving in England as an adult. Her career raises the question of whether, if you arrived on the social scene without a history but behaved and dressed as a lady and had enough money to sustain that lifestyle, you could carry it off. Perhaps – if like Robins you worked hard at it and were a consummate professional actress. St John Hankin's 1908 play, *The Last of the De Mullins*, has a heroine, Janet De Mullin, who has shaped an identity for herself and her illegitimate

---

[12] Ruth's diary, spring 1907, WL, 7RSJ/A/01/13, ff. 56, 58–9; Ruth's diary 3 September 1908, WL, 7RSJ/A/01/14, f. 64; Ruth's diary 10 June 1908, WL 7RSJ/A/01/14, f. 34, Thompson, ed., *Dear Girl*, pp. 117–18; Ruth's diary 15 December 1909, WL, 7RSJ/A/01/14, ff. 114–16.

[13] Ruth's diary 25 July 1908, WL 7RSJ/A/01/14, ff.52–3; Ruth to Eva 11 July 1908, WL, 7RSJ/G/02/06.

[14] Ruth's diary October–November 1908, WL, 7 RSJ/A/01/14, ff. 90–2, 97, 101, 104.

child as Mrs Seagrave, the widowed owner of a successful up-market hat shop; and she demonstrates to her lineage- and status-obsessed family exactly how it was done. The stage direction for her first entry notes, 'She is admirably dressed but her clothes are quiet and in excellent taste, dark in colour and plain in cut but expensive.' A hand-written note in the copy presented to the Lord Chamberlain's office for licensing, reads, 'It is essential that they [the clothes] should be made by a first-rate dressmaker in contrast to those of her mother and sister, which are cheap and shabby.'[15]

Bernard Shaw's play *Mrs Warren's Profession*, written over a decade earlier, in 1894, but refused a licence and performed only privately in London in 1902, shows how the construction or reconstruction of an identity might unravel. Mrs Warren, in her forties, is plainly of ample means and has sent her only daughter, Vivie, to Newnham to read Mathematics. Vivie first appears in a 'Plain, business-like dress, but not dowdy'; she is an 'attractive specimen of the sensible, able, highly-educated young middle-class Englishwoman'. Her mother, by contrast, is 'showily dressed in a brilliant hat and a gay blouse fitting tightly over her bust and flanked by fashionable sleeves'.[16] The showiness of her dress is matched by her manners; and the plot turns on the gradual revelation that she has made her money through prostitution and now manages a chain of brothels across Europe.

Constructing an identity as a lady needed not only money but its carefully directed spending, informed by an acute sense of the prevailing conventions of social behaviour in which dress and demeanour played key roles. Dress, sending immediate, emphatically visual signals, was particularly important. When Tom Ball, John Major's father, won his swimming competition dressed as a New Woman, the key feature of his costume was a pair of bloomers.[17] The Cambridge undergraduates demonstrating against the admission of women to full membership of the University in 1897 dangled a full-size straw effigy of a young woman, clad in outsize bloomers and riding a bicycle, from the first floor window of the bookshop opposite the Senate House, where the vote was taking place.[18] Yet 'rational dress', as it was known, even including divided

[15] Reprinted in *The New Woman and Other Emancipated Woman Plays*, ed. Chotia, pp. 223, 299; see also p. 85.

[16] Reprinted in *Plays Unpleasant*, one of ten volumes published by Penguin Books in honour of Shaw's ninetieth birthday, 1946, pp. 212, 218.

[17] Above, p. 3.   [18] Reproduced p. 139.

7 The dummy at the vote, Cambridge 1897

skirts or jodhpurs, never caught on in England before the First World War, precisely because it tended to attract the jeering crowds. In the 1890s Florence Exten-Hann and her mother, working-class socialists from Southampton, both 'rode bicycles and wore bloomers, but had to carry a skirt to put on when riding in a town for fear of being mobbed'.[19] It would take war work 1914–18 to begin the breakthrough in the slow process whereby trousers became acceptable garb for women.[20]

[19] Quoted Rowbotham, *Dreamers of a New Day*, p. 39.
[20] Diana Crane, *Fashion and its Social Agendas* (Chicago 2000), pp. 113–15, 118–20.

Managing skirts had not however deterred ladies or women from taking to the bicycle. Enthusiasm for it exploded among both sexes and all classes in the course of the 1890s. Clementina Black, Constance Garnett's sister, wrote in the *Woman's Signal* in 1896 that, 'The bicycle is doing more for the independence of women than anything expressly designed to that end'; and for the caricaturists of *Punch* the woman cyclist was an 1890s staple.[21] In the 1908 play, *The Last of the De Mullins*, the heroine, Janet, turns out to have begun the relationship with the young officer who becomes the father of her illegitimate child when they collide out bicycling. Her mother laments, 'Bicycle! I always said it was all through bicycling.'[22]

Women riders might not choose, or be able to afford, the specialist clothing advertised by firms such as Gamages, Lilley & Skinner or Burberry;[23] but there were ways of coping, once a bicycle without a cross-bar had been acquired. An ample guard for the back wheel was a useful basic requirement. Next was a skirt, some three to six inches off the ground, often gored and always loosely fitting round the hips. Under it some women might wear gaiters as well as stout stockings; and the skirt hem could be weighted, or have small elastic loops or stirrups sewn into it.[24] Such skirts with stirrups were the standard wear at Girton and Newnham. Girton had a College Cycling Club from 1894, while at Newnham the cause of the bicycle was greatly aided by the fact that Eleanor Sidgwick, Principal from 1892, rode and rode well.[25] Eva Slawson and Ruth Slate do not tell us what they wore to cycle, but they do add to our vocabulary a contemporary slang term for the activity. In 1908 Eva asked Ruth how her 'scorching' was getting on and ventured a modest boast about her own, 'I can now get on it, ride and get off alone! On Saturday I went to the library on it, but I generally dismount whenever I see an extra large cart or a small hill – my courage not being equal to either.'[26] Ruth was slower to learn, in part because the process became mixed up with the long-drawn-out and painful disintegration of her engagement to Walter Randall. But these

---

[21] Quoted Rowbotham, *Dreamers of a New Day*, p. 2; Kathleen E. McCrone, *Sport and the Physical Emancipation of English Women 1870–1914* (London 1988), pp. 177–85; above, p. 5.

[22] Hankin, *Last of the De Mullins*, ed. Chotia, scene 2, line 641.

[23] McCrone, *Sport*, pp. 239, 255.   [24] *Ibid*. pp. 237–9.

[25] *Ibid*. pp. 32 and 37; Phillips, ed., *Newnham Anthology*, p. 44.

[26] Eva to Ruth 13 July 1908, WL, 7RSJ/B/01/07, Thompson, ed., *Dear Girl*, p. 124.

complications yield the incidental information that a local firm was offering a good second-hand ladies' bicycle and some lessons in how to ride it for a total of 35 shillings.[27]

Women cyclists had thus to manage their skirts to ensure that inappropriate amounts of leg were not displayed. The same rule held for other sports like hockey, rowing and tennis. More abbreviated costumes could be and were worn in the gymnasium and swimming pool, but these spaces were firmly designated private spaces, whether belonging to schools or colleges, or when they offered women-only sessions.[28] In his 1881 novel *A Laodicean*, Thomas Hardy makes the invasion of this privacy a key episode in his plot, when the villain makes a hole in the wall of a gymnasium to enable him and his confederates to spy on the rich heroine at her exercises.[29]

Clothing the upper half of the female body was equally carefully addressed, whether on the sports field, on a bicycle, or in everyday life. The preferred garb was shirts, sometimes ties, jackets with unconstraining armholes, and always some sort of headgear, a securely anchored hat or cap. The Newnham and Girton hockey teams – and others – rejoiced in the kinds of caps which could still be seen adorning schoolboy heads into the 1950s and 1960s.[30] More generally, Diana Crane has argued that in England, France and North America by the late nineteenth century there were two distinct styles of female dress: the fashionable, which was constraining, elaborate, emphasising decorativeness and signalling dependence, and the alternative, which was tailored, un-frilly, less constraining, more practical in allowing vigorous movement, and copying key aspects of male styles, often including a tie.[31] The daughter of a corn merchant who went up to Newnham in 1908 to read Natural Sciences, recalled,

We wore almost a uniform of white blouse, and tweed coat and skirt. The blouse should be of 'nun's veiling' and the collar fixed with a plain rolled gold pin; but such blouses were expensive! When I wore my first, my clumsy spilling

---

[27] Ruth's diary 21 May 1908, 12 June 1908, 6 August 1908, WL, 7RSJ//A/01/14 ff.29, 35, 55; Ruth's diary 30 March 1909, WL, 7RSJ/A/01/15, ff. 59–62; she was still trying to master the skill at Woodbrooke in 1914, WL, 7RSJ/G/02/12 Ruth to Eva 6 and 25 October 1914.

[28] Crane, *Fashion*, pp. 114–16.

[29] Thomas Hardy, *A Laodicean: A Story of Today*, first published 1881, Book the Second, chapters vi and vii. I am indebted to Clare Pettitt for this reference.

[30] McCrone, *Sport*, p. 239; see p. 142.   [31] Crane, *Fashion*, pp. 101–9.

8 The Newnham hockey team, 1892–3

9 Newnham scientists, 1900

of acid in the lab. made large holes in the front which no darning would conceal. But it was still all right with the coat on; and not on the warmest spring day might that coat be removed, either at lectures or in the street, so all was well.[32]

Coats, skirts and blouses, whether of nun's veiling or not, were practical and economical. But however tight their budgets, Newnham students were also expected to change for dinner each night and had to have in addition some clothes to wear at social events. Although Mary Hutton had commented, 'There is no very brilliant dressing here', she regularly reported home to Dublin on the clothes she wore for evening parties and concerts, ringing the changes on shawls and trimmings to accompany her black silk skirt and grenadine tunic, and alternating them with her green muslin. At one point she wrote home urgently for a black velvet sash for this dress. The next year she added a Japanese silk dress and a polonaise to her resources.[33] (Grenadine was a silk and wool mixture, while a polonaise was an over-dress consisting of a body and an open skirt.)

Not only were coats or jackets *de rigeur* for Cambridge women students in the street and at lectures, so always were hats, a requirement which persisted at least up to the Second World War. As a Newnham student who came up in 1923 explained, 'You could go down to the river and have your country walk without a hat, but you had to have hats when you went into town, including lectures.'[34] Along with skirt length, hats and gloves were the key items of apparel marking a dividing line between ladies and respectable women, and just women. Early in Arnold Bennett's 1908 novel *The Old Wives' Tale*, the daughters of a prosperous draper, the sisters Constance and Sophia, stand at the window at some time in the 1860s watching Maggie, their servant girl, going out to meet her beau: '"No gloves, of course!" Sophia criticised. "Well you can't expect her to have gloves," said Constance. Then a pause as the bonnet and dress neared the top of the Square.'[35] It is worth recalling that some

---

[32] Phillips, ed., *Newnham Anthology*, pp. 77–8; See p. 143, Newnham scientists, 1908.

[33] NC Archives, Hutton Papers, the direct quotation comes from Mary Hutton to her sister Catherine, November 1875; see also Mary Hutton to mother 5 December 1875, Monday [December 1875] 13 February 1876, 5 March 1876, 24 March 1876, 4 April 1876, Thursday [November 1876], Mary Hutton to Lilla (a cousin?) 22 November 1876.

[34] Phillips, ed., *Newnham Anthology*, p. 165.

[35] Book 1, ch.1, 'The Square', p. 43 in Penguin Classics 2007.

of Olive Schreiner's experiences in being treated as not-a-lady in the 1880s resulted from going about without hat or gloves.[36]

Gloves seem to have been at least as important as hats, if not more so, as signals of gentility and aspirations to gentility. One of the major expenses at the funeral of John Baines, Constance and Sophia's father, was the provision, in effect gift, of a new pair of black kid gloves to every mourner who went to view the body before the service and burial.[37] Hannah Cullwick was both servant and wife to the Chancery barrister A. J. Munby, that obsessive observer of working women. Hannah's oscillation between the two roles was signalled always by changes of clothing and, in the wifely role, by the donning of gloves. Derek Hudson, Munby's biographer and editor, has commented that by the early 1870s 'Munby could no longer easily decide whether he wanted Hannah's hands to be rough and cracked, or smooth and soft. It was almost impossible to have it both ways, before the days of detergents and cheap hand-lotions' – and, he might have added, rubber gloves.[38] Hannah, for her part, hated the constrictions of gloves and long sleeves especially, as well as those of a floor-length skirt, remarking, 'That's the best o' being drest rough & looking "nobody" – you can go anywhere & not be wondered at.' In the end, she had her way, choosing for good the garb and lifestyle of a working woman.[39] By contrast, the clergyman's wife Mary Higgs, who in disguise investigated common lodging houses, an investigation published as *Glimpses into the Abyss* in 1906, considered that wearing the clothes of a working woman made her more and not less vulnerable.[40] This may, however, say something about her own sense of self and her behaviour when wearing them, a point to which we will return below.

Much of Hannah Cullwick's work as a domestic servant was dirty and required physical strength. In these respects women white-collar workers fared better; and it was easier for them to present a lady-like appearance

---

[36] Above, p. 79.   [37] Bennett, *Old Wives' Tale*, Book 1, ch. 4 'Elephant', p. 116.

[38] Hudson, *Munby*, p. 336; see also pp. 115, 320, 324, 339, 341, 378.

[39] *The Diaries of Hannah Cullwick*, ed. Liz Stanley (London 1984), direct quotation from p. 16. Stanley allows Cullwick to put her side of the story, complementing Hudson's account of Munby. The diaries of both can be consulted in their entirety on microfilm, *Working Women in Victorian Britain, 1850–1910: The Diaries and Letters of Arthur J. Munby (1828–1910) and Hannah Cullwick (1833–1909) from Trinity College, Cambridge* (Marlborough 1993). For Hannah in working clothes, see p. 146.

[40] Quoted in Nord, *Walking the Victorian Streets*, p. 232.

10 Hannah Cullwick sweeping and scrubbing, 1864 and 1865

at work, and even, if they chose, make the odd modest gesture towards fashion. Even so, their clothes had to be capable of coping with grubby offices, warehouses, or classrooms and playgrounds, and travelling back and forth to work, sometimes using the cheap workmen's trains. Shaw captured some of these considerations in describing Vivie Warren on her first appearance as wearing a 'Plain, business-like dress, but not dowdy'. The clothes of the woman white-collar worker might not look quite so much like a uniform as the clothes of the Oxbridge woman undergraduate, but like hers, they tended to be sober and above all practical. Nor were their wardrobes likely to include clothes for changing for dinner or evening parties. There might be something special for high days and holidays; but all the finery Ruth Slate could manage for her firm's annual party in June 1902 was a new blouse to accompany her coat and skirt and a large hat trimmed with marguerites.[41]

For a powerful consideration was cost. When Vivie Warren declared her determination to refuse any more money from her mother, once she knew its provenance, her mother retorted that the alternative would be 'toiling and moiling early and late for your bare living and two cheap dresses a year'.[42] Janet De Mullin explained to her aunt that, 'If I were a school teacher or a governess or something genteel of that kind I could only afford to dress like a pauper. But as I keep a shop I can dress like a lady. Clothes are a question of money after all, aren't they?'[43] Women white-collar workers could seldom fall back on the resources of a high-end milliner's and most had to make do and mend. It is worth remembering Cicely Hamilton's lament that during her short career as an actress her poor sewing skills put her at a disadvantage in providing her own costumes;[44] and Ruth Slate and Eva Slawson's letters and diaries make many mentions of work done to make, mend, refurbish and spruce up outfits.[45] Eva, summoned unexpectedly to undertake some work for her solicitor employer at his house on a Saturday in May 1907, was

---

[41] Ruth's diary 30 June 1902, WL, 7RSJ/A/01/08, f. 4.

[42] *Mrs Warren's Profession*, p. 278.

[43] *Last of the De Mullins*, ed. Chothia, p. 226; see also above, p. 138.

[44] Above, p. 60.

[45] Eva to Ruth 13 July 1908 WL, 7RSJ/B/01/07 and Ruth to Eva 11 July 1908 WL, 7RSJ/G/02/06 (dress-making); Ruth's diary 5 April 1899 WL, 7RSJ/A/01/02, Ruth's diary 10 November 1899 WL, 7RSJ/A/01/03, Ruth's diary 10 February 1900 WL, 7 RSJ/A/01/04, f. 2, Thompson, ed., *Dear Girl*, p. 26, Ruth's diary 20 August and 6 September 1900 WL, 7RSJ/A/01/05, ff. 115, 134 (all dresses trimmed and re-trimmed), Ruth's diary 22 January 1906 WL, 7RSJ/A/01/12,

distressed by her shabbiness: 'I bethought me of a big hole in the heal [*sic*] of my stocking which I fervently hoped would not show – my gloves were the very worst pair I possessed, indeed I intended throwing them aside at the end of that day ... My hat required re-trimming, the kindly rain having at sundry times and in divers places "rained upon it".'[46] In November 1910 Ruth set out to buy a new winter coat but lost her purse and the £2 it contained. Subsequently her father lent her £2 in order to get a coat; but the need to pay him back meant that she could not get the 'nice winter frock' for which she had also planned.[47]

The clothes of the woman white-collar worker were likely to be well-tended but also increasingly well-worn, their lives prolonged to and sometimes beyond their limits, and often covering a form with a certain physical fragility. A stage direction from Harley Granville Barker's 1910 play *The Madras House* conveys a general faded air. Mrs Brigstock was 'one would guess, a clerk of some sort. She lacks colour; she lacks repose – she lacks – one stops to consider that she might possibly be a beautiful woman were it not for the things she lacks. But she is the product of fifteen years or so of long hours and little lunch.'[48] Often Ruth Slate rushed her lunch in the City, seeking instead food for the spirit in a concert or sermon during the hour's break. Eva envied her access to such treats, not available close to her own office in Walthamstow, but worried whether on those days Ruth ate any lunch at all. In June 1908 Ruth weighed under 7 stones (about 42 kilos).[49]

There was another aspect of limited disposable income, seldom mentioned, but all-pervasive in its impact: body odour. As late as the 1930s Frances Lonsdale, daughter of the actor-manager Frederick, amused herself for a spell by working as the private secretary to the manager of a large manufacturing firm. One day she was charged with 'a task of special difficulty and delicacy' – how could the typists' pool, past or through which all clients had to walk, be rendered less smelly? 'I explained that not to smell is an expensive thing. One needs to own more than one dress which, too thin in the winter, is too thick in the summer, and also

f. 25, Thompson, ed., *Dear Girl*, p. 76 – she begins a dress-making class; Eva to Ruth 13 July 1908 pencil postscript, WL, 7RSJ/B/01/07 – making a dress.

[46] Eva to Ruth 9 May 1907 WL, 7RSJ/B/01/06.

[47] Ruth to Eva 10 and 17 November 1910, WL, 7RSJ/G/02/08.

[48] Barker, *Plays: Two, The Madras House (1925 revision)*, ed. Margery Morgan (1994), p. 131.

[49] Eva to Ruth 31 January 1906 WL, 7RSJ/B/01/06, Ruth's diary 15 June 1908 WL, 7RSJ/A/01/14, f. 36 – her actual weight was 6 stones 11 pounds.

many sets of underclothes, so that these can be frequently changed. Hot water and plenty of soap are also essential and not easily obtained in working class houses.' But her recommendations that salaries be increased and the workroom better ventilated were entirely ignored.[50]

White-collar women workers might therefore differentiate themselves sharply from working-class women in terms of skirt-length, long sleeves and those crucial social signifiers, hats and gloves. But those hats were likely to have been trimmed and re-trimmed, the gloves neatly darned in several places, the skirt hems showing signs of the repeated brushing and sponging needed to deal with the dirt and mud they invariably picked up, perhaps having lost their nap in places. If modish, the mode might be that of several years ago and the ensemble might smell more than a little stale. The wearers might be over-slender, pale and less than adequately nourished. Most observers, not only the playwrights of the day, were likely to be able to distinguish without difficulty between the respectable woman and the lady, just as Conan Doyle had Holmes and Watson unerringly place Miss Mary Sutherland as a shorthand typist by her clothes and their points of wear in the story 'A Case of Identity', first published in 1891.[51]

What else might identify a lady? For not every woman with a considerable disposable income chose to spend it on her clothes. One lecturer at Newnham recalled a discussion in the common room about the amount of space taken up by a dressing gown in luggage for a week-end visit. '"Oh, do you take a dressing gown?" said Mrs Sidgwick [the second Principal and bicycling enthusiast]. "I always wear my macintosh." And a macintosh was her usual garb by day too. As the sister of the Prime Minister [A. J. Balfour] she had sometimes to go to smart functions, but then, we were told, she used to borrow a dress.'[52] Nora Sidgwick's social standing trumped her clothes and crucially had bred in her another quality, the habit of authority. Entrusted early by her widowed mother with the responsibility for managing the family's estates and money, she also, from time to time, acted as her brother's hostess. All of this was quietly but effectively brought to bear as she

[50] Frances Donaldson, *Child of the Twenties* (London 1959, 2nd pbk edition 1986), pp. 136–40, direct quotation from p. 139.

[51] Initially published as a single story in the *Strand Magazine*, it became the third story in the collection *The Adventures of Sherlock Holmes*, published in 1892. I am indebted to Clare Pettitt for this reference.

[52] Phillips, ed., *Newnham Anthology*, p. 45.

came to manage first the financial resources and then all the affairs of Newnham.[53] Nora Sidgwick may have been a little out of the ordinary, with her financial skills and intellectual penetration – she was a very capable mathematician. But her example serves to dramatise the point that many people also expected a lady to be prepared and able to exercise authority effectively over other adults. It was a model which owed much to the structural importance of domestic service in the society as a whole. Was this woman able to manage/used to managing servants?[54]

The example of Nora Sidgwick brings us back to the necessity of considering demeanour and behaviour together with clothes and recognising that they were all three likely to interact in complex ways. It was suggested above that the sense of vulnerability experienced by the clergyman's wife, Mary Higgs, when disguised as a working woman, might owe something to her demeanour and behaviour, a suggestion strengthened by the realisation that middle-class women philanthropists in slum areas, however plainly, even shabbily dressed, were generally free from harassment.[55] When sketching Olive Garnett's relative freedom of movement about London, it was also suggested that evidence of demeanour and behaviour were particularly hard to come by; so much was taken for granted and escaped comment.[56] Such sparsity is equally the case in respect of that other signifier of social status, voice, including accent, vocabulary and grammatical structure. Phillip Waller has made an heroic attempt to pull together what can be said about this, which includes the point that, from Jonathan Swift onwards, observers had noted the sharper ear and greater sensitivity of women towards the linguistic environment in which they operated – and wished to operate.[57] Robert Roberts observed that publicans' and shopkeepers' daughters wanting to better themselves spent money not only on clothes, music lessons and commercial classes but also on elocution

---

[53] Sutherland, *Faith, Duty and the Power of Mind*, pp. 103–4.

[54] On the power and durability of this model see Summers, 'Public Functions, Private Premises', pp. 353–76, esp. pp. 355–60. I am indebted to Anne Summers for several fruitful discussions of this issue.

[55] Walkowitz, *City of Dreadful Delight*, pp. 52–9; for Mary Higgs, see above, p. 145.

[56] Above, pp. 77–8.

[57] P. J. Waller, 'Democracy and Dialect, Speech and Class', pp. 1–33 in P. J. Waller, ed., *Politics and Social Change in Modern Britain: Essays Presented to A. F. Thompson* (Hassocks 1987), esp. p. 16, n.68.

lessons.[58] Eliza Doolittle's wish to become 'a lady in a flower shop stead of sellin at the corner of Tottenham Court Road' launches the action in Shaw's play *Pygmalion*, written in 1912.[59] These clues apart, however, in exploring the exercise of social authority further below we have to keep reminding ourselves that there were additional dimensions which it is now near-impossible to see, or hear – or smell.

In nursing in general and in army nursing even more, a model for the exercise of authority grounded in the paradigm of domestic service was the dominant one. Annie Steele resigned from the Army Nursing Corps in 1891 after a report on her seven years' service included the comment, 'Satisfactory report on all points. Not being a lady, is unfit for promotion.'[60] It was precisely this kind of thinking which lay behind the two-track entry to nursing, one for potential matrons and sisters, the other for the rest, described above;[61] and behind the recruitment of 'ladies' to supervise women employees in government service, M. C. Smith to the Post Office in 1875 and Janet Hogarth to the Bank of England in 1894.[62]

Yet such authority could not be straightforwardly exercised in all situations. Matrons and sisters might command their nurses and over-awe working-class male patients; but male medical men were another matter. Nursing in general and army nursing in particular saw a prolonged battle before it began to be accepted that professional knowledge, expertise and experience could trump social standing and gender.[63] Even then the position and authority of women doctors was less secure than that of their male colleagues, insecurities cruelly exposed in the debate over the safety of the forcible feeding of women suffrage campaigners.[64] At the Bank of England, Janet Hogarth, clergyman's daughter and Lady Margaret Hall graduate, described the trouble she had to take as superintendent of women clerks, to manage and

---

[58] Above, p. 89.

[59] Act II (p. 38 in the 1946 Penguin reprint); Waller discusses Shaw's preoccupation with language and the models for Henry Higgins in 'Democracy and Dialect', pp. 1–6.

[60] Summers, *Angels and Citizens*, pp. 109–10.   [61] Above, pp. 48–9.

[62] Above, pp. 42, 107.

[63] Summers, *Angels and Citizens*, *passim*, but esp. ch. 3 and the career of Jane Shaw Stewart.

[64] J. F. Geddes, 'Culpable Complicity: The Medical Profession and the Forcible Feeding of Suffragettes, 1909–1914', *Women's History Review* 17:1 (2007), pp. 79–94.

humour her male professional supervisors. Her first boss 'was a mine of information and a constant delight; but he was dreadfully upset if we seemed to think the work too easy, or tried to go the pace'. Less patronising but also less avuncular were some of his successors, who would happily have seen the women clerks' department abolished.[65]

Within individual occupational groups, however, serious experience and demonstrable competence began gradually to make their mark, even in medicine and nursing. In army nursing Elizabeth Dowse had initially had the same experience as Annie Steele, deemed 'socially ineligible for promotion' at the beginning of her career in 1885. But she stuck it out and eventually broke through: by 1908 she was a Matron in Queen Alexandra's Imperial Military Nursing Service.[66] During World War I the arrogance and barely concealed hostility of the male medical establishment would drive the units of the Scottish Women's Hospital Group eventually to work entirely on the Eastern Front – where they would be welcomed with open arms.[67] Somehow, with a judicious mixture of demonstration, diplomatic pressure and contacts, Dr Louisa Garrett Anderson, daughter of Elizabeth, and Dr Flora Murray prevailed upon the military authorities to sanction a hospital for wounded and convalescent soldiers, staffed entirely by women, in London. Their success rates at Endell Street would stand comparison with the best.[68] Although these gains seemed to evaporate in the immediate post-war period, they did constitute a precedent and mark the beginning of a long slow process whereby ability, training, experience and the competence they combined to generate would come to match considerations of social background, status and gender – slowly eroding their importance and even, on occasion, outweighing them.

This process was slow indeed; and it would take most, if not all, of the twentieth century before the professional and occupational descriptors, doctor, nurse, teacher, writer, civil servant, manager, lawyer, would convey more and be used more commonly than the social and gendered descriptors, lady and woman. As Daisy Hay has recently reminded us,

---

[65] Courtney (her married name), *Recollected in Tranquillity*, pp. 154–5, from which the direct quotation comes, and p. 163.

[66] Summers, *Angels and Citizens*, p. 110.

[67] Leah Leneman, *In the Service of Life: The Story of Dr Elsie Inglis and the Scottish Women's Hospitals* (Edinburgh 1994).

[68] J. F. Geddes, 'Deeds *and* Words in the Suffrage Military Hospital in Endell Street', *Medical History* 51 (2007), pp. 79–98.

as late as 1960 Jessica Mitford, the committed Communist and radical amongst the six daughters of Lord Redesdale, wrote of her life with her first husband, Esmond Romilly, 'our style of behaviour ... the strong streak of delinquency which I found so attractive in Esmond and which struck such a responsive chord in me, his carefree intransigence, even his supreme self-confidence – a feeling of being able to walk unscathed through any flame – are not hard to trace to an English upper-class ancestry and upbringing'.[69]

The slow process of change, of the gradual move towards occupational rather than class- and gender-based descriptors was fed by multiple shifts in the social structure, including the absolute shrinkage of manual work in the economy and the reshaping and eventual decline of traditional patterns of domestic service. These can only be flagged but not explored at all here.[70] Nor was the process of change, albeit slow, a smooth one; instead it was uneven, jagged and syncopated. The demands of total war between 1914 and 1918 appeared to shake up the social and occupational structure and to create more opportunities for women with some skills and training. But peace and post-war economic slump brought some backlashes. As we have seen, marriage bars began to proliferate, attacks on 'the spinster' became shriller, openings for women graduates closed again.[71] For some of the women whose pre-1914 experiences we have tried to trace, life must have appeared to be going backwards and scope for choice and action narrowing in a number of ways. Again these reverses and caesuras can only be flagged, not explored.

Set against such a background of glacially slow and uneven movement, it is important not to overstate or to over-dramatise the shifts, the seeds of change in the experience of middle-class women in the period up to 1914. Despite all these caveats, however, identifying these seeds seems worth a try. In such an attempt, the experience of teaching as an

---

[69] Quoted from *Hons and Rebels*, Jessica Mitford's first volume of memoirs (London 1960) by Daisy Hay in 'Honourable Rebel', pp. 69–73, *Slightly Foxed: The Real Reader's Quarterly* 41 (Spring 2014), p. 72.

[70] A. H. Halsey, *Change in British Society from 1900 to the Present Day* (Oxford, 4th edn 1995), esp. pp. 40–1, table 2.1; Alison Light, *Mrs Woolf and the Servants* (London 2007, pbk 2008); Lucy Delap, *Knowing their Place: Domestic Service in Twentieth-Century Britain* (Oxford 2011).

[71] See above, pp. 40, 120–21; see also Susan Kingsley Kent, *Making Peace: The Reconstruction of Gender in Interwar Britain* (Princeton 1993); chs. 5–7 of Oram, *Women Teachers*; and chs. 10 and 11 of Pedersen, *Eleanor Rathbone*.

occupation is important. It allowed movement across the lady/woman divide, blurring its boundaries, extensively demonstrating the importance of training, of qualifications, of experience and competence. It offered some women opportunities to work side by side with their male colleagues, doing essentially the same jobs. Teachers exercised authority inside the classroom, with and sometimes over colleagues, and held their own with parents, managers, governors, even on occasion with Her/His Majesty's Inspectors.

As Chapters 2 and 6 above have shown, teaching at a variety of levels constituted one of the fastest-growing occupations for women in the late nineteenth century. It offered some career progression for them, a progression extended by the creation of maintained secondary schools in the wake of the 1902 Education Act. It is impossible to overestimate the importance of this legislation, for the changes it brought enabled the systematic intermingling of the daughters of artisans and skilled workers, of shopkeepers and small businessmen with the daughters of the surgery, the rectory and the manse, who were already teaching in the independent secondary schools for girls which had mushroomed since 1870. As we have seen, the Association of Assistant Mistresses dated real growth from their willingness to open their membership to women teachers in maintained secondary schools from 1904–5 onwards.[72] If we compare the reading, cultural concerns and pursuits of the women teachers in D. H. Lawrence's circle before 1912 with those of the St Hugh's graduates who aimed for teaching posts in London, the differences do not seem great.[73]

The one notable difference in this comparison is the greater frankness of the Lawrence circle about sexual curiosity and experiment. This may simply reflect back concerns which preoccupied Lawrence and his particular friends and thus subsequently Lawrence scholars, being a construct of a particular literature, primary as well as secondary. It may also, however, suggest that respectability might be less constraining than ladyhood, that a woman who achieved economic independence did not automatically then hanker to become, to be treated as, a lady. Neither Helen Corke nor Jessie Chambers seems to have harboured such ambitions; nor did such ambitions appear to figure among the aspirations of Eva Slawson and Ruth Slate. Moreover the gradual evolution of Ruth's and Eva's attitudes towards sexuality which

---

[72] See above, pp. 30, 123–8.   [73] Above, pp. 32–3 and 130–33.

brought Eva very close to the widowed Minna and Ruth to share a flat with Françoise Lafitte, an ardent advocate of free love, meant that they shared much common ground with the Lawrence circle.[74]

There are some signs that boundaries were becoming more permeable, that distinctions between ladyhood and respectability were beginning if not to blur, to soften. Those distinctions might remain real enough at the extremes. Hearing that evening dress was expected at some meetings of the Women's Social and Political Union, the WSPU, Nellie Best of Middlesbrough asked, 'Is it intended to debar servants, laundresses etc.?' In the *Labour Leader* Katharine Bruce Glasier offered the same comment on the deliberate decision of the WSPU to cultivate the social elite, although in less dramatic terms: '"the Society Women's Political Union" would be the honester interpretation of the WS and PU capitals'.[75]

Yet among women between the aristocratic and seriously wealthy (the upper class) and those who worked with their hands and bodies (the working class), and among the women of the 'middling sort' (lower middle, middle middle and upper middle), it was possible to find some solidarities, and shared activities and aspirations. Eva Slawson was initially intimidated by the self-assurance of the teacher Comrade Mrs Shimmins when she joined the ILP, but hung on and made her own mark.[76] Both she and Ruth Slate were also intimidated at first by the self-assurance of other students who had had more formal education when they began their studies at Woodbrooke. Ruth reflected, 'There is such an abundancy of spirits . . . in those who were at school until their twenties and then began on a "profession" which tells me plainly that in our cases a reservoir has been sapped.' Replying, Eva agreed that the college girls had more stamina for examinations, but 'I do think though we have the advantage in a much more intimate knowledge of the suffering side to life – of those who toil – and, I think, perhaps, a deeper appreciation of friendship.' The whole exchange prompted Ruth to broader reflection. 'I was particularly struck at Rowntree's with the

---

[74] See above, pp. 110–12; also the summary passages in Thompson, ed., *Dear Girl*, pp. 150–3, 160.

[75] Best in *The Woman Worker*, 25 September 1908, and Glasier in *The Labour Leader*, 27 September 1908, quoted in Sandra Stanley Holton, *Feminism and Democracy: Women's Suffrage and Reform Politics in Britain, 1900–1918* (Cambridge 2003), p. 37.

[76] Above, p. 126.

tired faded look of the forewomen there, most of them a little over thirty but had been working at the factory since they left school. The social workers, on the other hand, who had a jolly school-time and lots of choice as to the work they would take up, looked smooth and fair and healthy.'[77] After Eva's death, Ruth came close to irritation at the stress everyone laid on Eva's humility: 'Much of that humility was the lack of self-confidence both Eva and I have felt to be the curse of our lives & which has been unduly and unhealthily fostered in us by mistaken religious training & hard circumstances.'[78] By this time she herself was now numbered among the social workers, even if, as she implied, she more resembled the forewomen; and she worked in this field for the rest of her life. A boundary of sorts had been crossed.

More illustrations of boundary-crossing, sharing, might be found if we knew more about the non-Oxbridge women graduates. As has been noted, they considerably outnumbered the Oxbridge students, in 1900 approximately not quite 3,000 to 600.[79] Any hypotheses about their social relationships have to be tentative, however, pointing to another area where much more work needs to be done. We have only fragments of information about and analyses of the social composition and occupational destinations of students at universities and university colleges outside Oxbridge and these are seldom systematically broken down by gender.[80]

What little we do know about the social origins of these non-Oxbridge graduates suggests that they resembled the origins of women maintained schools teachers and clerks more closely than they resembled the social

---

[77] Ruth to Eva 7 February 1916 and Eva to Ruth 10 February 1916, WL, 7RSJ/G/02/14, 7RSJ/B/01/14, Thompson, ed., *Dear Girl*, pp. 291–3.

[78] Ruth's diary 24 March 1916, WL, 7RSJ/A/01/17, f. 15, Thompson, ed., *Dear Girl*, p. 300.

[79] Above, pp. 21–2. I owe the germ of these suggestions to a discussion with Felicity Cooke.

[80] R. D. Anderson, *Educational Opportunity in Victorian Scotland: Schools and Universities* (Oxford 1983), ch. 8; Anderson, *The Student Community at Aberdeen 1860–1939* (Aberdeen 1988); Lindy Moore, *Bajanellas and Semilinas: Aberdeen University and the Education of Women 1860–1920* (Aberdeen 1991), pp. 120–31. The work of Anderson and Moore on Aberdeen is the shining exception and suggests that more could be done with the surviving data than has been done in the handful of studies of other institutions; see Michael Moss, J. Forbes Munro and Richard H. Trainor, *University, City and State: The University of Glasgow since 1870* (Edinburgh 2000), pp. 76–8, 107, 109, 351, Fig. 1, and Eric Ives, Diane Drummond and Leonard Schwarz, *The First Civic University: Birmingham 1880–1980* (Birmingham 2000), pp. 54–5, 57–8, 61–6, 257.

backgrounds of the Oxbridge women. Some of the children, including some of the daughters, of artisans, skilled workers, shopkeepers and small farmers were beginning to find their way to a higher education, often locally, either to the old-established Scottish universities, or to the new university colleges which initially prepared their students for external London degrees. And a proportion of these women, far greater than the comparable proportion among Oxbridge women, went on afterwards to earn their own living. Often this was the reason for which they had gone to university, aiming for qualifications which would lead to a decent, secure, white-collar job, almost invariably teaching.

Although the direct evidence available so far is fragmentary, there is some indirect evidence of divergence between the social background and aspirations of the Oxbridge and non-Oxbridge women students, in the form of the differing attitudes of their institutions towards chaperonage. In Oxbridge the women's colleges and their supporters were struggling to insert ladies into a gentlemanly elite; elsewhere young adults of both sexes were sharing the kinds of social encounters which would continue into their working lives. As we have seen, the Oxbridge women's colleges were obsessive about requiring the presence of chaperons whenever their students were in public places in the University or received male non-family visitors in college. The rules about this were rigorously enforced until 1919 and eroded only gradually in the years between the Wars.[81] The authorities in the university colleges of Wales, Manchester and Durham initially fought to do the same but already by 1914 had largely lost the battle.[82] In the London women's colleges chaperonage appeared barely an issue,[83] as the women students at UCL and KCL lived at home or in lodgings. At UCL the committee overseeing the admission of 'ladies' to classes initially spent a great deal of time on devices to keep men and women separate both in lecture rooms and in their comings and goings, including a separate door for women and a rule that their lectures began and ended on the half-hour while those for men began and ended on the hour. But this entailed a duplication of resources which proved unsustainable in the longer term.[84] In Aberdeen there were no halls of residence before 1940 and women students who could not travel home each

---

[81] Above, pp. 135–6 note 8.   [82] Dyhouse, *No Distinction of Sex?*, pp. 192–7.

[83] Tuke, *History of Bedford College*; Sondheimer, *Castle Adamant*; Bingham, *History of Royal Holloway College*.

[84] Negley Harte, *The Admission of Women to University College, London: A Centenary Lecture* (London 1979), pp. 12–13.

day all lived in lodgings. Chaperons were never required at lectures; and after evening events and functions it was considered good manners for the men students to walk the women students safely home – behaviour which would have led to rustication or sending down in Oxbridge. An early Aberdeen graduate who went on to further work at Somerville College, Oxford was astonished to find she was not allowed to invite her male cousin to dinner, even though she was sharing a house with eleven other women students.[85]

This particular group of students undoubtedly made their own contribution to bridging social divides and sharing concerns and preoccupations as they lived together in Oxford. It seems a reasonable hypothesis that this happened elsewhere, either during student life or in the workplace, usually a school, although only more detailed work on the backgrounds, destinations and social lives of non-Oxbridge women students to the First World War and beyond will confirm or negate this. Unless great swathes of the institutional records of universities outside Oxbridge have been destroyed, it should be straightforward to test this hypothesis more systematically.

Far harder is any systematic attempt to discover whether such bridging, such sharing and intermingling, also went on among women journalists and writers. As Chapter 4 above has shown, they were drawn from a diverse range of social backgrounds, ladies and women together. Yet their Society and their Club brought them together, and although they might compete for 'scoops', their need to network was far greater than such a need among male colleagues and competitors. It is difficult, however, to work out how to look systematically for evidence of such networking and sharing; serendipity will have to serve. It would be the mid twentieth century – 1954 – before Vera Brittain could boldly title a book on women's employment *Lady into Woman*; and it would be at least another forty years before the possession of higher education and qualifications, or their absence, could be identified as creating key divisions between groups of women.[86] Yet the embryo of this transition is surely to be found in the experience of women white-collar workers, especially the teachers and writers, as the nineteenth century gave way to the twentieth.

[85] Moore, *Bajanellas and Semilinas*, p. 70. Sadly Moore does not give us her interviewee's exact dates as a student.
[86] Shirley Dex, Heather Joshi and Susan Macran, 'A Widening Gulf Among Britain's Mothers', *Oxford Review of Economic Policy* 12:1 (Spring 1996), pp. 65–75.

8 | *Some conclusions: degrees of freedom*

The 'girl graduate' had become such a stock character in popular fiction that in 1912 *Thersites*, the Newnham student magazine, offered an extended parody, 'The Girls of Luneham (with apologies to L. T. Meade)'. Two years later *The Fritillary*, the literary magazine of all five Oxford women's colleges, offered a very tongue-in-cheek review of *The Chesterton Girl Graduates*, yet another novel by L. T. Meade.[1] Yet for all the catchiness of the tags 'girl graduate' or even 'Girton Girl' and the scope for blue-stocking/bloomer-clad, bicycle-riding caricatures, the actual numbers of women graduates in the society of late Victorian and Edwardian Britain were tiny, in a total population which in 1911 numbered just over 42 million, slightly more than half of whom were female. Even fewer of them were in employment and economically independent, whether in the closed world of women's independent secondary and higher education, or forming a token presence in the upper reaches of government service. While we need to know much more about the non-Oxbridge graduates, where they were and what they were doing, the overall numbers of women graduates were still, in absolute terms, few. It is hard to argue that on their own they represented a real shift in the visibility of middle-class women within the society as a whole. It is even harder to argue that they constituted a serious challenge to established patterns of social behaviour.

Moreover the occupations in which were to be found those women graduates who did work tended to be heavily freighted with expectations of certain kinds of behaviour. Women teachers in independent schools, in universities, in the higher reaches of government service were expected to be ladies of a very traditional kind, unmarried, impeccably conventional in their behaviour, able to direct their staff and students but deferential to their governors and political and social superiors. The

---

[1] *Thersites* 6 June 1912; *The Fritillary* 62 (June 1914). For a selection of other novels, see above, p. 5.

enduring power of the image of the Lady Bountiful, dispensing charity, which shaped those posts available in government service and in social work complements and amplifies the point.[2] The only gestures permitted to them were a careful simplicity and practicality of dress – and bicycling, although, despite *Punch*, 'rational dress' aka bloomers never caught on. Whatever secret ambitions some of them may have harboured beyond the carefully coded signals of dress and recreation, it is hard to identify more than a handful of New Women in this company, except perhaps among the doctors. Among this tiny group a key factor was likely to be the amplitude of resources, usually family resources, which had sustained them through medical school and clinical training in the first place and provided some armour against rebuffs and setbacks. Time and again, having some money in the first place helped in the search for more resources and the construction of an independent lifestyle.

Was the New Woman then entirely a fantasy, a grim and utterly mysterious entity with which to titillate the senses, like Lewis Carroll's *Snark*?[3] Yet if we press on in a search for women beginning to challenge prevailing conventions of behaviour, we do not, unlike the Baker in Carroll's poem, 'softly and suddenly vanish away' or find that this happens to the objects of our search. Instead we begin to discover a situation of much greater complexity and uncertainty. The first signals of this come when we turn to women writers. The rise and rise of the popular periodical press did provide some new opportunities and attracted a more socially diverse group than did higher education and those occupations access to which depended on higher education. This of itself was a fertile breeding ground for nine days' wonders and media feeding frenzies.

In addition the very nature of the work demanded visibility. To sell the work of your pen, you had to become known. Greater public visibility was also greater exposure and could bring in its train fierce and sometimes condemnatory scrutiny. Some women writers embraced notoriety, finding it enhanced visibility. At the same time it was likely to limit the genres in which they wrote and was never cost-free in social terms. Aside from the pressures of private life, one offered oneself as a

[2] See above, pp. 50–54.
[3] See Carroll's repeated denials that he knew what the Snark, or its alter ego, the Boojum, represented in Martin Gardner, ed., *The Annotated Snark* (2nd edition London 1974), pp. 21–3.

prime target for attacks by the Grant Allens and the Mrs Humphry Wards of the world. It was not a route chosen by all. Having experienced the pressures actresses faced to conform to a different stereotype, that of the good-time girl or prostitute, Elizabeth Robins fought hard and ultimately successfully during her work in the theatre and then as a writer, to shape and to protect a public persona of impeccable social standing.[4] Elizabeth wrote for adults; Evelyn Sharp, who made some of her reputation and income from writing for children, fought even harder to protect her complex and distinctly unconventional personal life from the public gaze.[5]

A different kind of visibility, and one which would prove to have a more enduring impact, was that of mass presence. By 1914 this had already been achieved by the growing ranks of women engaged in white-collar work, shop assistants, nurses, telephonists and clerks, local government employees and, above all, maintained school teachers. Where graduates were present in the society in their tens, at most in their hundreds, these women workers were present in their thousands. If we are looking for signs of real change in the labour force and in social structures, they deserve much fuller scrutiny than hitherto they have received. With the exception of shop assistants, they were not obvious subjects for caricature and fantasy whether in pen and ink or in print, not smart, protected by their modest social status and their very ubiquity.[6] Yet their experiences, their opportunities for a modicum of independence make them earlier and more substantial harbingers of change than the handful of women graduates, even though similarities of background and working experience may have brought the young women who had attended the Scots universities and the new university colleges of England and Wales closer to the white-collar workers than to the Oxbridge women.

To claim that women white-collar workers were more plausible candidates for the label 'New Women' is not, however, to assert that they were New Women, hell-bent on challenging the status quo in social, sexual and marital relationships and behaviour. New opportunities to make a living without dependence on parents or husband brought women some choice, some additional freedom. What they did with this, what they could do with it, are separate issues. Anne Heilmann has argued that New Woman writing was 'a complex historical phenomenon which operated at both cultural (textual and visual)

---

[4] Above, pp. 61, 82, 84.   [5] Above, pp. 85–6.   [6] Above, pp. 89–90, 91–2.

and socio-political levels'; and later that New Woman fiction and journalism 'played a major part in contributing to the complex social changes which led to a redefinition of gender roles and a consolidation of the notion of women's rights at the turn of the century'.[7] It is easy to bat such a large claim away with the question, 'Where is the evidence?' More stimulating to consider is Clare Pettitt's tentative suggestion that one should explore whether the 'imaginary New Woman did help people ... to imagine the possibility, and then to recognise the emergence of the real thing ... the link between the imaginary and the historical is, in this case, a peculiarly fraught and interesting one'.[8]

All of us who deal in words, whether literary scholars or historians, would be driven to give up if we thought no-one ever listened. It would be foolish to suppose that either the women graduates or the women white-collar workers were unaware of the debate and discussion about the scope and opportunities open to them, the expectations and assumptions of society about their behaviour – a large part, if not the whole, of the media feeding frenzy. Ada Radford, a sketch of whose life illustrated the beginnings of this enquiry, was undoubtedly politically aware, as an early graduate, a friend of Constance Garnett, an acquaintance of Amy Levy, a contributor to the *Yellow Book*, an aide to the Russian revolutionaries, before ever she met and married the prominent Fabian and political scientist Graham Wallas. Yet, as we saw, the trajectory of her life is best described as that of a New-ish Woman. It is a tentative and qualified description which could also fit that prolific diarist and observer of literary London and Bohemia, Olive Garnett. She was fully *au courant* with debates on the institution of marriage and on the existence, or otherwise, of the New Woman. She contributed to the anarchist newspaper *The Torch*, run by the older children of W. M. Rossetti, and was an ardent supporter of *Free Russia*. In love with Stepniak, she was devastated by his death in 1894. Eventually she rallied and set off in the summer of 1896 to spend a long-planned year in Russia. The fruits of this in fiction were *Petersburg Tales* (1900) and *In Russia's Night* (1918). She never married and either from choice or from lack of family support she had not followed her school friend and later sister-in-law, Matty Roscoe, to Newnham. When her father died

[7] Ann Heilmann, *New Woman Fiction: Women Writing First-Wave Feminism* (London 2000), pp. 2, 41.
[8] Personal communication.

intestate in 1906 lack of resources meant that she had to quit the family home in Hampstead and make her home with one of her brothers. Living until 1958, she published nothing after 1918. Olive knew all about New Women and their caricatures but did not herself fit neatly into the stereotype.[9]

Clare Pettitt's seductive hypothesis about the possibility of a 'link between the imaginary and the historical' works best for the two young women clerks, Ruth Slate and Eva Slawson. The range and choices of their reading do suggest that its relationship with their hunger for new opportunities and urge to explore new patterns of living was a symbiotic one – each fed the other in complex ways. Ruth's diary entry for 28 May 1908 captured this: 'Read *The Story of an African Farm* in lunch hour. Am I presumptuous in feeling that *much* of what I have been thinking and feeling so strongly is here expressed.'[10] In the light of the reservations expressed above about Hardy's presentation of Sue Bridehead, I find myself wholly in accord with Eva's concern in 1915 about the likely impact of the novel on her half-sister Gertie, the militant suffragette – 'Hardy is like a great organ, but he plays in the minor key.'[11]

The Story of an African Farm was also an important text for D. H. Lawrence's friend Helen Corke; it is little wonder that W. T. Stead had hailed Olive Schreiner as 'The Modern Woman par excellence, founder and high priestess of the school'. Olive Schreiner, too, had experimented for a spell in not dressing as a lady.[12] The experiences of the two women clerks and of some of the maintained school teachers, like Helen Corke, allow us to develop the point further and to suggest that having to behave like a lady might have been more burdensome and constraining than simply the preservation of a respectable demeanour. Paradoxically there are also the first hints that training, qualification, the achievement of a professional or quasi-professional status might, over several generations, have a role to play too in reducing the importance of the social descriptors, lady and respectability, in diluting the part played in their construction, especially in the construction of the former, by gender.

---

[9] See above, pp. 8–9, 10–11; the two volumes of diaries 1890–95 ed. Johnson; and Sandra Kemp, Charlotte Mitchell and David Trotter, *The Oxford Companion to Edwardian Fiction* (Oxford 1997, reprinted 2007).

[10] WL, 7RSJ/A/01/14, f. 31, Thompson, ed. *Dear Girl*, p. 117, her emphasis.

[11] 4 August 1915, WL, 7RSJ/G/01/12; above, pp. 129–30, 133.

[12] See above, p. 79.

Again a key group are the maintained school teachers. Yet if these hints have not been misconstrued, they are only hints of a process just beginning. Its development is another story and another study, as women teachers' prolonged battle for equal pay and the battle of both women and men teachers for a fully professional status would show.[13]

Clear evidence of links between the life of the imagination and the lived life, of the kind yielded by Ruth's and Eva's diaries and letters is all too rare. Moreover not all the women who secured some independence through their work chose radically to reshape their lives in the ways that these two, or Helen Corke, or Dora Marsden, the teacher who became a suffragette, did. The comment of the clerk Elsie Barralet resonates here: 'I had a friend who was a suffragette and she did open my eyes to the poor deal that women were getting and I began to think in her direction although I never had any activities, but she did'.[14] Other women, like the teacher Lavinia Orton, mother of the novelist Richard Church, and the teacher Mary Hatch, supporting an invalid husband and five children, used their earnings and status to build family structures which reflected their own personal priorities.[15] The choices Lavinia and Mary made resembled those made by Ada Radford after her marriage to Graham Wallas, although the resources Ada brought to bear were inherited.[16] In looking at the modest independence brought to some middle-class women, either by family resources or by new opportunities to work, it is important not to imagine that such independence brought unfettered choice, an opportunity to make brush-strokes on a blank canvas. The resources were modest; and while the opportunities for employment were beginning to change, much else in these women's world was not; social attitudes and conventions in particular moved with different rhythms and each woman had to make her own decisions and choices in trying to navigate among them.

Jose Harris has suggested that in this period the shifting pattern of women's roles was 'fraught with ambiguity, contingency and tension'. She continues, 'The most important characteristic of gender roles in the 1900s was not simply that they had changed in a particular way but that, by comparison with the early and mid-Victorian era, the very

---

[13] Above, p. 126 and Tropp, *School Teachers*, chs. xii–xiv; cf. also the impact of registration on the status of nursing after 1920, Abel-Smith, *History of the Nursing Profession*.

[14] BLSA, C707/216; see above, pp. 102–3.   [15] Above, pp. 128–9.

[16] Above, pp. 9–10.

nature of those roles was increasingly contested and uncertain.'[17] In the four decades up to 1914 the conventions and constraints on female behaviour might appear looser, tempting some women to push against them; but there was always uncertainty about whether particular barriers would yield and some proved remarkably resilient, particularly those concerning personal and sexual relationships. Instead of assuming economic independence equalled unalloyed freedom, it makes sense to see it as bringing middle-class women what in the twentieth century the novelist Iris Murdoch would characterise as 'degrees of freedom'.[18] They had some enhanced scope for action but always with boundaries and limitations; no choices were without costs. The relationships thus between the caricature of the New Woman and its attendant rhetoric, and the actual lives of middle-class women in the period, are complex and nuanced. Labelling these women as either New Women or failed New Women is a profoundly ahistorical activity. Such women's lives and the uncertainties and challenges they faced provide routes of entry for the historian into complex, often untidy and not easily classifiable realities. These women, just like their male contemporaries, were people with a diversity of expectations and ideals, who, insofar as they were able, made diverse choices, using what freedoms they had to try to shape and to assert priorities of their own choosing.

How then finally might we use the New Woman media feeding frenzy of the 1890s and the questioning in the surrounding years as a means of exploring shifts in British society as a whole? The New Woman caricature is best seen as a vivid reflection of turmoil and uncertainty. It is not a crystallisation of change already accomplished, rather it is a sign that change was beginning. The numbers of white-collar women workers arriving on the scene cry out for fuller investigation and scrutiny, of the kinds only the Oxbridge graduates of the period have so far received. In the course of such an enterprise, it should be possible also to pursue more of these white-collar workers into the ranks of campaigns for the vote and other causes, the women's movement in its broadest manifestations. We have put a few faces, names and histories to women who

[17] Jose Harris, *Private Lives, Public Spirit: A Social History of Britain 1870–1914* (Oxford 1993), pp. 25, 31; cf. also Angelique Richardson, *Love and Eugenics in the Late Nineteenth Century: Rational Reproduction and the New Woman* (Oxford 2003, pbk 2008). pp. 7–9.

[18] A. S. Byatt, *Degrees of Freedom: The Novels of Iris Murdoch* (London 1965), pp. 9–11.

joined organisations, marched, demonstrated, evaded the census enumerators, chose or eschewed militancy, behind the conspicuous leader-
ship of people like the Pankhursts, the Pethick-Lawrences, Millicent
Garrett Fawcett, Teresa Billington Greig, Catherine Marshall, the
Wolstenholme Elmys etc. It would be good to be able to add more
faces and names to those not in the front rank, not immediately attracting the attention of the press and the authorities. We might then begin to
understand more about the growth of mass female political engagement
and activism in Britain, its extent, its nature and its limitations, in the
decades after 1900.

Sources and select bibliography

Manuscript primary Sources

British Library
Additional Manuscripts (BL Add Mss), 61927, 61928 and 61929, correspondence between Mathilde Blind and Richard Garnett
Sound Archives (BLSA) C707/21, C707/143, C707/216, C707/300, C707/368, C707/406
Metropolitan Archives, Clerkenwell (MA)
Skinners' Company Schools' Committee Minute Books
Archives of Newnham College, Cambridge (NCA)
Hutton Papers
Wallas Papers
Archives of the Skinners' Academy, Stamford Hill
Papers relating to the Skinners' Company School for Girls
The Women's Library (WL), at the London School of Economics
7RSJ, the diaries and correspondence of Ruth Jones, née Slate, and Eva Slawson

Printed primary sources

Barker, Harley Granville, *The Madras House* (1910) in *Plays: Two*, ed. Margery Morgan (London 1994)
Bennett, Arnold, *The Old Wives' Tale* (first published London 1908)
Bondfield, Margaret, *A Life's Work* (London 1949)
Boulton, James T., ed., *The Letters of D. H. Lawrence*, vol. I, *1901–1913* (Cambridge 1980)
Chambers, Jessie, *D. H. Lawrence: A Personal Record* (3 editions, London 1935, 1965, 1981)
Church, Richard, *Over the Bridge: An Essay in Autobiography* (London 1955)
Collet, Clara, *Essays on the Economic Position of Women Workers in the Middle Classes* (London 1902)
Corke, Helen, *D. H. Lawrence: The Croydon Years* (Austin, TX 1965)
In Our Infancy: An Autobiography (London 1975)

Garnett, Olive, *Olive & Stepniak: The Bloomsbury Diary of Olive Garnett 1893–95*, ed. Barry C. Johnson (Birmingham 1993)

    Tea and Anarchy! The Bloomsbury Diary of Olive Garnett 1890–93, ed. Barry C. Johnson (Birmingham 1989)

Girton College Register 1869–1946 (Cambridge, privately printed for Girton College 1948)

Girton Review (GR) [the College's magazine for former and current students, printed three times a year for private circulation]

Gissing, George, *The Odd Women* (first published London 1893)

Gordon, Mrs J. E. H., 'The After-Careers of University-Educated Women', *Nineteenth Century* 37 (June 1895)

Hamilton, Cicely, *Diana of Dobson's* (1908), ed. Diane F. Gillespie and Doryjane Birrer (Peterborough, Ontario 2003)

    Life Errant (London 1932)

Hankin, St John, *The Last of the De Mullins* (performed 1908), reprinted in Jean Chotia ed., *The New Woman and Other Emancipated Plays* (Oxford 1998)

Haramundanis, Katherine, ed., *Cecilia Payne-Gaposchkin: An Autobiography and Other Recollections* (2nd edition Cambridge 1996)

Hardy, Thomas, *Jude the Obscure* (London 1895)

Hughes, M. V., *A London Girl of the 1880s* (Oxford 1946, paperback 1978)

Lawrence, D. H., *The Rainbow* (first published London 1915, Cambridge edition ed. Mark Kinkead-Weekes, 2 parts, 1989)

Levy, Amy, *The Romance of a Shop* (1888), ed. Susan David Bernstein (Toronto 2006)

Marshall, Mary Paley, *What I Remember* (Cambridge 1947)

Martindale, Hilda, *From One Generation to Another* (London 1944)

Morley, Edith J., ed., *Women Workers in Seven Professions: A Survey of their Economic Conditions and Prospects* (London 1914)

Nelson, Carolyn Christensen, ed., *A New Woman Reader: Fiction, Articles and Drama of the 1890s* (Peterborough, Ontario 2001)

A Newnham Anthology, ed. Ann Phillips (Cambridge 1979)

Newnham College Club Letter (NCCL), [Annual Letters of The Old Newnham Students' Club, begun in 1881, printed for private circulation]

Newnham College Register 1871–1971, vol. I, *1871–1923*; vol. II, *1924–1950* (2nd edition Cambridge, published for Newnham College, 1979)

Our Chronicle (OC) (The magazine of the Skinners' Company School for Girls), copies held in the archives of the Skinners' Academy, London

Persean, The (the magazine of the Perse School for Girls, Cambridge), copies held in the archives of the Stephen Perse Foundation, Cambridge

Roberts, Robert, *The Classic Slum: Salford Life in the First Quarter of the Century* (first published Manchester 1971, paperback 1973)

Shaw, G. B., *Mrs Warren's Profession* (1894, first performed privately 1902)

Somerville College Register 1879–1971 (printed in Oxford for the College)

St Hugh's Club Paper (privately printed in Oxford for St Hugh's College)

St Hugh's College Register 1886–1959 (published for the College, Oxford 2011)

Stronach, Alice, *A Newnham Friendship* (London 1901, reprinted in the series *Victorian Novels of Oxbridge Life*, ed. Christopher Stray, Bristol 2004)

Thersites, the magazine of the Newnham students, copies held in the Archives of Newnham College

Thompson, Tierl, ed., *Dear Girl: The Diaries and Letters of Two Working Women 1897–1917* (London 1987)

Wallas, Ada, *Daguerrotypes* (London 1929)

Weibel, Kathleen, Heim, Kathleen M. and Ellsworth, Dianne J., eds., *The Role of Women in Librarianship 1876–1976: The Entry, Advancement and Struggle for Equalization in One Profession* (Phoenix, AZ 1979)

Octavia Wilberforce: The Autobiography of a Pioneer Woman Doctor, ed. Pat Jalland (London 1989)

Wootton, Barbara, *In a World I Never Made* (London 1967)

Secondary works

Abel-Smith, Brian, *A History of Nursing* (London 1960)

Adams, Pauline, *Somerville for Women: An Oxford College 1879–1993* (Oxford 1996)

Anderson, Gregory, *Victorian Clerks* (Manchester 1976)

Anderson, R. D., *Educational Opportunity in Victorian Scotland: Schools and Universities* (Oxford 1983)

The Student Community at Aberdeen 1860–1939 (Aberdeen 1988)

Ardis, Ann, *New Women, New Novels: Feminism and Early Modernism* (London 1990)

Beard, Mary, *The Invention of Jane Harrison* (Cambridge, MA 2000)

Beckman, Linda Hunt, *Amy Levy: Her Life and Letters* (Athens, OH 2000)

Bell, E. Moberley, *Storming the Citadel: The Rise of the Woman Doctor* (London 1953)

Bernstein, Susan David, *Roomscape: Women Writers in the British Museum from George Eliot to Virginia Woolf* (Edinburgh 2013)

Berry, Paul and Bostridge, Mark, *Vera Brittain: A Life* (1995, 2nd edition London 2008)

Bingham, Caroline, *The History of Royal Holloway College 1886–1986* (London 1987)

Black, Alistair and Hoare, Peter, eds., *The Cambridge History of Libraries in Britain and Ireland*, vol. III, *1850–1900* (Cambridge 2006)

Blake, Catriona, *The Charge of the Parasols: Women's Entry into the Medical Profession* (London 1990)

Bostridge, Mark, *Florence Nightingale: The Woman and her Legend* (London 2008)

Bush, Julia, *Women against the Vote: Female Anti-Suffragism in Britain* (Oxford 2007)

Caine, Barbara, *English Feminism 1780–1980* (Oxford 1997)
Victorian Feminists (Oxford 1992)

Clarke, Peter, *Liberals and Social Democrats* (Cambridge 1978)

Copelman, Dina, *London's Women Teachers: Gender, Class and Feminism 1870–1930* (London 1996)

Crane, Diana, *Fashion and its Social Agendas* (Chicago 2000)

Cross, Nigel, *The Common Writer: Life in Nineteenth Century Grub Street* (Cambridge 1985)

Crossick, Geoffrey, *An Artisan Elite in Victorian Society: Kentish London 1840–1880* (London 1978)
'From Gentleman to the Residuum: Languages of Social Description in Victorian Britain', in Penelope J. Corfield, ed., *Language, History and Class* (Oxford 1991), pp. 150–78
ed., *The Lower Middle Class in Britain* (London 1977)

Davidoff, Leonora and Hall, Catherine, *Family Fortunes: Men and Women of the English Middle Class, 1780–1850* (2nd edition London 2002)

Davidoff, Leonore and Westover, Belinda, eds. *Our Work, Our Lives, Our Words: Women's History and Women's Work* (Basingstoke 1986)

de Bellaigue, Christina, *Educating Women: Schooling and Identity in England and France 1800–67* (Oxford 2007)

Delap, Lucy, *The Feminist Avant-Garde: Transatlantic Encounters of the Early Twentieth Century* (Cambridge 2007)

Donoghue, Emma, *We Are Michael Field* (Bath 1998)

Dyhouse, Carol, *No Distinction of Sex? Women in British Universities 1870–1939* (London 1995)

Eltis, Sos, *Acts of Desire: Women and Sex on Stage 1800–1930* (Oxford 2013)

First, Ruth and Scott, Ann, *Olive Schreiner: A Biography* (London 1989)

Garnett, Richard, *Constance Garnett: A Heroic Life* (London 1991)

Geddes, J. F., 'The Doctors' Dilemma: Medical Women and the British Suffrage Movement', *Women's History Review* 18:2 (2009), pp. 203–18

Glynn, Jenifer, *The Pioneering Garretts: Breaking the Barriers for Women* (London 2008)

Haight, Gordon S., *George Eliot: A Biography* (Oxford 1968)

Harris, Jose, *Private Lives, Public Spirit: A Social History of Britain 1870–1914* (Oxford 1993)

Heilmann, Ann, *New Woman Fiction: Women Writing First-Wave Feminism* (London 2000)

Heller, Michael, *London Clerical Workers 1880–1914* (London 2011)

Holcombe, Lee, *Victorian Ladies at Work: Middle-Class Working Women in England and Wales 1850–1914* (Newton Abbott 1973)

Hosgood, Christopher, '"Mercantile Monasteries": Shops, Shop Assistants and Shop Life in Late Victorian and Edwardian Britain', *Journal of British Studies* 38:3 (July 1999), pp. 322–52.

Howarth, Janet, '"In Oxford but … not of Oxford": The Women's Colleges', in M. G. Brock and M. C. Curthoys, eds., *The History of the University of Oxford*, vol. VII, *Nineteenth-Century Oxford, Part 2* (Oxford 2000), ch. 10

Howarth, Janet and Curthoys, M. C., 'Origins and Destinations: The Social Mobility of Oxford Men and Women', in M. G. Brock and M. C. Curthoys, eds., *The History of the University of Oxford*, vol. VII, *Nineteenth-Century Oxford, Part 2* (Oxford 2000), ch. 14

Hudson, Derek, *Munby: Man of Two Worlds. The Life and Diaries of Arthur J. Munby 1828–1910* (London 1972)

Jeffreys, Sheila, *The Spinster and her Enemies* (London 1985)

John, Angela, *Elizabeth Robins: Staging a Life* (Stroud 1993, paperback edition 2007)

Evelyn Sharp: Rebel Woman, 1868–1955 (Manchester 2009)

Kamm, Josephine, *Indicative Past: A Hundred Years of the Girls' Public Day School Trust* (London 1971)

Kemp, Sandra, Mitchell, Charlotte and Trotter, David, eds., *The Oxford Companion to Edwardian Fiction* (Oxford 1997, reprinted 2007)

Kent, Susan Kingsley, *Making Peace: The Reconstruction of Gender in Interwar Britain* (Princeton, NJ 1993)

Sex and Suffrage in Britain 1860–1914 (Princeton, NJ 1987)

Koven, Seth, *Slumming: Sexual and Social Politics in Victorian London* (Princeton, NJ 2004)

Lancaster, Bill, *The Department Store: A Social History* (London 1995)

Law, Cheryl, *Suffrage and Power: The Women's Movement 1918–1928* (London 1997)

Leary, Patrick and Nash, Andrew, 'Authorship', in David McKitterick, ed., *The Cambridge History of the Book in Britain*, vol. VI, *1830–1914* (Cambridge 2009), ch. 4

Livesey, Ruth, *Socialism, Sex and the Culture of Aestheticism in Britain 1880–1914* (Oxford 2007)

McCrimmon, Barbara, *Richard Garnett: The Scholar as Librarian* (Chicago 1989)

McCrone, Kathleen E., *Sport and the Physical Emancipation of English Women 1870–1914* (London 1988)

McWilliams Tullberg, Rita, *Women at Cambridge* (2nd edition Cambridge 1998)

Mangum, Teresa, *Married, Middlebrow and Militant: Sarah Grand and the New Woman Novel* (Ann Arbor, MI 1998)

Martindale, Hilda, *Women Servants of the State* (London 1937)

Miller, Jane, *Seductions: Studies in Reading and Culture* (London 1990)

Mitchell, Sally, *Frances Power Cobbe: Victorian Feminist, Journalist, Reformer* (Charlottesville, VA 2004)

Moore, Lindy, *Bajanellas and Semilinas: Aberdeen University and the Education of Women 1860–1920* (Aberdeen 1991)

Morgan, Simon, *A Victorian Women's Place: Public Culture in the Nineteenth Century* (London 2007)

Niven, Mary M. *Personnel Management 1913–1963* (London 1967)

Nord, Deborah Epstein, *Walking the Victorian Streets: Women, Representation and the City* (Ithaca, NY 1995)

Oldfield, Sybil, *Spinsters of this Parish: The Life and Times of F. M. Mayor and Mary Sheepshanks* (London 1984)

Onslow, Barbara, *Women of the Press in Nineteenth-Century Britain* (London 2000)

Oram, Alison, *Women Teachers and Feminist Politics 1900–39* (Manchester 1996)

Pedersen, Susan, *Eleanor Rathbone and the Politics of Conscience* (New Haven and London 2004)

Peterson, Linda H., *Becoming a Woman of Letters: Myths of Authorship and Facts of the Victorian Market* (Princeton, NJ 2009)

Prochaska, F. K., *Women and Philanthropy in Nineteenth Century England* (Oxford 1980)

Pugh, Martin, *The March of the Women: A Revisionist Analysis of the Campaign for Women's Suffrage 1866–1914* (Oxford 2000)

Richardson, Angelique and Willis, Chris, eds., *The New Woman in Fiction and in Fact: Fin-de-Siècle Feminisms* (London 2001)

Robinson, Wendy, *Pupil Teachers and their Professional Training in Pupil Teacher Centres in England and Wales 1870–1914* (Lampeter 2003)

Rose, Jonathan, *The Intellectual Life of the British Working Classes* (London 2001)

Rowbotham, Sheila, *Dreamers of a New Day: Women Who Invented the Twentieth Century* (London 2010)

Edward Carpenter: A Life of Liberty and Love (London 2008)

Sanderson, Michael, *From Irving to Olivier: A Social History of the Acting Profession 1880–1983* (London 1984)

Schwartz, Laura, *A Serious Endeavour: Gender, Education and Community at St Hugh's 1886–2011* (Oxford 2011)

Scott, M. A., *The Perse School for Girls: The First Hundred Years 1881–1981* (Cambridge 1981)

Sondheimer, Janet, *Castle Adamant in Hampstead: A History of Westfield College: 1882–1982* (London 1983)

Spalding, Frances, *Gwen Raverat: Friends, Family and Affections* (London 2001)

Vanessa Bell (London 1983)

Stetz, Margaret D., *Facing the Late Victorians: Portraits of Artists and Writers from the Mark Samuels Lasner Collection* (Newark, NJ 2007)

Gender and the London Theatre 1880–1920 (High Wycombe 2004)

Summers, Anne, 'A Home from Home – Women's Philanthropic Work in the Nineteenth Century', in Sandra Burman, ed., *Fit Work for Women* (London 1979), pp. 33–64

Angels and Citizens: British Women as Military Nurses 1854–1914 (London 1988)

'Public Functions, Private Premises: Female Professional Identity and the Domestic Service Paradigm in Britain 1850–1930', in Billie Melman, ed., *Borderlines: Genders and Identities in War and Peace 1870–1930* (London 1998)

Sutherland, Gillian, 'Education', in F. M. L. Thompson, ed., *The Cambridge Social History of Britain 1750–1950* (3 vols. Cambridge 1990), vol. III, pp. 119–69

Faith, Duty and the Power of Mind: The Cloughs and their Circle 1820–1960 (Cambridge 2006)

The Education of Girls: The Contribution of the Skinners' Company 1890–2010 (London 2010)

Sutherland, John, *The Longman Companion to Victorian Fiction* (2nd edition London 2009)

Thirlwell, Angela, *Into the Frame: The Four Loves of Ford Madox Brown* (London 2010)

Todd, Selina, *Young Women, Work and Family in England 1918–1950* (Oxford 2005)

Tomalin, Claire, *Charles Dickens: A Life* (London and New York 2011)

The Invisible Woman: The Story of Nelly Ternan and Charles Dickens (London 1990)

Thomas Hardy: The Time-Torn Man (London 2006)

Tropp, Asher, *The School Teachers: The Growth of the Teaching Profession in England and Wales from 1800 to the Present Day* (London 1957)

Tuke, Margaret, *A History of Bedford College for Women 1849–1938* (London 1938)

Vlaeminke, Meriel, *The English Higher Grade Schools: A Lost Opportunity* (Woburn 2000)

Walkowitz, Judith, *City of Dreadful Delight: Narratives of Sexual Danger in Late Victorian London* (London 1992)

Waller, Philip, *Writers, Readers, & Reputations: Literary Life in Britain 1870–1918* (Oxford 2006)

Whitelaw, Lis, *The Life & Rebellious Times of Cicely Hamilton* (London 1990)

Wiener, Martin J., *Between Two Worlds: The Political Thought of Graham Wallas* (Oxford 1971)

Wild, Jonathan, *The Rise of the Office Clerk in Literary Culture 1880–1939* (Basingstoke 2006)

Worthen, John, *D. H.* Lawrence: *The Early Years 1885–1912* (Cambridge 1991)

Zimmeck, Meta, 'Jobs for the Girls: The Expansion of Clerical Work for Women 1950–1914', in Angela John, ed., *Unequal Opportunities: Women's Employment in England 1800–1918* (Oxford 1986), pp. 153–77

Index